The Irish
Patient

Paul Byrne

This is my true story. I've changed some names but the events remain as I experienced them.

Paul Byrne

Published by Paul Byrne
Publishing partner: Paragon Publishing, Rothersthorpe
First published 2016
© Paul Byrne 2016

ISBN 978-1-78222-421-1

Book design, layout and production management by Into Print
www.intoprint.net
01604 832149

Printed and bound in UK and USA by Lightning Source

HELLO, MY NAME IS PAUL BYRNE. I was born on the 12th of February 1974 in St. Sebastian's Hospital, Co. Dublin.

I do not know what weight I was. As I never asked my mother.

I came from a very poor family. Although at the time I did not know that.

I was baptised Paul Eric Byrne in the Holy Family Church, Kill O' The Grange.

I lived in St. Jude's bungalow on Pottery Road.

My sister Lesley was born on the 12th of April 1976 in the same hospital that I was born in.

I remember that we only had one TV channel at the time - RTE One.

But that was normal back then for most Irish families.

I remember the attic of our bungalow was infested with rats and there were holes in the ceiling and you could see their eyes.

I did not think that this was unusual at the time until many years later.

The council would only put rat poison around the outside of the house.

My childhood at the time was very happy. Like most Irish children.

I do remember at the time. That when my ma went to work.

That my da, who was supposed to be looking after me, would leave me on my own and take my sister with him as she was two years younger than me.

But I did not think this was unusual until many years later.

I first went to primary school in late August early September 1978.

It was Johnstown Road near Watsons in Ballybrack or Cabinteely. I'm not quite sure.

My mother later told me that she was crying when she was letting me go into school that day but I could not remember back then.

When I was not in school, as I said, I was often left on my own for many hours.

My mother would tell how to tell the time on the hands of the clock so I knew what time to turn on the telly; it was either 3.30pm or 4.30pm. I'm not quite sure when the children's programmes would come on.

In late 1978, either September or November I'm not quite sure, a new TV channel came on called RTE Two. So we now had two TV channels to watch but I think RTE Two was only on for a couple hours a day at first.

One time I remember I was on my own and there was a knock at the front door. I answered and there was a Garda; he asked me was my mother or father in and I said no and then I closed the door. When my mother came back later that day she gave out to me for answering the front door.

I also remember I used to fall asleep around eight or nine in the evening especially when the news came on because it was very boring for a kid.

One evening my da broke the front window. I think he must have knocked at the front door but I could not hear him because I was fast asleep. When my mother came back she gave out to me.

I remember my da's friend Christy used to have a green fishing boat parked outside our house.

When my sister was there we would both play in it together for hours; sometimes a friend of mine from Macintosh Park would call down to me and he would also play in it. I cannot remember his name.

I also remember that my father had a van which he used to sell sweets and vegetables from. I'm not quite sure if it was together or separately.

One day we were heading down to Co. Wexford and I could see the road as there was a rusty hole in the floor I was always scared that my foot or my whole body would fall through it.

My da also had a coal truck, maybe not at the same time. It was an old English truck where you could sit on the engine in the driver's compartment; obviously it was covered by a metal cover but you could feel the heat from the engine and appreciate it in winter especially.

When there was little or no coal on the flatbed the children would jump up on it. Which I thought was great as a kid.

My da also fixed cars and even took out whole engines and painted cars with a spray gun mostly as a hobby. I think he actually enjoyed it. He was always very good at those sorts of things.

I think the pop band 'The Boomtown Rats', coincidently since our bungalow was full of rats, used to keep their drum kit in the spare room of the bungalow. I used to try and play the drums. My mother told me that during the summer they would all sit out in front of the bungalow, including Bob Geldof.

Although I did not realise who they were at the time and did not until many years later.

One night I think around early January 1979 a man came to our house looking for my da; he asked my mother could he borrow the car she said yes. He must have been a friend of my da's.

I remember it was snowing. I think he drove up to my grandmother's where he was staying.

I'm not quite sure. My mind is very foggy about that.

I don't know what exactly happened but my da gave out to my ma for letting that man borrow the car.

I'm not sure whether we all walked home in the snow except for that strange man.

I remember 1979 was a particularly cold year as there was snow on the hills and ditches even in May.

I also had a strange tricycle with a very long handlebar at the back of the tricycle which my mother could push. It also had a big basket.

Which my mother would use to carry peat briquettes, firewood and many other things from Hardy's Shop in Cabinteely Village.

My da told that there were only three of those tricycles in the whole of Ireland.

He said that they were made in West Germany at that time.

I remember going on a fishing trip in Christy's green boat. We were in Dun Laoghaire Harbour and then we went out into the Irish Sea. It was a beautiful summer's day.

It was either July or August 1979. The weather had picked up by then.

We got a lot of mackerel mainly and when we got home my da fried the fish and he asked would I like some and I said yes and it was really nice.

My mother and I would mainly go to Mass at St. Brigid's Church in Cabinteely Village.

I also remember when the Pope came to Ireland in September 1979.

We did not go to visit him in The Phoenix Park. But I remember watching some of the visit on TV.

I wasn't happy about this because there were no cartoons on TV; as a kid that's all you want to watch as most other things are boring

It wasn't till years later that I realised how important the Pontiff's visit was.

One day my auntie Brigid came up to visit us and when we were coming back from Hardy's shop a Traveller asked my auntie did she need a hand carrying the peat briquette on my famous tricycle and she said no. I think she was frightened of them.

All the travellers were across the road from our bungalow. That was a long time ago. Then they left and there were just empty fields and many years later they built houses there and they still are till this day.

I also remember there was a tar pit as I called it near our house which one day my sister pushed me in, catching me totally by surprise. I got tar all over my hair especially and the upper part of my body.

I then pushed my sister in but she was expecting that to happen and only got tar on her hands.

There used to be some factory with people like lab technicians near our house.

I went in there for help to get the tar out of my hair. They tried but weren't very successful.

Then I went to my mother and she used Johnson's baby oil and it was brilliant. It got all of the tar out of my hair. I was very relieved as I thought I would have tar in my hair for the rest of my life.

As 1979 drew to an end and into early 1980, my mother told me that we going to be moving house shortly and going to a place called Shankill which I didn't know much about.

I remember they had already started digging the foundations for the new building that was going to replace our bungalow.

One day a teenager or young man, I can't remember, tried to trespass around where the new trenches had been dug.

I told him that he was not allowed to go near there. He told me to 'shut my gob'.

This was the first time I had ever really heard bad language and I still remember it till this day.

Shortly before we moved to Shankill I told people in my school class that I was going to leave soon.

But I wasn't sad that I was going as I was only a kid.

I can't remember too much about the day we moved, only that there was a big dumper truck and there were many men.

The dumper truck was full of our belongings.

All I remember was that the back garden was muddy from the wet weather.

This was in March 1980.

My grandad was there putting up new light bulbs.

I just remember walking a long road in the front of our new home on my own.

After we moved in, there were mice running up and down new bare stairs; you could hear their feet on floorboards on the stairs.

I was actually scared but I don't think I told anyone.

Eventually my dad killed all of them and that was the end of that.

I don't remember going to school for several months as I had to enrol in a new school.

Eventually I started to make friends with the new neighbours.

My best friend then was Keith; he lived in the house beside me.

I did not know at the time that my mother was expecting a new child until one day she was doing the washing up and she told me or someone to call for an ambulance; then her waters broke and the ambulance came and took her away and we stayed in my best friend's house until my da arrived and we told him what happened.

My new brother was born on July 4th 1980 also in St. Sebastian's Hospital, Co. Dublin.

I can't remember much about the day we went to visit him, only that it was in the morning and the weather was beautiful and my da said high to our neighbour Helen.

That's all I can remember.

My new brother Alan must have got baptised about a month later also in Holy Family Church, Kill O' The Grange, Co. Dublin.

I enrolled in a new primary school call St. Anne's in Shankill.

It was separated into a boys and girls school.

I can't remember who the new lady teacher was. It was first class that I was in and I made more new friends from different parts of Shankill.

But most of them I did not know where in Shankill they exactly lived until years later.

I started to enjoy school again.

I almost forgot, when I started going to school my mother would walk me up.

Then one day my mother started talking to this lady who was bringing her two daughters to school as well.

I thought they were twins, not identical but the same age, but I only found out years later that they weren't twins but sisters; one of them is the same age as me; her name is Hazel and her other sister is Donna, who Hazel later told me was exactly a year and a day older than her.

Their mother had this old-fashioned pram that carried, I think, their much younger sister, I'm not exactly sure.

Occasionally from time to time we would all walk together to school.

These girls went to the girl's part of St. Anne's school which as I mentioned was separated at that time.

From then on for many years I would often bump into these girls in shops or out walking.

The last time I saw Hazel was July or August 1986. When we were both on our summer holidays, she was with her friends heading down to the beach. I think she called out my name but I pretended I didn't hear her. I wasn't being rude. I was just shy.

The last time I saw Donna was in the summer of 1987; she was at the caravan shop. When I said hello to a friend of mine called Stephen. He was extremely rude to me and I never spoke to him again. She just looked on in amazement and said nothing. He actually lived near her. She just wanted to keep her nose clean and keep out of trouble and who could blame her.

I also remember when John Lennon got shot on December 8th 1980.

I was up in my grandparents' and I said it to my uncle who was four and a half years older than me.

I also remember filling a bucket full of clay for the Christmas tree to stand up in that Christmas in 1980.

I remember wetting myself in class. My mother gave out to the teacher. But it really wasn't her fault.

Many other boys wet themselves but most of us grew out of it.

I just remembered, I'm not quite exactly sure I think it was around February or March 1981 or could have been February or March 1982, I just don't know. The only way I could be sure would to request my medical records from St. Sebastian's Hospital. Somehow I never bothered to request my medical records from St. Sebastian's Hospital till this day.

I had this pain in my stomach. My teacher Mrs O'Toole brought me home and told my mother that I was not well. If this is accurate it must have been nearly 1982.

My mother called for an ambulance; then I was brought in.

I think I was kept in for about a week. I remember being very lonely and bored and I would walk up and down the corridor in my bare feet as I had no slippers. I don't recall relatives or anyone visiting me while I was there except my mother who came in once or twice the last time to bring me home.

Years later I would look back on this and feel none of my relatives cared; maybe they were just too busy working or something else. I felt like I was just an orphan with no family; maybe I'm feeling sorry for myself.

I can remember the weather; as I looked through the window it always seemed to be raining. I was treated the same as most of the patients. One morning one of the nurses said to me I was half asleep when she was checking my temperature but I remembered nothing but I know she was telling the truth. Sometimes the doctor would come and press his hand on my abdomen and asked did that hurt I must have said no. I think he was checking for appendicitis.

I also remember the television; you had to put in 50p if you wanted to watch something; there was this patient who had his leg in traction. I remember watching Mass on the TV.

One thing that happened and still disturbs me till this day. When I was having my bath and went back to the ward. I decided to go back when I went in the bathroom; the nurse was washing one of the young female patients; she was probably the same age or a little older than me.

When I walked in, the nurse she roared at me. I quickly got out of there.

Now I'm going to try and explain why I did that. When I would be at home, my mother would bath me and then after me my sister. When my ma would be bathing I would go in and talk to her - this was perfectly normal as we were all one family.

That is why I went back to the bathroom where the nurse was bathing the other patient. I just did it automatically without thinking because I knew no better as I was only a kid back then.

Before you jump to any conclusion I'm not a pervert or anything like that.

I had absolutely no interest in girls at that time and even if the most beautiful woman in the world was having a bath I would have taken no notice and just walked out.

As I have said before, I had not gone through puberty yet.

This would not be last bad thing to happen to me in a hospital; in fact things would get a lot worse.

In early 1981 I was preparing for my First Holy Communion.

I remember going to confession for the first time.

Then my mother bought me my first suit. It was May 1981.

But she could not afford to buy my leather shoes which were very expensive back then. She had to get a loan from my Grandad to pay for them.

After going to Mass and receiving Holy Communion I had my dinner in my grandparents'.

I think I made about 20 pounds in money altogether from all of my relatives.

I actually remember leaving all my money behind and I thought I had lost it for ever. But I got it back the following week to my relief.

I remember going on my first summer school tour; it must been around June 1981. We went to Dublin Zoo. I spent a lot of First Holy Communion money on chocolate and sweets. I nearly made myself sick. That's greed for you. I even had to give away some of my chocolate bars to classmates on the bus.

Around this time they started building new private houses across the road from our housing estate where there was some land.

As kids we all had great fun playing on this building site.

I can't remember much about the summer of 1981; it's a bit a daze.

When I returned to school in September 1981. I started 2nd class and our new teacher was Mrs O'Toole and she must have been at least 60 years of age.

I remember she had a kind of tremor or shaking in her head and body.

My mother told me one day she had been in a car accident and that is what caused it.

My mother told me never to laugh at her condition.

But she didn't have to tell me that anyway because I didn't think it was funny even though I was still very young and only a child.

The first day I started class there were two boys messing in the class room. I had never seen them before.

I'm not sure whether they were kept back or not. I never ever asked them.

Their names were Alan and Keith.

For the first few weeks I had no school books because my mother hadn't got the money; after a while Mrs O'Toole would give out to me about it.

Eventually my mother met me in the schoolyard and gave me the money to give to Mrs O'Toole and she could buy the books for me.

In those days sometimes if you gave your money to teacher she or he would get your school books for you.

When I came in from the schoolyard and gave the money to Mrs O'Toole and told her what it was for, she went into a rage and nearly ate me alive.

I told my mother what happened when I got home. I can't exactly remember what she said to me.

I don't know whether it was days or a week or two later Mrs O'Toole gave my new books to me.

When I got my new books I used to love doing mathematics; I don't know why.

But Mrs O'Toole complimented me on it.

A month or two later, I'm not sure, I got my first pet dog. I called him Ben.

The only problem was he used to follow me to school nearly every day and sometimes he would come into the school.

The Principal gave out to me and told me to send my dog home; I tried my best. I had to pick up stones and throw them at him. I felt really terrible for doing this but I had no choice.

Around Christmas 1981 there was a song by 'The Human League' called 'Don't You Want Me?'. My mother loved that song and still does to this day.

When I went to the shops my dog would follow me; I was always very scared he would get run over by a car.

He used to chase after the schoolgirls on roller skates and they hated me and my dog for that.

What I remember about January 1982 was the now infamous snowstorm.

I can remember the gale force winds and very heavy snow which as a schoolkid I thought was great.

I remember the clothes pegs were covered in thick ice.

They said it was the worst snowstorm in 50 years but, as with every weather phenomenon, they always said that.

Also one day when it was snowing my dog was jumping up and down in the back garden at the clothes' line and he tore the sleeve of my mother's jumper.

One day my mother and I had to go up to Quinn's Grocery Shop in Shankill Village as there was a rumour he had fresh milk which was in short supply due to the bad weather.

There were people all getting their fresh milk; eventually we got ours which we poured into fizzy drink bottles.

When the snow eventually disappeared in just one night I was devastated because now I would have to go back to school.

I cannot remember too much about early 1982; only my da used to saw down trees at the woods near the train tracks.

Which most of the local children called Vietnam.

C. I. E as it was called then was building the electric power lines for what would become the Dart.

So my da got the job to fell some of the trees near the railway tracks I think.

At around this time I think I had my first sexual experience. Although I did not know at the time and not until many years later, this would come back to haunt me and later destroy my life forever.

I began having erections although I did not know what they were at the time.

Sometimes they would last a couple of hours. I think I had three or four - I'm not exactly sure.

I thought there was something wrong but I never told my parents because I was too embarrassed.

The only time I said something was to a friend in class at school.

His name was Philip; I said to him, does your willy ever get real big? He said no.

I said no more and thank god I don't think he ever remembered me asking him that embarrassed question.

Only in 1995 when I was in St. Gregory's Hospital, Co. Dublin did I read an article in a magazine.

The man who was being interviewed by a journalist - I think it was in the U. S. A. - must have been famous but I had never heard of him.

He was telling the journalist about his personal life like what I'm doing now and said the same thing happened to him at the same age. That day I knew actually what he was talking about.

But that's in the future tense.

After that episode things returned to normal. I forgot all about it and life was great again.

A little later on in the year my dog Ben died. My neighbours found him dead in a water drain.

Where they were building the new houses across the road.

I was devastated when they told me. I was trying my best not to cry. I had to hide the tears from everyone.

Till this day I blame myself. Because many months before, I'm not sure exactly when, I touched his nose with a red hot poker straight from the kitchen fireplace.

I have kept it a secret till today. A week or two before he died he was getting violently sick; it might not have been from the poker but I can't be 100% sure.

All that I know is that he never got his injections because my parents could not afford it.

I kinda knew he was going to die but I was still in shock.

I think my da buried him.

Many nights after that I could not sleep properly because I thought he was going to come back from the dead and somehow kill me.

But after a few weeks this worry went away.

But till this day it still disturbs and may always will.

After that in the summer of 1982 I began hanging around a group of slightly older lads.

These were what you would call a gang of toughs

Their names were Mark and Alan, and a few other guys that I can't remember.

We would be hanging around the housing estate and beach skimming stones and so on.

One day that I remember I was with Karl and a few other lads. When some lad on a bicycle was passing near us and Karl threw a stick right between the spokes of the wheel and he fell off in front of the bicycle and his nose was bleeding.

Then a few minutes late the boy's mother came up to us and gave out but Karl basically told her to get lost.

We were all totally fearless in those days and basically thought we could do whatever we liked within reason.

I remember going into Karl's house and I thought he was rich; his parents had a washing machine and tumble dryer and when he opened his fridge it was full of cakes and fizzy drinks and other luxury goods. I was astounded by this.

My mother never even had a washing machine at that time.

Later on that summer something happened to me. I might not be alive today to talk about it.

One day near the sewage plant which had no walls or fences in those days I was being chased by a group of lads.

I decided to take a short cut across the sewage plant. I thought the sewage in the ponds or whatever was only the depth of tiny puddle so I decided to cut across it.

The moment I stepped on it I sank straight in it.

I must have been more than waist deep in shit literally.

I was slowly sinking into it. I kept shouting for help! But nobody heard me.

I decided if I was going to get out alive I would have to do it myself.

With all of my strength I managed to get out.

I know it's a terrible thing to say but many years later I wish I had died that day.

I would have gone straight to heaven hopefully as an eight year old child.

But I was still in great health and still had a lot to live for.

When I got out of the sewage I had to make my way home without getting spotted so I decided to go through fields near the cliffs has they were full of long grass so nobody would see me.

I managed to make it through I think to where they had nearly finished the new houses near my parents. There was this little laneway that you could walk up through and my house was only less than halfway up the length of the road.

I knocked on the front door and my mother was astonished. I told her what had happened to me.

So she ran me a bath and told me to take off my clothes before I came into the house.

I did this and I only had my underwear on. Then I noticed some of the neighbours coming up the road and they saw me. They did not know what had happened to me and just went on with their business.

All my clothes had to be thrown away as they were just too filthy to wash.

I had my bath and everything was okay again and life went back to normal again.

In early September I went back to school again. It was 3rd class; our new teacher was Mrs Murphy.

Who I always thought wore a lot of make-up and I wasn't imagining things because many years later I was talking to a lady called Clare who is three years younger than me. But she told me she remembered the same teacher and she said the exact same thing as me.

A few weeks after starting school again Mrs Murphy was talking to my mother about me and then, after my mother left, she turned nasty towards me and told me to get into class which I did very fast.

Then came Halloween; as far as I can remember the weather was very good for that time of year.

I can't remember too much about treats. I got only a small husk of coconut which I thought was amazing because I had only seen them on films.

The next thing I remember was Christmas 1982. I think I got an electric train set. Which was the best Christmas present I had ever got until then.

Until my brother Alan put it in the bathroom sink and it never worked again and he also scribbled biro all over my da's football programme for a Shamrock Rovers and Liverpool FC friendly match that my da had given me as a gift and which I think I still have to this day.

The next thing I can remember was my 9th birthday on February the 12th 1983.

I think I got around 15 pounds altogether from all of my relatives.

Around that time I decided to go my neighbour's back garden with my friend Anthony who was a few years younger than me.

We found paint in their back shed and I opened the tin. I decided to do a little painting so I painted a pair of furry boots on the inside and the shed door. Then I also painted the back kitchen window including the glass. After that I put the paint away and calmly went home and said nothing.

Then a few hours later there was a knock on my old front door.

It was Anne and someone else; somebody had squealed on me.

I knew Anthony had talked and told them who was mainly responsible - me.

But somebody might have backed up his story, but don't really know and can only speculate.

Obviously I got into a lot of trouble for this.

My da gave all my birthday money to Anne and also wanted to smack me but she told him not to do that and he didn't.

The next thing I know was it was around April when my little brother Alan hurt his big toe.

The watchman, called Dan, ironically in the now nearly finished building site, tried to suck out any dirt that was in his big toe.

I don't really know whether he did or not.

But everything was okay.

I remember the weather at this time of the year was unusually warm and dry. In fact as I remember that was overall the warmest and driest year ever recorded in Ireland.

Around the same month my mother used to work as a cleaner I don't know where.

But as usual my sister, brother and myself were left on our own because my da was not there.

I remember I used to love fried bread made with cooking fat which gave it that extra flavour.

Anyway maybe that day, I'm not quite sure, my mother got a lift home from her supervisor who just happened to be my friend's mother who went to the same school as me by coincidence

My mother was shocked by our appearance because we had dirt on all of our faces but I did not notice that because we were only kids.

A few days later in school I got talking to my mother's supervisor's son Tomas and told him I saw his mother with mine.

We got talking and I went to his house in Shanganagh Grove; that was my first time there.

Then I said do you want to call down to my house and he said yes; he had a bicycle but I had none at the time so I said can I borrow your brother's or sister's bike and he said yes.

So we cycled down to my place and I said let's go to a friend of mine Karl; it started to get late and I said I will have to get my tea. Which was my favourite stew which my ma was a connoisseur of.

So he said how will I get home? I said Karl will cycle home with you on the other bike and he said okay.

I thought nothing of this and had my stew; sometime later there was a knock on the front door - it was Tomas and his mother.

He told me that Karl had never got home with him and had taken the other bike with him; they later found it abandoned on the road.

His mother asked me where Karl lived and she drove me in the car and, like the eejit I was, I showed her where his house was.

For many years after that Tomas' mother always had it in for me as if I was always leading her son astray, as if he had no mind of his own.

Maybe the next day Karl and a few friends found me and confronted me about ratting on him where he had lived. It was in the same laneway were my escapade from accident in the sewerage plant the previous year had been, where the new houses were now nearly finished.

I thought he was going to beat the crap out of me but he didn't; he just pushed me against the wall of the laneway and threatened me and left me, to my relief.

But after that he and his friends became my arch enemies for about nearly two years.

Around the same time of year in school, myself and my friend and a couple others - I can't remember who exactly, were sent down to the Principal of the girls Mrs Fenton.

I was poor at English and I think the others were too. I think we would go once a week to improve our English.

We would have to learn 20 new spellings every week on a sheet of paper we took home to learn; and then we brought the sheet of spellings back and we had a spelling test.

I actually enjoyed this as every week I think I got 20 out of 20 and she would give us these lovely sweets that I had never seen before so that was a pretty good incentive.

One week I forget to bring back my spellings sheet and she accused me of not learning them.

I told her this was untrue and that I had simply forgotten to bring back the sheet which I had left at home by mistake.

She said in a stern manner, Master Byrne you never learned your spellings did you?

So we all did the spelling test and when the next week came she apologised to me as had got full marks and she gave me some sweets.

The one thing that I remembered when I was trying to improve my English with Mrs Fenton was how to pronounce 'knife'. Which I always pronounced with the K when reading - she told that this was a silent K and I always remember it till this day.

I was never good at English even at that age and I regarded it as a foreign language because I'm Irish. I still suffer today with very poor English grammar and probably always will.

Even writing this book is very difficult because my grammar is terrible.

I occasionally would see some of the girls in that part of the school as I have mentioned. I remember seeing Hazel the odd time and kind of knew who she was. But I did not know any of the others.

I remember a little over four years later I asked were Mrs Fenton was and somebody told me she had died from a heart attack. I was in shock.

Even though we had our differences I still had a great deal of respect for her and always will.

R. I. P Mrs Fenton.

My sister made her first Holy Communion in May of 1983. At St. Anne's Church, Shankill.

I remember the weather was dull but dry. My auntie Anne had the made the First Holy Communion dress for my sister as a present for her and she did a brilliant job like a top fashion designer.

It was still done in the traditional style but her dress was unique as it was one of a kind.

My grandmother Rita was there which was very unusual as she very rarely left her house because she had very bad bronchitis brought on by heavy smoking and other respiratory problems and of course my grandfather was there but he was in much better health.

I'm not exactly sure where we went to have dinner; it could have been my grandparents' but I can't be 100% sure.

I remember in June my friends would go on little adventures. Once I decided to go up into the Dublin Mountains. There was me, Stephen and Anthony who was few years younger than us.

At that time two of the neighbour's dogs would follow me everywhere - one was called Prince and the other Major.

So there were three of us and two dogs. First we managed to get to the Silver Tassie Pub in Loughlinstown; there was an old abandoned VW Camper Van which we played in for a while then we got bored so I went and asked the barman for a pint of water as I had no money and he gave a pint of tap water which was for free. Which I thought was like I was a full grown man having a pint.

Then I said let's try and follow the stream up into the mountains so we went under the famous Viaduct in Loughlinstown and kept going and eventually lost track of the stream.

I could see the hills in the distance, the famous smelting tower and lead mines that would be our ultimate objective.

As we got on up further into the hills we started to encounter very sharp and thorny bushes which had lovely flowers but that a false illusion of beauty.

My friends were complaining about how sharp and prickly these thorns were and they were very sore and so was I but I said nothing I think Anthony was wearing shorts but I don't think that made any difference.

We were all in pain but eventually we got out of them.

Then we encountered lots of cattle; they were everywhere and my friends were frightened because these cattle were huge to us as we were only small children.

These cattle were like huge dinosaurs. I even thought they might turn and attack us but they didn't thank God. I think my other friends thought exactly the same thing.

I think Anthony started to cry and was trying to play it cool and I acted like I wasn't scared but I was.

Eventually we got out of that tricky situation.

Then we ended up in this big field which of wheat or some other crop.

As we were walking the farmer or owner came out and gave out to us for walking in the middle of the field; he said we should be walking at the edge of the field because we were destroying some of his crops.

I wanted to explain to him that I don't think I was ever on a farm before and I knew nothing about crops. This was all entirely new to me and my friends.

But I said nothing. Eventually we got off the farm and ended up in a wooded area.

We were kinda lost but eventually we got to the smelting tower and lead mines and spent a while playing there.

I had always seen this place from a distance, many miles away in Shankill; this was the first time I had ever walked to it.

It was like climbing Mount Everest.

Then I said we better start getting home as our parents might be wondering where we are.

At first I thought we were making good progress but everything started to look the same - the roads the forests and so on. Then I said to the others we must be walking around in circles.

No matter how hard we tried we kept going back to the same place over and over again.

Then we asked a man for directions; he was painting his bungalow.

I said I'm lost, I'm looking for directions to Shankill. He gave us directions but we still got lost.

Then we saw a woman and a man with a car. I told them that we were lost and that we were from Shankill.

They had an older boy who must have been their son.

They said, is it alright if we drop you at St. Anne's Church? I said that will be fine as I always knew my way in Shankill as this is a great landmark

So we all managed to get into the back of the car, the two dogs and the three of us and her son. So it must have been a bit cramped but didn't bother us.

So when we got dropped off at St. Anne's we made our way home.

It was after 4pm in the late afternoon we had been gone since about 9am.

My ma and da were there and I thought they were going to give out to me but they didn't and I said nothing and had something to eat and was glad to be back home.

A few years later I told my mother what had happened to us.

***

The next adventure was a trip through Woodbrook Golf Course; it was in the same month.

I don't really know how we got out to Bray walking along the golf course but as we got to the end of the golf course, I said we better turn back. So we walked back across after we came out of it.

We ended up climbing over this wall and ended up in Shanganagh Grove.

As I said, I was first here in April but this was a totally different way of entering it.

As we walked through Shanganagh Grove we came out into Quinns Road where I saw two of my school friends playing marbles.

One was called Peter who was from the same school as me and then he would become my best friend for the next several years.

The other boy was also called Paul he was always bright and intelligent.

Then I went home with my friends Anthony and Stephen.

The next adventure was also in the same month.

This time my friend Patrick and his two brothers decided to head out to Superquinn in Bray.

I robbed a chocolate bar and they might have done as well but I'm not quite sure.

Then I decided to head home and I made the mistake of telling them not to mention to my mother that I was out in Bray.

Of course they did the complete opposite and the moment I got to my house and my mother opened the door they told her straightaway that I was in Bray and they might have mentioned I robbed a bar of chocolate.

I of course said it was all lies and had I gone into Bray by mistake.

I don't think my mother believed me but she didn't punish me and that was the end of that.

It was the hypocrisy of these so-called friends of mine that really annoyed.

If for example it had been the other way round and they told me not to say anything to their mother I would have kept my mouth shut because everybody would call you a rat. So you would never say anything even if they robbed the whole shop.

The next thing I remember being on my summer holidays in 1983.

One day I remembered going to the beach for swim. It was a beautiful summer's day.

There were of course a lot of people there. This was unusual for me as I was quite conservative and never liked appearing in semi-naked in pubic.

I couldn't swim but I tried and enjoyed myself then I got dressed and went home.

My da one day said he was going to hire a boat at Bulloch Harbour in Dalkey.

It was in August and it was a beautiful summer's day.

I asked if my friend Anthony could come along and he said yes.

We went around Dalkey Island and then landed on Shanganagh beach.

There was kind of thin high cloud around the top Killiney Hill it was quite unusual I mentioned to my da and he said it was heat haze. Never before or since have I seen anything like it on Killiney Hill.

I really enjoyed that day.

Then I started 4th class in September 1983 my new teacher was I think was Mr Sayers. He had grown a beard that summer so he looked a little different.

The weather was still great one day the Captain of Dublin football team arrived with the Sam Maguire Cup it must have been late September I think his name was Tommy Drumm.

I'm not sure whether we got our photos taken or not.

Also in September my ma asked what did I want for Christmas I said a racer which is what we called a bicycle with five or more gears.

When we were down in Dun Laoghaire my ma asked me to show what bicycle I liked in the bicycle shop.

I showed which one it cost over a hundred pounds which was a lot of money back then but that was actually one of the cheap ones. That bicycle shop actually no longer exists I think it went of business over 25 years ago.

Then shortly afterward she told there was no such thing as Santa Claus.

I still believed in Santa Claus up until then. I don't remember been in shock I just had to except it. I wasn't devastated or anything. You can't believe in Santa Claus forever unfortunately that's just life.

So every week my ma paid weekly instalments on my bike until the week before Christmas.

Around the same time an incident occurred that I can obviously remember.

I had written out a poem. But it wasn't original I had memorised from a poem in a school book a few years previously.

I wasn't trying to cheat it was the first time I had ever learned to memorise a poem in my life and I have never ever since done that.

I can still remember the poem exactly today.

Straight away Mr Sayers knew it wasn't original and that it was a copy and so did the boy beside knew.

I broke down crying for a few minutes. After that nothing was said of it.

I can't remember too much about Halloween in fact it's very vague for some reason. I don't know why.

Christmas 1983 was of course when I got my first proper bicycle that my mother had bought for me out of her very low income.

I was of course delighted I couldn't wait to start cycling around the block that Christmas morning.

I can actually remember what the weather was like it was nice crisp sunny morning I think the temperature got up around 7 degrees Celsius that afternoon.

I think we went for dinner on St. Stephens Day to my grandparents. We used to do this most Christmases but I never mentioned it till now.

My uncle had a portable black and white TV in his bedroom where we would mostly watch children's programmes and he would rob my grannie's Cadbury's milk chocolates she hid in her wardrobe.

My sister would be with me and sometimes my cousin David I think we used to eat the whole box but we never felt sick. The chocolates were much nicer back then like everything else.

Every Christmas my sister and I would always get a large Selection Box from our grandparents; we thought this was amazing.

January 1984 I started calling up to my friend Peter in Quinns Road on my new bicycle.

Later that January the weather got colder and there was snow on the hills.

So after school we decided to go up to the hills and play in the snow.

He knew a much quicker way to get up there than I.

When we got up there we had a great time sliding and playing the snow.

When it was getting dark we decided to head home. Because we were walking on back roads of Dublin there was no street lighting. I can remember seeing the car headlights and there were light precipitations that looked like snowflakes.

I had a feeling that night it was going to snow.

So when I was going to bed I looked out the window and it began to snow and it was sticking on the shed roof and garden. I actually saw one of my neighbours walking down the lane snow.

I was looking forward to tomorrow with excitement. The next I could not wait to play in the virgin snow.

Everything was so crisp and clean. Most people were still in bed.

So after a while I called up to my friend Peter. We decided to head down to football pitch at the end of Quinns Road. There were plenty of other kids there I was also joined by my other friend John who lived beside Peter.

When I started talking about the air temperature John looked at me with bemusement and laughed at men and turned to Peter who might have laughed as well.

So we were playing in the snow and a while later I said I better head home.

So when I started to walk and this girl and another girl started following me.

Then one of the girls said to me can I go with you Paul?

I had never seen this girl before in my life. I was in shock and she kept on following me and kept on saying can I go with you Paul? I was very scared too.

All I could think was how does she know my name? Peter's young brother Graham happened be walking near me so I pretended I couldn't her saying this I was starting to get more and more worried I started walking faster and faster; then when I got out of the football pitch I began to run in case she would follow and find out where I lived.

It wasn't till over a year later I found out her and her friends name.

Her name is Niamh and her friend is Elaine. I did not know their names at this time and I have never told anybody about this until now.

I hoped that would be the last I would see of any of them again and so after a while I forgot all about and put it behind me.

I used to start to call up to my friend Peters at this time and he became my best friend on and off for the next several years.

Although you may not think this, 1984 was probably the best year of my life. I wish I could have stayed in that year for the rest of my life and stay ten forever but unfortunately life does not stay still for anyone.

I almost forgot in 1984 the GAA celebrated its 100th Anniverary so they got an artist to start a mural on one of the walls were you could sit and have a little shelter if it was raining everybody in the class got a chance to paint although I thought I got a bit raw deal for some reason everybody got a lot more to paint than me and it wasn't in my imagination. I don't know that happened but as a kid you say to yourself that was unfair but I never complained about it.

The next big event was my tenth birthday on February 12th 1984.

It was really the only time that my da was kind to me.

He bought me to dinner in Dublin city centre I think the restaurant was called New York, New York I remember the bun burgers were lovely covered in sesame seeds.

Then he bought me a speedometer for my bicycle and a lock and steel chain linked also for my bike.

That is the fondest memory of my father.

When I got back the following few days he put the speedometer on my bicycle. So now I knew what speed I was going at.

I used to have great fun going down the hill near Clifton Park I used to get up to speeds of 35 MPH.

I know that doesn't sound much but to me at the time it was like travelling in a car at over 100 MPH.

Back at school things went along fine as usual.

Then one day I'm not exactly sure what month it was probably between March and May 1984.

I was walking out of school minding my own business one day when I heard a girl's voice saying can I go with you Paul.

I looked around and it was Niamh she was on her own this time. This time there were many other school kids around and she kept on saying it in front of everyone. I tried to ignore but she wouldn't stop.

I was very embarrassed; eventually when she had gone one of the lads who was a year older than me said, is that your girlfriend?

I said no I don't have a girlfriend. I don't know what you're talking about.

I know this sounds terrible I was going to beat her up but I couldn't find her so I gave up.

Please forgive Niamh. Thank God it never happened.

I had absolutely no physical attraction to girls at this time because I had not gone through puberty.

I'm not making excuses it's just a fact. Even if it was the most beautiful girl in the world I would have had the same reaction.

Niamh was beautiful and still is.

After that I had forgotten everything and life returned to normal.

It was the June Bank holiday weekend 1984.

I remember going down to Gorey on the diesel train. I kinda knew what the weather was going to be like for the weekend, mostly very wet. That evening as we were going down it was beginning to cloud over.

My late auntie Bridget was there on 1 Arklow Road the house no longer exists as when my auntie passed away it was sold and knocked down.

Nearly every year we would go down to Gorey on June bank holiday weekend as my mother is from that area.

My grandad Tommy was still alive at this time but I think he had mouth or throat cancer from smoking the pipe he was in a lot of pain and he would only have a couple of months to live.

He always drank heavily; he was especially fond of whiskey but this time it had a more medicinal quality in order to kill the pain.

I think it rained most of Saturday and my auntie made bacon, cabbage boiled potatoes and ice cream and jelly.

Which we all enjoyed I remember get my feet wet because I was running through the long grass in the back garden.

I remember seeing U.S. President Ronald Reagan on TV in Ballyporeen, Co. Tipperary; my grandad saw him taking a sip of a pint of Guinness and complimented him on it.

Even then as I knew nothing of politics he was only visiting Ireland to get the Irish American vote for the upcoming election.

When we came back on the Bank Holiday Monday when we were walking down to the house I saw a so-called friend of fiend Michael hanging around at the concrete slabs square near the bus stop for the number 58 bus he wasn't waiting for the bus he was just hanging around there.

We never really liked each other even though we were in the same class at school. We were the total opposite of each other. We would later become bitter enemies and still are to this day.

In early July as I was on my summer holidays 1984. My grandparents decided to take my sister and myself for a week each.

They took my sister for the first week and then me.

When I was there my aunt and uncles would give me pocket money and I would always spend on it on HB Feast Ice pops which I loved. I think they were only 20p at the time.

Then one day my auntie Anne took me and my cousin David to Stillorgan Cinema we went to see Indiana Jones and The Temple of Doom.

We got the 46A from Holy Family Church, Kill O' The Grange to Stillorgan.

I remember buying a can of diet coke and brought it into the cinema it was the first time in my life that I drank a can of diet coke.

After the film we waited for the 46A outside St. Gregory's Hospital.

Never did I know that this so-called hospital would haunt me forever.

Several years later there was a woman showing ever article of clothing that she bought in the shops to my auntie. We thought she was mad and tried our best not to laugh.

When we got back I'm not sure if it was that day or another my uncle was spraying in the back garden with water and I was cycling my cousin David's BMX bike when I was passing by on the bike my cousin started spraying me with water he thought it was funny.

I got fed up of this and turned off the water at the bath tub; then my uncle and cousin came down and my cousin said to me, what did you turn off Michael's water for because you kept spraying water at me.

Then he pushed me and I pushed back and a fight started we had each other in a head lock and then he started pulling my hair.

I said to myself only girls do this and decided to do the exact same thing to him.

Then my uncle Joe heard the commotion and broke up the fight.

I sat down in the sitting room and was trying my best not to cry with my grandmother and said nothing then after a while I calmed down.

The next morning lumps of hair started falling out. I was starting to get worried. I thought I was going lose all of my hair. But eventually it stopped. It was of course because of that fight with my cousin David when he was pulling my hair.

I remember around this time on TV a new series called V was on then

Then on Sunday there was an outdoor Mass across the road at the green. I'm a little ashamed that when the Mass was on, there was this teenager who might have had a physical or mental handicap; he was making all sorts of funny faces I was trying not to laugh at him. I kept mentioning him to my uncle he was trying tell me to keep quiet.

Only a few years later did I know that this was wrong and that I should not be laughing at him.

But I was too young to understand at that time.

After the Mass was over, there were mostly cakes and buns; it seemed all the people were like savages and by the time me and my uncle got to the tables there was nothing left. So much for Christian Charity.

My grandad had kept a few buns for us after the Mass was over. So everything was okay.

I almost forgot to mention that me and my uncle stayed in the mobile home every night while I was staying there. That was in the back garden.

I think I nearly wet the bed every night because the toilet in the mobile Home had been taken out for repairs.

I don't know if my uncle knew or not, but he said nothing. I tried my best not to move at night in case he found the bed wet and I always waited for him to get up first.

One day my auntie was washing the sheets from the bed and was hanging them out on the line; I was afraid she would say something but never did.

I also remember there was an earth tremor which was very unusual but I never felt it was around 8am in the morning.

My grand uncle used to come down most days to eat his lunch as he worked in Premier dairies in Monkstown which is no longer.

He told my grandmother, who was his sister, that he felt the tremor that morning when he was sitting on his bed.

The weather that summer of 1984 was great I started calling up to my friend Peter regularly now as we became better friends.

I remember the miners' strike in England was always on the news and Arthur Scargill the union leader.

I started school again September 1984 I think my new teacher was Mr Cotter who became the school principal at that time or a little later I'm not quite sure.

He had two jobs - he was principal and teacher. Mr. Cotter is still very well known today although retired a few years ago.

One day we were doing drama and when it came to my turn I just couldn't stop laughing I was in hysterics. Mr. Cotter gave out to me and told me to sit down for some reason I couldn't take it seriously.

Later that month my grandad Tommy passed away from cancer.

My ma sent me and my sister on the 58 bus to St. Fintans Park Kill O' The Grange to stay with my auntie Patty.

She took my baby brother Alan with her down to Gorey on the train.

I had to share a bed with my old enemy David but to my surprise we didn't fight - in fact we got on very well.

My sister slept in the spare room as she was the only girl and needed her privacy.

I remember my auntie made an apple tart and it turned out very well; it was really nice.

The weather was strange: one day was nice and next day there were hail showers and another morning it was frosty as the shed roof was covered in frost.

Another evening some young lads came around the door selling cakes. I had seen these guys before because they used to call around Shankill as well.

My auntie bought round cake like a Swiss roll. I made a vulgar joke about it and my cousin said it looked like a piece of shit.

He told his mother and she just laughed it off.

One day the Gardai knocked at the front door to tell my auntie that my grandad Tommy had passed away.

She thought my cousin David had gotten into trouble with the law.

I had to hold back the tears when I heard the news.

A day or so later I was up in my grandparents who only live ten minutes away and I saw my da with Christy and I told him that grandad had passed away.

For some reason both me and my sister missed my granda's funeral - only my baby brother got to see it.

Shortly afterwards my sister and I went down to Gorey to meet up with the rest of the family.

Most of my family's relatives from England and America were there.

I remember one night I had to share a room with my auntie Bridget I had to sleep in tiny couch it had two armrests at each end it was the most uncomfortable night of tossing and turning I was exhausted the next morning.

Then one evening everybody was invited up for dinner in the Guest House where my auntie Tess was staying - everybody was invited except me and my auntie Bridgit. It would not be the first time I was left out and it wouldn't be the last.

I only remember a night with my uncle Larry - I had to share a bed with him but at least I got some sleep.

Then I went home.

The next thing I remember was Halloween 1984. I went up my friend Peter in Quinns Road.

That evening we were going to light a few old mattresses on fire in the thorny bushes near Foxes Grove.

But these smart girls knew what we were up to. I don't even know who they were but they obviously lived around the area.

Their persistence was amazing - we just gave up.

Then we decided to dress up as coalmen by putting soot on our faces and carrying a big black bag which we filled with apples and nuts. I actually think I might have called to Niamh's house in Shanganagh Grove but I didn't know that at the time until a few years later.

Then we went to a bonfire - I think it was in Foxes Grove.

I think a month or so later I was hanging around with Peter on Quinns Road when some lad and sister were going to the shop. Peter hated the lad for some reason and was calling him names and then a fight broke out between them near Bojangles Hairdressers - I kept out of it.

But then his sister who must have been two or three years older than me suddenly grabbed me by the hood of my duffle coat and swung me around. I know it sounds funny but I was totally taken by surprise.

I was humiliated even though I had done nothing wrong as usual - then they both went into the sweet shop. I said to myself she's not going to get away with this so I took off my coat and waited until they came out and I hit her and crushed her snowball that she bought in the shop.

There were a lot of older boys sitting on the wall including Peter's older brothers - they must have thought I was crazy.

They did not know the full circumstances.

I then said to Peter that we better get out of here before we get into trouble.

We both hid behind the wall at Foxes Grove for a while until the heat died down.

In December my da decided to get the ferry to Holyhead in Wales to buy Christmas presents mainly.

I remember getting up around 6am or so and we got the Dart to Dun Laoghaire.

The Dart was only running since July 23rd I think. It was the first time I had travelled on it - I remember how clean it was and space age. I actually saw my friend David's sister from Shanganagh Grove waiting at the Dart station in Shankill - she was going to school.

When we got out at Dun Laoghaire the sea was very rough – in fact there must have been a force 8 or 9 gale blowing and the boat was going from side to side.

I remember walking on the deck with my father and brother and nearly getting blown away - that's how stormy it was.

When we got to Holyhead we had dinner. I had plaice and chips which I later regretted eating.

After that we went to Woolworths and my da bought these bumper cars with their own round circuit like at the carnival and he also bought me for Christmas this kind of Space Invaders console and he must have bought other presents too. I almost forgot he also got Toblerone bars.

Then when we got the ferry back it was really stormy and I started to get sea sick as did many of others - it was the first time I had experienced this.

Every minute I wanted to throw up - I kept running to the toilet but they were filthy and full of sewage which made me even more sick.

It only calmed down when we got into the shelter of Dun Laoghaire harbour.

I remember that night when I got home I was eating my Tobler one bar in bed before fell asleep.

Also in December maybe later in 1984 the CB Club had its Christmas party there in the Sunny Bank in Bray.

The Sunny Bank no longer exists. When we were there, a Scottish couple owned the place at that time but they sold it and moved on.

My da and his friend Stephen founded it in the early 80s.

My ma and sister and brother and I got the bus out to Bray. I remember the weather was cold with heavy sleet at the time.

My friend Roger happened to be on the bus as well - his father Mick was also a member of the CB Club - he was also going to the party.

I never mentioned them before but these parties were great as they were specially for the children of the members. It was just one great Christmas Party.

We had rice crispy cakes, sweets, fizzy drinks and many other delights.

Then my da's friend Stephen would dress up as Santa Claus and give us all presents.

We also had musical chairs and other fun games too and maybe watched a film on the big TV which had a video player which was hi-tech in those days.

I also remember my da told me that he and a few friends drove up Mount Kippure and it was covered in heavy snow. I was disappointed that he didn't ask me if I wanted to go because I wanted to see the snow.

Christmas 1984 I got my Space Invaders game console which I played after dinner in the sitting room then I must have fallen asleep for an hour or so which was very unusual for me.

I think on St. Stephen's there was a snow shower in the morning - this was the closest thing to a white Christmas since living in Pottery Road when my sister was with me.

In January 1985 there were a few days of heavy snow or maybe more. I remember talking to my old friend Keith who I had fallen out with the previous year.

Then one night I was watching the snow falling in the ray of light at the lamp posts in the early hours of the morning but I think the temperature was already beginning to rise.

The next day by the middle of the afternoon the snow began to melt slowly but surely.

After the snow melted we all went back to school.

In February the weather became very cold - there was a strong Siberian wind blowing which would last the whole month.

There was snow on the lower levels of the hills for the entire month.

I remember calling up my friend Peter and went down the field near the end of Quinns Road and in the field there was this huge puddle covered in thick ice - we had great fun sliding on this.

My birthday was of course on the 12th of February 1985 I was 11 but I can't actually remember anything about it for some reason.

I think there was an article on RTE News about pike fishermen on frozen lakes on the West of Ireland.

The lakes in the West froze over much easier than the East because they were settled from the bitter east wind.

I can't remember much about March.

In April my da and I started cycling a lot. I remember the weather was dull and cold when we would cycle up to my grandparents.

I remember going through the housing estates of Ballybrack.

One day my mother was gone with the rest of the family and my auntie to the Carnival in Shankill Village.

My da starting kicking in the back door as he had no patience. I'm not sure; I think he kicked it in.

When my ma came back we told her what had happened. But amazingly she was calm about it.

Later in April there was this ocean-going steamer going from Dublin to Dun Laoghaire harbour and back again if you wanted to.

We got on in Dublin and went to Dun Laoghaire and I really enjoyed it.

I remember talking about The Embassy World Snooker Championship trying to find out what score it was.

It was of course the most famous final of them all between Steve Davis and Dennis Taylor.

I remember going back on the 58 bus and my da said: can you hear the old ladies talking about the snooker?

I remember watching the snooker that night. When it came to 17-all.

How nerve racking it was. It was edge of the seat stuff and of course when Dennis Taylor potted the black ball and won by the narrowest margin ever it must have been 12.30am.

My da and I were both going for Dennis Taylor.

But I would become a Steve Davis fan forever and he still is my hero till this day.

The next big month was May. I remember there was this man in a suit who would come every year and asked us to collect money for the Wheelchair Association of Ireland.

I would always try my best every year even though I was shy. I would try and go to as many houses as I could. It wasn't easy.

The people in the posh houses were usually the meanest - you would be lucky to get 5p, very rarely more than 10p a tine. They would sometimes interrogate you like The Gestapo and ask you what it was for and what you were being sponsored for.

I think I did a sponsored run or walk, I'm not quite sure.

I remember my da said something to me which at the time I did not understand.

He said do you know that the man who asked you to collect the money for The Irish Wheelchair Association keeps most of the money for himself and gets you to do all the work?

It wasn't till years later that I copped on to what he said and he was right.

I was taken for a complete eegit not for the first time and not for the last.

This remains one of the saddest and most horrible times of my life.

Once a week there was swimming and if you didn't go you were sent sometimes into a different classroom.

I remember being in Mr Sayer's class and my friend Patrick was there too.

After we came in and had just settled down, there was a knock on the classroom door and I saw two girls. It was Niamh and her friend Elaine.

They came in and I could not believe it - just my luck I said.

I just hoped they don't see me. So I turned around quickly and buried my head in my arms and pretended to be studying a book that I just grabbed from the bookshelf that was close to me.

A few minutes later somebody handed me a piece of white paper.

I opened it and it was a love heart with an arrow going through it saying Niamh loves Paul.

I was really embarrassed and pretended I didn't get it or acknowledge it.

I hoped Niamh would give up but she didn't. A minute or two later I got a second piece of white paper saying the same thing and when I looked around she was smiling with her beautiful perfect white teeth.

I just wanted the earth to open up and swallow me. I kept looking at the clock but it just seemed to stand still. I kept saying to myself and to the clock: please speed up so I can go home but it wouldn't.

Then she sent me another piece of paper with the same thing again. I became very angry and said to myself I'm not putting up with this.

Then I did something that at the time I didn't care about because I had absolutely no interest in girls whatsoever. But I always will be deeply ashamed of doing it for the rest of my life.

I wrote: I'm really sorry but Fuck Off. I know that's really horrible but I didn't care at the time because I had not gone through puberty yet - I'm not trying to make excuses though.

I never ever even used foul language in my life back then. I don't even know how I even spelt it. I must have learned it off obscene graffiti on walls.

It must have smashed her heart in two. I can't even imagine how she felt.

That was the end of our romance forever.

How can I even apologise for something like that. I just can't.

She must have left the class quickly when it ended because I didn't see her till next September but it was of course all over forever.

I sometimes see Niamh on the TV now and again.

I remember reading something on her in an article.

She actually is a feminist. I can't actually blame her - don't flatter yourself says you.

To be honest she is much better without me. She is also very intelligent and still looks great, far better than me. But that wouldn't be difficult.

If only I had been a year and half older things might have been a lot different - we might have been married today with lovely children but it never happened.

I think that same day coming out of school I met my da on his new Dawes bicycle. I never told him what had happened and not anyone till this day.

My da and I, and sometimes my sister, started cycling a lot that summer.

On my summer holidays we would cycle down to Wicklow and sometimes Shillelagh.

I can also remember Live Aid - it was July 13th 1985 and we cycled up to my grandparents and watched some of it there but I did not seem to realise how important this big music charity event was until many years later.

I remember late that month there were these massive thunderstorms. Which I had been expecting all day as it been a very dry day.

That night beginning at approximately midnight the thunder and lightning started - every few seconds there was a lightning flash, every few seconds it was the most tremendous thunderstorms that I ever experienced then and since. It lasted the whole night until about 8am nonstop.

I did not sleep a wink that night. I remember getting up the next morning and talking to my da about and it was on the news on the radio.

They were saying what damage it had done across the country.

They said it was the worst thunderstorm in 50 years. But to be honest, they always said that about every weather phenomenon.

I remember getting up early and leaving the house at about 8am - my da and I were cycling down to Foulksrath Castle in Co. Kilkenny and an An Oige Youth Hostel.

I think we cycled through the Wicklow Mountains near Lugnaquilla, the highest mountain in Leinster. We could not cycle up some of hills as they were too steep so we had to walk up them.

Then we cycled the longest stretch of straight road in Ireland so my da said.

Then we entered Carlow Town and had something to eat. I remember Blockbusters was on the TV I'm not sure if this was my first time seeing this on TV.

Then we cycled into Co. Kilkenny and asked for directions then we reached Foulksrath Castle.

I remember I did not sleep a wink that night because I was too warm and the blankets were too itchy.

Then we had breakfast and it was a kind of burnt - I did not eat much because it was horrible.

I remember it was raining that morning. I was complaining of a sore back.

My da was not impressed. I think we cycled all the way back to Dublin.

I remember getting home and my da was giving out to me because of my complaining of my sore back.

I think my mother had brought my brother Alan to the dentist in the health centre in Patrick Street in Dun Laoghaire that day.

I vaguely remember later that month that my da and sister and I went cycling again, only this time I think into the Wicklow Mountains and I think we stayed in two hostels.

I think one near Ashford Co. Wicklow as far as I can remember where the food was burnt as usual, by my da's cooking and again I did not sleep a wink that night as it was too warm and the blankets were itchy.

Then we went further into the Wicklow Mountains where we stayed in what my da said was an old army barracks.

I remember there were a lot more people in this hostel including many young women but I stayed most of the day in the dormitories or whatever you called them because I was too shy.

That night I did not sleep a wink again because it was too warm and the blankets were too itchy as usual.

That morning the breakfast was burnt again as usual and I couldn't eat it.

I remember cycling from the place. It was a beautiful morning.

The incline of the hills was very steep and I got a little scared because of the high speeds and bends. When we got on the dual carriageway, my da started talking to this German tourist who was cycling in the same direction as us.

That's all that I can remember.

The next big thing was school in September 1985. It was 6th class, my final year in primary school and our new teacher was Mr Sayers again.

I began to feel uncomfortable as they were trying to mix both the girls and boys schools together.

But 5th and 6th class were spared at this time.

It also dawned on me that the entire schoolyard was mixed. I really felt uncomfortable about this as I was shy and still had no interest in girls at this time.

I also remember seeing Niamh - this also made me feel uneasy.

So I tried to avoid her for the entire last year of school there.

I became good friends with Evan who I think was from Shrewsbury Road which was a little bit posh.

He was also conservative but not as much as me.

I remember later in September the new neighbour who had just moved in, in early May.

Who did not like me. Asked me for a fight which I wasn't interested in, not because I was scared but because I had no real interest in it.

I used to see him training and shadow punching and I knew he had taken up martial arts which he would later use on me.

One day my neighbour John who I was playing with said to me: are you afraid of him? I said no I'll fight him when the time is ready.

I'm not exactly sure but maybe a day or so later my sister came in and said Stephen wants to fight you. I probably said maybe another day. Then she said: are you scared of him or something? I said: no. She said: you are aren't you? No I'm not.

I was left with no choice but to go out and fight him.

He really got me on a bad day. Unusually for me I was very tired - I was watching TV and I didn't want to get out the chair.

But I was left with no choice. So I went up the road and we started fighting. He got me down on the ground by using his lower leg which I knew he learned from martial arts.

When he got me on the ground he started punching me in the face. Eventually I had enough and said I give up.

When he let me back up I was going to start on him again but I said no to myself because I knew I would not win this fight.

From this day my life would change forever. I wanted nothing more to do with anybody because when he was fighting me everybody was against me. Which I never forgot.

From that day on I was going to be a loner and be a perfectionist.

So that night I was thinking of everything that happened to me. It must have taken hours for me to get to sleep. I could not stop tossing and turning - my mind was racing.

So the next morning I decided to be a perfectionist.

I started to go to bed at exactly midnight every night and get up at exactly 7.30 am.

I would get into my pyjamas at five to twelve then say my prayers and go to bed at exactly midnight then in the morning I would get up at 7.30 and get dressed and say my prayers and make my bed with no creases - this either took exactly 10 or 15 minutes. Then I went down for breakfast and finished my breakfast at exactly 8.00am. I'm not exactly sure what I did next. I would give myself exactly 15 minutes to get to school. I'm not sure whether it was exactly 8.50 or 9 am when I arrived in class.

I would do this exact routine every day. During lunch breaks I would hang around with Evan.

We would mind the junior and senior infants in the playground.

I did this on purpose so I wouldn't have to mix with the older girls in school.

The next thing I remember was Halloween. I did not go around trick or treating. Because I was a perfectionist and did not consider it appropriate then.

But I remember when I was giving out the nuts and apples, my enemy Stephen called at the door - even though he had a mask on I knew it was him. I pretended I didn't notice him and gave him some nuts and apples.

I said to myself: the cheek of him.

The next thing I remember was late November or early December.

The UK Snooker Championship was on - Steve Davis versus Willie Thorn.

I was in bed and my da called me down - he was gloating because it looked like Steve Davis was going to be beaten.

He was 13-8 down and Willie Thorn was clearing the colours; then he missed a blue off the spot and I had a feeling this might be the turning point and it was.

I said nothing to my da because I wanted secretly for Steve Davis to win and he did - he won 16-14.

I was delighted because he was my hero and still is.

The next big thing was Christmas 1985. I remember I wanted to get a digital watch for Christmas.

My da brought me to Lawrence's Jewellers in the Ilac Centre.

I said I had never heard of them before. He said to me that they were one of the most famous Jewellers in Dublin.

Then I showed which watch I would like it was a Casio digital watch.

Which I got on Christmas morning. I got my new watch.

My sister had got Barbie dolls or something for Christmas from Santa Claus.

I don't remember too much that Christmas.

Then January 1986 came. This was going to be the most perfect year for me because I was a perfectionist.

Starting from the 1st of January I would be as perfect as possible, go to Mass at exactly 8am every Sunday and polish my leather shoes on a Saturday so I would be in pristine condition for Mass the following morning.

This happened every week to perfection. I don't think I ever used any bad language at all at that time.

I hoped this would go on for the rest of my life until I passed away from natural causes.

I was an orthodox Roman Catholic so I never took paracetamol for headaches or anything or any other medication. I very seldom got headaches so I was okay - this was all because of my strong religious views.

But it would all end in catastrophe for me but I never knew that would happen.

Sometimes I would call up to my friend Evan - he had an Commodore 64K computer that was cutting edge at that time. I noticed how wealthy his family were and his da worked in the Guinness Brewery. I think he had a good job because many years later I saw him on TV.

In February 1986, I remember the weather was very cold like in the previous February in 1985. A strong easterly Siberian wind was blowing again for the whole of that month. I remember I used to walk up on the back roads of the Dublin mountains and there used to be some snow on the side of the road. I think this was the second coldest February of the twentieth century in Ireland. I think Powerscourt Waterfall froze over this February, or it might have been in February 1985.

I remember walking along Shanganagh beach that month and there were little streams of water that had frozen on the cliffs. One of these days I was passing at the end of Quinns Road and for some reason the steps to the beach were missing and needed repair, so it was dangerous. I saw one my friends Peter who was with a group of other lads and when they saw me they started throwing stones at me. So I turned back.

I remember calling up to my friend Evan that same month a few times but he was never in. And I remember the little field beside the house where he lived was always covered in frost all day. So this would give you an indication of how cold it was that month.

Then in March, I started looking for frog spawn for some unusual reasons and there was this pond past the sewage plant, near the beach and I found some spawn though I cannot remember what I put it in. However, I remember that I had it in a bucket in my bedroom and I was hoping that the tadpoles would come out but only a few came out and the rest were dead. So I emptied the bucket down the bath and that was the end of it.

I remember going up in the lashing rain and there was snow on the hills to Evan's in March, that same month, and he had a microscope. I had some of the frog spawn with me for some reason and we were trying to look at it, but it wasn't that good. Later that afternoon his mother gave me a lift home. She was very kind. And I said, 'Thanks.'

Then in April the Chernobyl Nuclear disaster happened. I remember hearing it on the news and there was another strong easterly wind blowing again. I knew that that would blow a radiation cloud from there to Ireland, which is what exactly happened. I was a little concerned, but not too bothered about it.

Late April, I started sending letters to different public companies around Dublin including Jacobs and the Irish Commissioners for Lights, but I cannot recall the others. A week or two later I got a response; I thought this was great as I was only a kid. And it was full of interesting information from these enterprises.

Then in May, one late evening or night when I was starting to go to bed, certain things began to happen to me which were biological changes in my body. But at the time I did not understand this. I started having erections, then there were these funny feelings in my body and then this white stuff came out. I did not know what it was at the time until a few days later. I hoped this would be the last of it, but it happened the next day when I was going to school. I had an erection which lasted for hours. Even though it was the summer and it was warm I had to wear a long duffel coat to hide this as I did not want anybody to see it. So when I got into school, I had to sit down, but I felt really uncomfortable and I could do nothing about it. This erection would last for hours but it was beyond my control. I would feel really uncomfortable in class but I said nothing to anybody. Then I went home that day and the same problem happened that night again and this went on for I am not exactly sure how long, maybe several days or a week or two. I could not concentrate in school or even do my homework. After a few days of this happening to me I began to realise what the white stuff was. I said to myself, this is how women must get pregnant, but I never said anything to anybody.

When I was making my Confirmation I had an erection which lasted for most of that day for hours. I felt really uncomfortable, but said nothing to nobody.

Within about two to two and a half weeks, I began to get interested in women and girls for the first time in my life. I remember seeing something on the television; it was about this woman who was being photographed by male photographers and one of the men touched one of her breasts. This was the first time I noticed anything like this in my life.

I remember going out to the shed and I found a book with a picture of two beautiful women in bikinis. This was the first time that I had noticed anything like this before. Also, at this time I stopped going to Mass because I felt like I was a total hypocrite and did not deserve to be there. It wasn't because I didn't believe in God, it was because I was totally ashamed.

I started masturbating around this time. Then it must have been around late June, I saw this topless woman in a newspaper and I said to myself that this is the most beautiful woman I have ever seen. Her name was Carol Anne Stevenson. To me she was the greatest glamour model I had ever seen, before, or since, and I still have a picture of her in my bedroom to this day.

Around this time I started hanging around with my friend Darren as we were both on our summer holidays. I remember he used to buy bars and sweets in the local caravan shop and I was amazed by how much spending money he had because I could not afford any of these luxury items. Sometimes I would ask him for a bar of chocolate and he would give me one. He must have thought that I was a nit of a miser but he didn't realise that I hadn't got the money.

Many times when we were in the caravan shop we used to make fun of the guy that worked there. I remember his boss had an old Land Rover and when he was in the caravan talking to his friend, me and Darren found some Marmite and put it around the foam under the seat cover and when he found out, he chased after us but we were sitting up on a high wall at the end of the road that I lived on, and he gave out to us and we laughed because we knew he could not touch us.

I remember sometime in mid August, one of the girls from my school called out my name. She was with a group of my friends who must have been heading down to the beach. I was still shy at this time and pretended that I didn't hear her. Her name was Hazel and I'd known her for many years before. Then I began Secondary School in early September in 1986, in St. Brendan's College, Woodbrook, Bray, County Wicklow. I remember some of the guys were making fun of me because I hadn't got my school tie with the rest of the uniform. I told them that this was because the school uniform shop had none of those school ties left in stock until a week or two later.

All through that summer that had gone by, I still had the same sexual problems and I kept looking at pictures of topless and semi-naked women but my conscience was already bothering me though I could do nothing about it as it was beyond my control.

Starting school in September / October went okay but not brilliant. Around Halloween, I called up to my friend Peter on Quinns Road and that night we went out for nuts and apples, and we dressed up as coal men like I did in Halloween 1984. We put soot on our faces and carried around these big black bags to collect our nuts and apples. We obviously went to see the bonfire in Foxes Grove.

The next morning, I noticed hair growing around my private parts which I kind of knew was pubic hair. I was ashamed but I could do nothing about it. Around this time, me and my friend Peter would go in his father's truck to where he lived in Rathfarnham, near HB. I think he had a pig farm. We used to go around different catering companies collecting pig slop and sometimes we would go to Ballyogdan and throw the rubbish into a waste dumping ground.

We used to do this roughly twice a month. Then the next big thing was Christmas 1986. I remember having to go up to the Shankill Barbecue Centre to buy a Christmas tree for my mother. I used to be fairly good at picking out the best Christmas tree there was there. I remember carrying home from the Barbecue Centre and the pine needles used to dig into my hands, so every five or ten minutes I used to have to take a rest as my hands were sore. I did not realise that I should have been wearing a pair of gloves, but eventually I got the tree home to my mother and she was delighted with it.

I remember going out to Superquinn in Bray with my father to pick out a snooker table. He chose a five by two and a half foot snooker table. I said I wanted a bigger one, like six by three. But he said that I wouldn't have the room for it as my bedroom wasn't big enough. We got the snooker table delivered and hid it in the back shed so that my younger sister and brother would not find out about it because they still believed in Santa Claus. So on Christmas morning, I got my brand new snooker table and I was delighted with it as I loved snooker at that time. It wasn't until a few months later that I realised that the snooker table was of poor quality as the cushions were made out of some material for insulated windows and they fell apart one or two months later.

I remember a couple of days before Christmas and my friend Ian said to me, 'See you next year.' I thought that this was very funny. Then in

January 1987, I remember one day the weather was very cold and I knew that it was going to snow that day, and it did. The snow actually lasted at least one week at a minimum. I remember some of the water pipes in the house froze from the cold and some of the water in the taps – perhaps cold or hot – because they were frozen.

I remember during that cold snap walking by Shanganagh stream near the woods where I live today, and it was a full of slushy snow and I realised how cold it was at that time. Then after a week or so, the temperature rose and snow melted away and I went back to school.

The next big thing was my birthday on February 12th 1987. I was 13. I think I got money for my birthday from my relatives and my parents.

My brother Graham was born on March 14th 1987 in St. Sebastian's Hospital, County Dublin. I did not go into see him in hospital as I was left to do most of the washing up and other things, while my dad and sister went into see my mother and baby brother.

I don't remember too much about my baby brother when he was brought home other than the fact that he was like any other new-born baby.

In later '87 I remember getting tonsillitis. I had to go to my GP in Ballybrack Village for antibiotics to clear it, which worked. When I was staying at home at the same time minding the house and helping my mother look after my baby brother, I missed roughly two weeks from school. Then when I was going up to the shops with my ma's shopping trolley I saw my school principal and a guy I knew at school in a car who was calling down to my mother. My principal jumped to the conclusion that I was mitching from school, but I wasn't and when I went back to school, he didn't believe me.

I don't remember much of the school term. Then I got my holidays in early June 1987. At this time I started to make a serious effort to change my immoral lifestyle. I think every second week or so, I would have a bath and start afresh on that Sunday evening, not to masturbate any more by sheer willpower alone. Normally I would last no longer than about three days and then I had to give into my feelings or temptation, and I was back to square one.

The next big thing I remember was late July 1987, when an old enemy of mine Michael beat up my seven year old brother Alan. My brother told me what had happened to him, so I told him that I would get Michael and his friends for doing that.

I found one of Michael's friends Jason, who I kind of beat up. I said to him, 'Tell Michael and the rest of those guys that they are dead as well.'

Then Michael and his friends started hanging around where I lived and I think they called at my front door to find if I was in the house. My mother must have said, 'No.'

One day I said to Michael, I will fight you on the 1st of August as it's the beginning of the new month. Well he didn't really understand what I was talking about. Eventually, he and groups of other lads would hang around where I lived for hours and I got sick of this. So I think it was around 31st of July, or the 1st of August 1987, I went up to Quinns Road football pitch and we started to fight, but for the first time I noticed when I was punching him, my fist would go into his flesh and it was like hitting blubber. I began to realise that this was not making any impact on him whatsoever. Then I also began to realise that this guy must have been at least three or four stone heavier than me and when he was hitting me, I could really feel the blows as I was a lot slimmer than him. Then eventually I said that I had had enough.

After that, it must have gone on for months. He must have told every single person that I know and didn't know that he had beat the crap out of me, and was boasting about this to everybody as though he was a heavy-weight boxing champion. Not even a newspaper or a TV ad or the internet today could spread this information as fast as he did, because when I went back to school in September 1987, one of my friends Brian said to me, 'Did Michael beat up you up in a fight?' I said nothing about this. Then I realised that he had been bragging about this to everybody.

Even if it had been the other way around and I had beaten him up, at the most I would have told one or two people and said nothing else, because it wasn't really worth talking about.

I remember that there was a song out at the time by a group called Morris Minor and the Majors, called Stutter Rap. They made fun of a Beastie Boys song called No Sleep till Brooklyn. I thought that this was a brilliant song and so did many of my friends.

Starting that year in September 1987, most of my school friends and I would crack jokes about each other and slag each other about our appearances, where we came from, but I really enjoyed this and so did all my friends as we did not take school seriously and we were a bunch of dossers without a care in the world.

I used to call up to my friend Ronan in Foxes Grove. Then in Halloween 1987, we went to see the bonfire which was across the road and lit some fireworks. I noticed one of my friends' sister who was very good looking. She used to have long blonde hair, and I used to call with Ronan to her house and Ronan would ask to see her brother and I used to like this because she used to tell us to wait at the door and we would be talking to her and enjoyed this because I was attracted to her but I said nothing and she didn't know.

The next big thing was Christmas 1987. I must have got money from my mother as a present. I still had the same sexual problems that I had since puberty at the age of twelve. My conscience was still driving me mad but I could still do nothing about it.

Back in school in January in 1988 I don't remember anything unusual. School went on as before. I can't remember much about my 14th birthday on February 12th 1988. My dad bought me a birthday cake in Blakes in Stillorgan which I thought was great. I really enjoyed it.

Around that time I used to call up to my friend Ronan to play snooker. He had a small four by two snooker table in his attic. I really enjoyed this as in our conversations we used to talk about The Beatles, about their songs and how great the Sgt. Pepper's album was.

I remember George Harrison released the Cloud Nine album in November 1987. The first song was I Got My Mind Set On You. Then he released the second single in early January 1988 called When We Was Fab. I remember talking to Ronan about how great this single was and how good the video was as well.

Around March my da was doing TV aerial jobs. He used to bring my uncle Michael with him. But he didn't like this because he had to pay my uncle.

So he decided to get me instead.

I told him I didn't want to go because I had made other arrangements to see my friend Ronan which I had already done the day before.

But my da didn't care. So I had to go whether I liked it or not.

I remember going to the TV aerial shop in Bray near the River Dargle.

I remember waiting in the car for ages for him to come out of the shop. When he came out with aerial parts we went down to Kilpedder in Co. Wicklow I think.

The weather was dull and dreary and cold. I remember standing on the roof of the house even though I was scared of heights. My da I think knew this but didn't' give a damn.

He would be shouting to turn the aerial this way and the other way. He had no manners and was always rude and never said thanks but he was always like that anyway.

Then when we finished we went to New Vale in Shankill.

I kind of knew the family in that bungalow as the lady's sons used to be in St. Anne's School.

The lady there kind of recognised me again - as usual I was standing on the roof turning the TV aerial this way and that and again my da was shouting abuse at me.

I remember the lady was complaining about the reception on the TV set as the picture quality was poor and she was right. I actually saw it for myself but I don't even know I got down there to see it for myself.

As the old saying goes the customer is always right. Eventually she was happy and we left.

Then we went home it was dark by now. We got to the back lane of our house but our house was several houses down the lane.

So my da untied the ladder and steel poles from the rack of the car.

I carried a few poles down the lane on my shoulders. I put them against the back wall of our garden.

I waited a while for my da who I assumed would come down the lane with the other poles but he never did.

I decided to put the poles that were against the wall into our back garden where I neatly put them in the corner of our house. Then I decided to go up the lane to see where my father was.

As I was going up the lane I met him coming down and he said, where were you, and I said I thought you were coming down the lane with the other poles.

Suddenly out of nowhere he hit me a punch in the stomach and slapped me in the face.

It was the punch that did the damage. I never felt anything like it before.

I couldn't breathe. I thought I was going to die. I could not stand up straight - the pain was that bad.

It must have taken at least ten minutes, maybe more, until I could stand up straight but not properly.

Years later I found out that I was winded.

I then remember making a pot of tea and pouring it out for my da. Then I broke down crying. I don't think he said sorry - there is a very slight possibility that he might have.

But my da never apologised to anyone no matter what he did as he had no conscience whatsoever.

I never told my ma until years later.

That night I was afraid to go to sleep in case I died from internal injuries as my stomach was very painful.

By the morning most of the pain had gone.

I can actually remember some of the songs that were out around that time - one was by Eighth Wonder the song I'm Not Scared. I used to love the video to this as Patsy Kensit was the lead singer and I thought she was beautiful. I thought she was a natural blonde.

It wouldn't be for over 20 years or more that I found out she wasn't.

In those days I thought that any woman that had blonde hair was really a blonde even if it was dyed as I was still innocent enough or stupid.

I remember Pink Cadillac by Natalie Cole which I thought was a brilliant song. Although I had no idea at the time that it was written by Bruce Springsteen.

Then in April I remember helping my da building 'his' shed as he called it, even though I did most of the work.

One day I told him several times that I wanted to go to the bathroom and that I would be back in a couple of minutes.

When I got back he said where the hell were you and I told him I had to go to the bathroom.

He grabbed a piece of 2" by 4" and went to hit me with it and I could see him grinding his teeth together. Then he just held back from doing it.

Then another day or it might have been the same day he said something to me but I did not hear what so he said: are you deaf or something? I said no.

Then I was going to be smart with him by saying the same thing back about what had happened to me when I wanted go to the bathroom. But I thought I better not or he will kill me.

I remember around this time my da would buy British tabloid daily papers. I will not mention the name of that newspaper - it hasn't been in circulation in Ireland for many years.

The women in these newspapers were beautiful. I remember one woman who was naked but the photo of her was taken at her side and she had the most beautiful legs I had ever seen. She was gorgeous.

The caption was Legs 11. I had never heard of this phrase before but I now know it is related to darts.

There were many other beautiful glamour models. I know I shouldn't say this but I would masturbate looking at these beautiful women. I'm not trying to condone such behaviour and I never will.

What I did was wrong and my conscience still bothers me to this day - that is probably the main reason that I'm so ill now.

Most of these British tabloids are gone, well in Ireland anyway.

But most of the damage is done now and it is too late.

I have no problem with full-grown men looking at these filthy photos but the problem is that many schoolboys, including myself, saw all of these images too and will be forever tarnished. Some teenage boys have no problem looking at these images and that is their choice. Only God can judge, not me.

By early June 1988 I got my summer holidays. I remember going down to Gorey, Co. Wexford, with my two brothers and sister and of course my mother.

We stayed for the Bank Holiday weekend. I remember my auntie Bridget saying to me one day that I looked like an old man. I never forgot that and shortly after that I decided to make probably the most important decision of my life.

When I got back home I was going to make the biggest effort to mend my ways. I planned to take up cycling for most of the summer holidays and I know I shouldn't say this I was going to cut down on the number of times I would masturbate during the week and eventually give it up altogether.

Start praying and give up watching TV and looking at newspapers and magazines because of the immoral content and filth forever until I died.

This would require a super human effort - all or nothing. I did not know it but it would lead to my eventual downfall and rapidly declining health, which is declining every day including now and tomorrow until my early premature death shortly from now. That is why I'm trying to write this book so that you will understand why I'm the way I am and why every-thing went so horribly wrong and that no other person shall ever suffer like me and die.

I just got a flash back: I remember cycling down to Wicklow Town sometime in June. I was trying to rekindle the feeling when I had got cycling with my father in June 1985. Well to get back to the story, the gear shifter or the thing where the bicycle chain goes got in the spokes of the wheel and got mangled up.

I had to get off the bike and walk around with it until eventually I found a shop - I'm not sure what kinda shop, I don't think it was a bicycle shop but I asked the person in the shop could he fix it and he said yeah.

I was delighted when he fixed it. I of course paid - I'm not exactly sure how much, no more than ten pounds. I'm not sure if he gave me a receipt or invoice.

I would always carry money on me in case of emergencies like.

That was all of the money I had saved from Christmas and my birthdays.

Well after I went home and thought nothing of it. Then a week or two later I got a bill in the post from that shop saying I did not pay for the repair.

I was annoyed at this because it was totally untrue.

So the next day I cycled down to Wicklow to the shop and told him I had already paid and that he should check his records properly; in fact it might have been a woman instead, well they believed me and that was the end of that.

I remember starting to write a diary on when I took up cycling beginning I think on June 21st or June the 22nd 1988. Which I threw out in the bin later in early October.

I remember cycling late in the evening. I must have left the house at around 9pm that evening because it was the longest day of the year - it was still very bright out and I must have got back at around 10.30pm.

I did this for a couple of evenings each day recording the amount of miles I cycled.

Then I began cycling in the afternoons at around 2.30pm or 3pm. I remember seeing my woodwork teacher Mr Dutton standing at the roadside on the hard shoulder of the dual carriageway over the Dargle River. I don't know what he was doing there to this day. I don't think he was waiting for anyone to pick him up. I never asked him.

I think I put my hand up to him.

I began by cycling down to Newtown Mount Kennedy and back and some days down to Wicklow Town and back.

I really was enjoying doing this. This was like the good old days.

One day in early July I got a puncture. I had no puncture repair kit or bicycle pump.

For some bizarre reason at that time I would deliberately do this - I'm not exactly sure why.

I think it had something to do with my new crusade to change my life forever.

I remember walking for several miles all the way through Little Bray and into Shankill and back home but it didn't bother me in the slightest.

For most of July I did this. I think I had one rest day.

Then in late July I remember cycling through Newtownmountkennedy and I saw two teenage girls and I heard one of the girls paying me a compliment. I think he's gorgeous or something. I know you are thinking 'he really thinks a lot of himself' and you're probably right. But that's what she said and it wasn't in my imagination either.

I said nothing but of course I enjoyed the compliment - these sorts of compliment would gradually become less and less as time went by.

I remember around this time that Michael Jackson was on his Bad tour. I think he did two concerts in Pairc Ui Chaoimh in Cork.

But I did not go of course because I had no tickets.

I think my auntie Anne and my cousin Jacqueline went to those concerts, not exactly to the same and they did not know each other.

I think in early August I got my hair cut because I had let it grow very long.

In St. Fintans Park were my auntie Patty lived I remember my ma and I and some of my brothers went into visit her at that time.

When I got my hair cut my da said I looked like Steve Davis - that was a very big compliment from my da.

Beginning sometime in August I started cycling further to Arklow.

These trips would take up most of the day because I started my journey very late in the day.

So sometimes I would not get back till half seven or eight, then I would have my tea - mainly tomato sandwich or snack crisps and a few Rich Tea biscuits.

Late in August I got a puncture outside of Arklow on the way home. I got a puncture which was a serious problem. So I walked for a couple of miles and called into a bungalow and asked could I leave my bicycle there and the man said yes I said I will come back tomorrow to collect it. I remember my hands were freezing from the cold as it had been raining heavily for most of the day.

I heated my hands near his boiler and then left.

Then I remember thumbing for a lift - these two women pulled over and asked me where I was going. I said Shankill. They said they could give me a lift to Wicklow Town and there might be a bus there that I could get to Shankill. I said okay.

These women appeared to be very religious when I was talking to them. Then when I was getting out of the car they gave me religious pamphlets which were pictures of our Lord. I thought they were Jehovah Witnesses.

But it wasn't till a couple of years later that I realised they weren't and that they were Roman Catholic like myself.

Well when I got to Wicklow I went to the Garda station and asked where I could get the bus to Shankill. They said the last bus would be leaving within a few minutes and they told me where to get to it.

I made the bus with a minute or two to spare. I hadn't got enough money on me and the driver said that's okay - I gave every penny I had.

He dropped me off on the Dublin Road in Shankill. I got home and told my mother that I was playing with Peter in Quinns and had left my bike there and she believed me.

I think I threw the pamphlets with the pictures of our Lord in the bin in the mistaken belief that this was from Jehovah witnesses - I know I shouldn't say this rubbish.

I have always regretted doing that till this day. Sorry God.

The next day I had to go down to Arklow for my bicycle. So I waited for the bus in Shankill beside St. Anne's church on the Dublin Road. I seemed to be waiting forever but eventually the bus came.

I got to Arklow and walked to the house where I had left my bicycle.

I said thanks to the man. As I had no puncture repair kit or pump for that matter I walked with my bicycle and thumbed for a lift as well.

A man pulled up and asked where I was going. I said Shankill and he said I'll give you a lift to Wicklow Town.

When I got talking to him I said I will give you money for petrol if you give me a lift to Shankill and he said how much have you got. All I had was five pounds so I gave it to him and he said I will give you a lift to Bray Dart station. I said okay.

When I got there I said thanks.

When I was in the Dart station I had to try and persuade the man who checks the tickets to let me on the Dart with the bicycle. I said I was only going as far as Shankill and he said okay then.

I recognised his face as I had been there many times before. I have not seen that man for, it must be, over 20 years or more. He must have retired.

But eventually I got home and told my ma the same story as the last time, that I was in my friend's, Peter's, and got my bicycle back - she believed me.

This would be the last time ever that I would cycle as far as Arklow.

In the last two weeks of August late in the evening after cycling I would jog up and down the long football fields of Shanganagh Cliffs to make myself extra fit.

In August also I was beginning to unwind my looking at topless women for what I thought was for good.

I remember seeing Maria Whittaker and Karen Brennan together naked in The News of the World newspaper - they were gorgeous.

I also remember seeing Diane Willoughby but she was not naked but wearing a lovely dress in an Irish Sunday Paper - she was beautiful - also that was earlier in the month.

I'm not trying to make excuses for myself but these women don't seem to realise what sort of an effect they have on men and especially teenage boys.

I know they are trying to make a living like anybody else.

But in my case my conscience was driving me mad and still is to this day.

It is probably the biggest reason why I am so ill at the moment and getting worse every day towards my eventual death.

Religious and moral beliefs have always played a pivotal role in my life even at the age of eight or nine.

But at least then I had not gone through puberty and I was in great health and I had absolutely no interest in girls of my age or women until puberty or the catastrophe.

By about August 27th or 28th I gave up looking at topless women in the newspapers.

I know I shouldn't say that I would never masturbate again until I died from natural causes.

I think I started school on 5th of September - my 3rd year.

I remember my da giving me a lift and I accidently knocked the radio off because it was precariously wired to the front console or whatever you call it.

I could see the anger in my da's face. I think I said to him it's just an accident. I thought he was going to kill me.

When I got out of the car I met my friend Peter from Quinns Road. I told him what had happened to me when I cycled down to Arklow.

He joked: if you had brains you would be dangerous.

I still kept cycling after I got home from school but the days were closing in fast and by the end of the month it was pitch black dark by the time I got home and my bicycle was literally falling apart because it could not handle all the exercise I was getting out of it.

Every evening I would spend ages repairing it.

During September I started praying more each day; gradually the amount of time I was praying was going into hours, also I was worrying a lot because my conscience (from all of my dark past). I just wanted God to forgive me.

One evening I remember I threatened to kill myself by cutting my wrist with a sharp kitchen knife in front of a picture of the Sacred Heart because I was still getting erections and I wanted it to stop.

I know now that was totally wrong what I did but I was so upset at the time that I did not realise it was wrong.

But I refrained from killing myself.

By early October my bicycle was a complete wreck. I had to give up cycling and I threw out my diary of all the places I had cycled to and how many miles I did.

The last thing I remember watching on television was some of the 1988 Seoul Olympic Games.

After that I never watched TV again for moral and religious reasons so that I would never never see naked or topless women again.

At this time I began to live in a world of my own.

I started praying more and more in front of religious pictures in the house and I thought nobody saw me.

But my mother did and so did my sister. I did not find out about this until many years later.

I could hardly make it to school on my bicycle because it was in bits; the back wheel would come loose and the tyres would rub on the back forks. I even had a spanner with me to try and keep it on the road.

I was also praying more and more at school. I thought nobody saw me. But as I said it wasn't until many years later that I found they did.

I would be praying in front of religious pictures of Our Lady and the Sacred Heart also in school.

After each class was over.

The praying started to get more and more out of control.

I'd be praying in the bath but I would never look at my body for moral reasons; even when brushing my teeth I would also do the same; it must have taken half an hour or more to brush my teeth.

Then I could not stop washing my hands in case of germs. They have a name for it: OCD.

But I had never heard of it at the time.

When I was in my bedroom I would pray sometimes till 2am or 2.30am in the morning and get up at 7am and still be late for school; sometimes I would not get there till nearly 10am.

This went on into November; then one day the Career Guidance Teacher asked me what was wrong.

I broke down crying and said I let God down, my family down and my country down. I don't think she really knew what I was talking about.

Then about a week later I think my name was called on the intercom; it said will Paul Byrne go down to the Principal's Office.

I thought to myself that's unusual, maybe I'm in some kind of trouble.

So I went down and I saw my mother there. I said to her what are you doing here.

She said there is a taxi waiting outside; I said where am I going? I thought maybe I'm getting a lift home.

But when I got into the car my mother said something about St. Gregory's.

I started to get worried because everybody local knew of this place as a mad house.

When I was being driven, the driver got a little confused and he took us to some school with a similar name. I said that's got to be the place with some relief but when my mother asked someone there, they said it was the wrong place.

Now I started to get worried; they were taking me to St. Gregory's Hospital.

When I got to reception I was begging my mother not to sign me in. I said I will change my ways. But she signed me in anyway.

I was brought down to St. Ludwig's Ward - St. Anne's I think.

I thought that they were going to put me in straight jacket or give me an injection to calm me down but to my relief they did neither.

I was taken into a room where there were beds.

I became friends with a lad from Co Wexford not far from where my mother was from. I think he was the same age as me. His name was Cormac.

That evening the doctor checked my heartbeat and pulse and few other things.

Then one of the nurses - I think her name was Toni - asked me to give a urine sample. Which I had never done before. I was afraid that they might find sperm in my sample.

But they didn't. Thank God.

I never said any of these things to her so she was totally unaware.

I almost forgot I literally came into hospital with the shirt on my back. When I came into hospital all I was wearing was my school uniform and a light bomber jacket until my mother came in with a change of clothes on either Saturday or Sunday.

I remember when I came back into hospital again in the following year that one of the former patients was slagging me that I was wearing my school uniform; she did not seem to understand my mitigating circumstances and I said nothing.

I only realised many years later when I was a patient of St. Bernard's Hospital, Dublin, that nearly all the same nurses that I saw there were the same ones.

I had no idea that they must have been on a six-month rota system where they were transferred from St. Bernard's to St. Gregory's. I reckoned they must have been there from July 1st 1988 to December 31st 1988 and then back to St. Bernard's.

Toni said to me: your fingers are very long. I took no notice of this comment and then she said do you play the guitar? I said no I wish I did.

Then she said how do you keep them so clean?

I did not tell her that I had stopped biting fingernails when I started getting very religious. I let them grow naturally.

She never knew any of these things.

The first night I stayed in hospital I could not sleep. I was tossing and turning and the nurse came in and said if you don't go to sleep I will have to give you a sleeping tablet.

So I pretended to be asleep by keeping my eyes closed and staying as still as possible and it worked.

I had fooled her and I did the same thing every night until I was discharged. I never slept a wink in the whole time I was there - that was the longest time I had gone without sleep.

It's very easy to fool the nurses because they are not good at their job; in fact they are terrible to say the least.

The reason why I did this was that I did not want to take any sleeping tablets for strict religious reasons.

But those six nights of insomnia would be nothing compared to what would happen to me several months later.

I later found in my medical records that they said I slept fine every night which is a load of absolute rubbish. I'm telling you now I did not sleep a wink for those six nights I will put my hand on a bible and stand before God on judgement day and he will validate my true story.

The nurses are totally and utterly negligent and incompetent, ignorant, stupid and arrogant.

This view of mine will never change until I am dead shortly. When you begin to read you will certainly understand everything that I tell you because it is the absolute truth.

I remember one day one of the staff asked, did I want to go bowling? I said I had no money because I had not even got a penny on me as I was always broke.

She said all you need is one pound. I said I haven't got any money. I think she thought I was a miser.

I remember when I first arrived I was planning my escape but I soon realised I had very few options as I had not even got my bus fare home and I had no other place to run to. I thought about running up into the Dublin or Wicklow mountains but I gave up on that idea because the weather at the time was very cold.

Some time during the weekend, either Saturday or Sunday, Toni asked Cormac and me: did we want to go for a walk to Blackrock; we said yes.

I remember the weather was dull and very cold. I wore no jacket for my bizarre religious reasons although they did not know that.

I spent all that time shivering from the cold. I remember when we got to Blackrock Toni asked me did I want to go and buy a bag of chips. I said no; she kept persisting; I still said no; then she gave in.

The reason I did this was because of my orthodox Roman Catholic view not to eat processed foods and also to watch my weight but she did not know any of this because I said nothing.

I only found out many years later that in my medical records they wrote all this stuff about my appearance and personal hygiene.

Every evening or day a nurse would come in and - I did not know it then - but these were the most caring and best nurses that there were to be in St. Gregory's because from then on they never gave a damn how you were.

I'm not exaggerating; I'm just stating a fact.

When any of the nurses asked how I was, I pretended everything was fine that there was absolutely nothing wrong with me and that it was all just one big misunderstanding and that I just wanted to go home as quickly as possible. I said that to every nurse that asked me that question.

They had no idea what was really wrong with me.

I was too embarrassed to tell them what was really wrong with me (because I was just a teenage boy). That my private parts were at me and that my conscience was driving me mad.

Because they would be laughing at me and my parents would find out.

So I kept my mouth shut.

There's a lot of things that doctors and nurses don't know about no matter how well they're trained or how many years of experience they have.

To be honest they haven't got a clue.

The day I got discharged was the 29th of November because my grand-mother had passed away.

I only wanted to leave the hospital for several hours but there was miscommunication with the doctors and my mother had to sign my discharge papers.

I don't remember too much of the funeral.

The next day after the funeral I started going back to Mass for the first time since early May 1986.

I started going twice every weekday and five times on a Sunday.

I remember in early December I woke and I had ejaculated sperm. I was very upset but I could do nothing about it as it had happened in my sleep. It was what they call 'a wet dream'.

My ma did not send me back to school until after the Christmas holidays.

I could not stop praying; it got worse and worse.

After they would close the church door, I would be praying outside it. This would happen even if it was raining.

Then I would go around to the side of the church where I would try and hide in the corner so nobody would see me.

But some people must have seen me because years later in my medical records it was mentioned. I found out but I did not know it at the time as I was living in my own world.

I went to Midnight Mass on Christmas 1988 - my first time which I really enjoyed.

Christmas Day went off okay.

I think on St. Stephen's Day my ma invited the neighbour across the road for dinner for some reason. I got a bit jealous about how well he was being treated. Shortly afterwards I said sorry to God as this was un-Chris-tian of me and that I was a bit of a hypocrite because I was meant be so religious in the first place.

Then back to school in January 1989. Things had not changed. I was still as religious as ever.

In fact things started to get worse; I decided to try my best not to use the toilet at all in school because I wanted to be as perfect as possible and for religious purity reasons.

I tried my best not go to the toilet until I got home from school but no matter how hard I tried I could not hold it in any longer and I wet myself in school and sometimes cycling home.

Of course the boys in school would laugh at me but I didn't care because I was living in my own world.

I only found out years later that the teachers mentioned it to my ma which I discovered in my medical records.

This time I went to Naomh Theodores and then straight into St. Gregory's Hospital, Co. Dublin.

I did not bring too much baggage with me as I thought I would not be staying long.

This would become a more and more regular pattern; when the nurse checked my belongings she said in a 'smart Alec' remark: is that all.

I said yes because I thought I would not be staying long.

These sorts of smart comments would become more and more common from most, if not all, of the nurses that I would see throughout my stay in hospital.

I started to act more and more normal to give the impression that everything was okay.

So I could get released from hospital and it worked a treat.

It never seemed to occur to the nurses or doctors that I was only pretending to be wonderful and that everything was okay and that I was cured.

With all their years of experience (including the 'great' Dr. Lorcan O'Driscoll Mulhern) no-one knew that I was making complete fools of them, which wouldn't be difficult to say the least as they are a bunch of idiots, very well paid ones at that.

My birthday was on the 12th of February. I was 15 years of age.

I went home that day for my birthday, and then I came back in the evening.

When I was down in the coffee bar with some of the other patients, I was drinking some sort of orange juice when we were all told to go up to the ward on the intercom.

I think I was complaining about as I said we had at least another half hour at least.

When I got in the ward the staff nurse said there is somebody in the room to see you. I started to get worried. I thought I was in some sort of trouble.

When I came into the room it was dark; then the other patients in the room, who I hadn't seen, started singing 'happy birthday to you, happy to you'.

I was taken totally by surprise as I had totally forgotten about my birthday.

It remains to this day the only time I really felt touched by what had been done.

It really is the fondest memory I had of the place; mostly everything else was terrible.

I remember then we had to bring leftovers from the party into the kitchen where the Alzheimer's patients mostly were.

I did not realise until many years later how ill these patients were; they had to wear nappies and they couldn't even remember their names.

The staff nurse who came with me did not realise it was my birthday and when there was no one around she gave me a kiss on the cheek.

I remember something days earlier but did not cope at the time because I was a little stupid; when I would be sitting down watching TV she would pay me compliments. I thought she was only being nice to me but then one of the patients Clare said to her: you're only saying that because you like him.

Then I just realised why she kissed me on the cheek.

I'm not complaining because she is beautiful and I liked her a lot and still do to this day.

I remember something else: the only time anybody in St. Gregory's ever took blood samples from me properly without nearly killing me was when I went in on my first admission in November 1988 and the nurse there wasn't an employee of St. Gregory's as such because she was one of the nurses from St. Bernard's Hospital, Dublin. Because I recognised her later in St. Bernard's when I was admitted there in 1994.

One day in February 1989 when I was in St. Gregory's, the nurse there was supposed to be taking my blood but I could tell she was not really bothered by her attitude.

The syringe tore into my arm and it was sore. I know it was an accident but she never said sorry or anything as if nothing had happened. I think she might have said oops.

This was typical of every time from then on. Not one nurse or doctor for that matter in St. Gregory's could take blood properly; they are all like butchers and I'm not the only one with that complaint because the last time I was there in St. Gregory's in 2006 the same incompetent bastards were there because one of the female patients there said the same thing as me.

She said she regularly donated blood and never experienced anything like it.

Well back to February 1989 the only good thing was I made a few temporary friends.

One was Killian who really wasn't much of a friend at all.

I met some lovely friends including Alison, Audrey, Laura, Dorothy and Belinda. All of these young ladies were very good looking - this would be the closest I would have to a boy girl relationship sort of thing.

In the beginning of March I had hurt my arm by jumping over some chairs in the games room in the St. Ludwig's Ward, St. Anne's in St. Gregory's Hospital on my last day there.

I could not sleep a wink for three whole nights so I decided to go up to St. Sebastian's A&E, Co. Dublin.

I remember getting up there at around 8pm because I looked at the clock there - that's how I remember.

I had the mistaken belief that an emergency 24hr hospital was meant to be open 24hrs a day because I was only a stupid teenager and I lived in a world were nurses and doctors looked after their patients and did an amazing job but I was quickly brought to reality not for the first time and it wouldn't the last either.

So I must have waited half an hour or hour and this nurse came down and said don't you know we're busy - it's not the fact that she said it, it's the way she said it. It was her attitude – you'd think she was the only person in the entire world that had to do a bit of work.

She had no compassion and was extremely rude - this should have been my first wake-up call.

I remember she had an American accent. I was going to be smart and say why don't you go back to the United States if that's your attitude but I kept my mouth shut as usual.

I was told to come the next day.

Maybe I'm wrong but I thought nurses and doctors were meant to look after the sick and ill.

Or else I'm thinking of some other occupation.

I thought this was just a minor bad experience but I was sadly wrong - it would get a lot worse, a hell of a lot worse, in days to come.

Never in my life again will I have any respect whatsoever for doctors or nurses - they are the laziest, rudest most ignorant, vindictive, spiteful, cruel, uncaring lot of fucking scumbags.

Up until then, despite all the bad I had got from that shower of bastards,

I still held them up on a pedestal like saints or gods.

But they are nothing more than the devil in disguise and I'm not exaggerating in the slightest as you will read and learn from my horrific experiences at the hands of these monsters as it just gets worse and worse.

Everything I tell is the absolute truth - I will put my hand on a bible on judgement day when I meet my maker.

In March I started attending York Road in Dun Laoghaire. I think the place is full of apartments now.

I met a new friend from Ballybrack called Richard.

There was also Belinda who I just mentioned; she was also from Ballybrack.

Some of the other girls were there too including a beautiful young lady called Diane, also from Ballybrack, whom I have never seen since 1989. I don't know whatever happened to her.

I began to have a little bit of a relationship with Belinda.

This would be the closest thing I had to a girlfriend in my life.

We would chat and have a laugh.

One day in York Road we were sending each other messages in wrapped-up paper.

She kept giving me more and more compliments. I tried to reciprocate but I had not enough words left in the pile.

I could see the disappointment in her reaction and could well understand.

I wish now I had made more of an effort with Belinda but as usual I missed the boat again.

After finishing attending York Road in April sometimes Richard would call up to me on his bicycle and sometimes I would call up to him.

At the same time I was back at school preparing for my Inter Cert.

By this time I was starting to cut down on the amount of praying and so on.

This would have dire consequences for me later which would be the end of my life forever.

One day coming home from school I went in to prayer in St. Anne's Church, Shankill, Co. Dublin.

When I was outside I started praying near the corner of the church when suddenly I was falsely accused of peeing in the corner by the Parish Priest's Housekeeper. I said nothing and went to get my bicycle when another person appeared and she told her that I was in the corner of the church which was totally false. I said nothing as usual and the woman believed her story; as I was cycling away I was crying because all I was doing was praying.

This was totally untrue; even if I wanted to pee I would not pee in a corner of a Roman Catholic Church no matter how much I wanted to go. I wouldn't even dare do on church grounds because that is totally and utterly morally wrong.

But this was not the first time I had been falsely accused of something and, as you read this, it definitely wouldn't the last; in fact it would get a lot more sinister.

All of my life I have had to put up with this.

By late May I was starting to get aroused more and more because I had not masturbated by now for 9 months and I knew I could not hold out much longer.

I would have big erections at night but I managed not to masturbate yet.

I had a feeling that I just might get the Inter Cert exams out of the way.

I did my Inter Cert exams. I think I finished on the 22nd of June. I thought I did reasonably okay.

I knew my days were numbered. I managed to hold out till the end of the month, then all hell broke loose.

What I'm about to tell you next is disgusting and horrifying and explicit and something from which I have never recovered. I don't have much longer left to live so that's why I'm telling you this true story about me so that this may never happen to anyone else.

Please God.

So on the night of June 30th 1989 my ordeal began.

Starting that night I started getting aroused and masturbating all the time because I had gone ten months without doing this to my body. I'm not trying to make excuses, I'm just telling the truth.

What I did and what I have done since is utterly and morally wrong and is a grievous sin against God and man.

So on the night of the 30th June I started getting aroused and masturbating all the time during the night, sometimes rubbing my penis against the mattress as if I was making love to a woman.

I checked on the internet and a website said men sometimes do this when they are masturbating. I did not know this until tonight when I was doing research.

I thought I was a total pervert but that does not make it right.

Well as I said I did this all night and I never got a wink of sleep.

This happened the next night and the next night and so on.

Obviously I was getting more and more exhausted and my quality of life was deteriorating rapidly.

Also for the first time in my life my hair began to start to fall out - the same night I started doing these disgusting things.

After masturbating my scalp would get hot and itchy and my hair would darken in colour and get greasy; this had never happened before in my life but it would last forever, including now. I can't do a thing about it; for the last 25 and half years I have been trying to tell the doctors about it but I have been too embarrassed until the last two months.

Every time before that all they kept saying was that it was male pattern baldness or generic baldness or that I was imagining things or I had illusions about losing my hair.

I kept telling them they were wrong. I know what's really causing it but they never listened and my GP keeps saying the same thing but maybe in a few weeks I will tell the real reason. All this time I have been losing my hair but none of the so-called doctors would listen to me.

I did try for the first time in 1994 in St. Bernard's Hospital to find out what was really wrong with me; in mid-late July I tried to explain to Dr. Caitlin O'Larkin Devlin.

She judged me and tried suggesting I was looking for attention or something else on my mind.

But years later I discovered in my medical records what she said, which I have with me now today in her exact words:

He believes that his hair is falling out because he is playing with himself sexually but has only told one or two members of our team about this and as such it may be unwise to mention it.

Many thanks for facilitating an early appointment.

Yours sincerely,
Signed
Dr. Caitlin O'Larkin Devlin

Dr. Caitlin O'Larkin Devlin, MB, MRCPsych,
Registrar to Professor Liam O'Mullen Davis

I never told her that; she came to her own conclusion. I was trying to tell her what was really wrong with me but she did not believe me.

I have tried to trace her and I think I know where she is working if you can call it working - what a joke.

She should be assessed herself.

I'm so exhausted at the moment I can hardly type this down but I'll give it a try:

Registration:
Name:
Address:
Sex: Female
Registration Date:
Registration Type:
Primary Qualification:
Description:
University:
Conferral date:

So back to where I began after about a week of absolutely no sleep whatsoever. By the second week of July, I was totally burnt out. My eyes were paining me and my hair was greasy and dirty and falling out.

I thought about going to my GP Dr O'Dempsey O'Driscoll but I was trying to work out the pros and cons.

I said I will ask him for sleeping tablets but already knew they would not be strong enough for my severe condition and he might start asking questions about how it started.

I was afraid he might find out the truth and that it would be extremely embarrassing and humiliating and that he might send me to Naomh Theodores and they might ask more embarrassing questions and then I would be sent to St. Gregory's Hospital.

They would put me on sleeping tablets and I knew even then that they wouldn't work and after another couple of weeks without sleep they would realise this is serious and if they found out what was really causing it I would be in serious trouble because of the embarrassing circumstances and my parents would find out.

So I decided to stick it out. I gradually got tired and more tired and more and more hair began to fall out; my eyes were also starting to pain me a lot more. I hated any sunshine as my eyes were sensitive to light and I stopped combing my hair because large amounts would come out in the comb so I said I better start trying to reserve as much hair as possible.

I also noticed my nose starting getting little dimples in it - normally I only saw this in very old people.

My complexion also began to take a turn for the worse; normally I had a very clear complexion but now my face especially began to show signs of ageing as more blotches appeared on my skin and I also noticed dark shadows appearing under my eyes. I knew this was from exhaustion but I could do nothing about this and I told no one.

Not even my mother.

As I was the eldest in the family my mother was too busy looking after the rest of the family and so did not take much notice of me because she was too busy.

I rarely went outdoors as I began to realise my grotesque appearance and that I looked like an old man even though I was 15 years of age.

Also my interest in women came back again with a vengeance so I was always looking at the glamour models in the newspapers.

I also found some of my da's old magazines.

I began school in September 1989 - 5th year. I had gone over two months without a wink of sleep by now. I was a physical wreck. I was totally burnt out.

I had no interest in school whatsoever because I was finished. I told no one about this.

As you can guess I officially finished school on the 22nd of June 1989, the day I finished my Inter Cert.

I don't think I ever did any homework or study. I didn't want to be there anymore.

Some days, especially during physics or chemistry, I would just put my head into my arms because I was totally exhausted.

Also around this time my interest in the Third Reich came back also with a vengeance.

After reading several books about these things, I began to think about Gotterdammerung, or the end of the world for those of you who don't what I'm talking about.

How Hitler's world had ended in total destruction. I began to notice the similarity to my situation in which my whole life would end in catastrophe.

I used to get these Third Reich books in the library; that was about the only time I really went out anywhere because I was really shockingly aware of my drastic appearance.

Then one day I read about a soldier in the German army - I can't remember his name but in his biography he said he ran away from home because of his abusive father and he joined the German army in 1914 at the age of 16.

This gave me an idea - my 16th birthday was only a couple of months away by coincidence.

So I decided to come up with a plan.

I was trying to figure out how I could create the same situation for myself.

So I decided I would be real evil like a real Nazi.

So I decided to be abusive towards my sister on purpose so eventually I would get kicked out of the family home.

By early November I had not slept a wink for months so my health was getting worse day by day.

One evening when my parents went to the shop I threatened and pushed my sister against the fridge. I didn't hurt her but that doesn't make it right.

Then I remember saying to her if you tell ma or da it will be your word against mine and they won't believe you.

When they got back she told them what had happened; she told them what I said and they did believe her so I was wrong and I got my come-uppance, which I deserved.

These threats went on for the next couple of months, maybe two or three times a week. I was now in total self-destruct mode where there was no turning back from oblivion.

I also remember just before Christmas looking at a Third Reich books in the library when I saw two of my neighbours Elaine and Amanda; they were a few years younger than me. I remember them laughing at my appearance - that must have been how ugly I was. But they had no idea what kinda of hell I was going through; and sure, how would they know as God would only know what you are reading; they didn't know anything about wretched health.

One thing I have learnt from all of my experiences: never really judge a person unless you know exactly what they have been through.

I don't remember much about Christmas 1989 - only by now I had gone without a wink of sleep for six months. I was finished but I still carried on, now giving the impression that somehow I could carry on my total path of self-destruction.

I got a telescope from my da for Christmas; it was worth no more than 5.99 pounds; it was absolute rubbish; you could see better through an empty toilet roll. I'm not exaggerating.

Years later my brother would slag this and say how crap it was and I totally agree with him.

By January 1990 things were getting even worse
I had now gone for over six months without a wink of sleep.
I remember one day in January I went into my sister's room and she started screaming get out. I didn't even touch her.
Then there was a knock at the door; it was Larry O who used to sell clothes mainly on the HP.
He looked at me like I was some kind of mass murderer; he heard the screaming and had assumed that I was somehow behind it and that I had tried to do some sort of harm to my sister, which was totally false as I've said before and I will again. I was blamed for something that I hadn't done.
The reason why I was in her room was to teach her a lesson that she had no business going into my bedroom anytime she felt like, so I said how do like me being in your bedroom?
I never screamed when she was in my bedroom but that didn't seem to matter.

At around this time Naomh Theodores Community Mental Health Service in Co. Dublin began to receive information about my aggressive behaviour at home.
I only found this out years later in my medical records but I kinda had an idea they knew.
But with Naomh Theodores, they only hear what they want to hear.

By February 1990 I had gone for seven months without a wink of sleep.

Then one day my da drove me into St. Gregory's Hospital under duress with my arm twisted behind my back.
He signed me in.
When I got into St. Anne's St. Ludwig's Ward you could feel the hatred, especially from female members of staff.
You could cut the atmosphere with a knife.
I knew straight away they knew about my abusive and threatening behaviour towards my sister and mother.
But if you are meant to be a good nurse or doctor you are not supposed to show any dislike towards any patient whether or not you like that individual; whether he's a saint or a murderer, you are supposed to treat them exactly the same because you are supposed to be a professional healthcare provider, nurse or doctor.

But as you already know, they let their true feelings about you show plain and clear.

It was like I was some sort of woman beater and that I was the lowest form of scum on the Earth.

It was like being a mass rapist or child molester thrown into a maximum security prison full of hard criminals who were going to kick the shit out of you.

I didn't want to be there in the first place.

I'm 100% sure the whole week I was there not one nurse or doctor asked how I was.

In fact I saw very few, if any, of the so-called staff except for one student nurse who every day that she was supposed to be working, if you can call it work, picked on me for the slightest misdemeanour.

You could feel the hatred from her. I knew exactly how she felt about me: that I was a woman beater and an ugly bastard and it's not in my imagination and I'm not exaggerating.

I never told anybody that I could not sleep a wink and to be honest nobody gave a damn.

As I have said before not one nurse or doctor asked me how I was.

By now I had not slept a single wink for over seven months and one week.

I was burnt out and my hair looked like I had not washed it for ten years.

They probably assumed I had poor personal hygiene or to be really honest they didn't give a shit.

Now I'm about to write something a little controversial and it's up to you whether to believe it or not.

I am now 100% sure I was discriminated against on grounds of my gender or as the feminists would call sex discrimination. If a woman or 16-year-old girl who was aggressive towards a brother or father, a lot more aggressive and maybe even in a severe case attacked someone in the family with a knife. Then, the father or husband would admit the teenage girl or woman into the hospital and she would have been treated a lot better than me and that wouldn't be difficult.

Because none of the nurses, male or female, would have judged her because they would have said she's only a woman and that she couldn't hurt her husband or son because they are stronger because they are male.

The worst they would have said is we will have to give her something to control your aggression towards members of your family so they would put her on medication and monitor her.

If a 16-year-old girl had her hair falling out and all of her hair was dirty and greasy and looked like it hadn't been washed for ten years and never looked as if it had been combed, the nurse would have said to that patient what is wrong with your appearance because she is female and it's much more to a young woman.

Also if she hadn't slept a wink for nearly seven and a half months, my God how did you get dark circles and bags under your not even 16 years of age eyes, you poor dear.

Can you tell me what is wrong with you? Because you really look terrible and that teenage girl might start telling that she couldn't sleep a wink, since July 1st 1989 in my case, and that her hair starting falling out and it was all greasy and itchy then that nurse would say this sounds very serious I will make sure to mention it to the doctors and your team.

But in my case nobody gave a shit.

When I was in hospital in February 1990 that student nurse pestered me every day that I was there.

I knew she hated my guts but there was nothing I could do about it.

I just wanted to get out of there as quickly as possible.

I never actually saw any nurse check to see whether I was awake or asleep.

I never slept a wink the whole week I was there. But nobody cared.

Because I wanted to get out of there as quickly as possible.

I tried to pretend everything was okay.

I celebrated my 16th birthday there if you can call it that.

They managed to give me a birthday cake which they did for any other patient who happened to be in that hospital on their birthday at the time.

I was absolutely miserable. I never enjoyed any birthdays since because I'm very ill.

I just wish it would be all over and that I can get out of this horrible nightmare of a world forever because basically I'm just living a kind of existence.

Sometimes when we were meant to come to the ward in the evening or it could have been sometime in the morning or afternoon, I would say to the some of the other patients that we won't go up.

I know I shouldn't have really been doing that but I just wanted to get out of there as quickly as possible so they would use this as an excuse to discharge me and it worked.

This happened most of the week that I was there.

I remember on several occasions, this particular student nurse would come down to the coffee shop and say to me you're behind this, as if none of the other patients had minds of their own or that I had brainwashed them, which is a load of rubbish.

I said I don't what you're talking about. She said you do alright.

Sometimes the staff nurse Martin would be with her but he kept his mouth closed.

Also I remember some of the patients would be making jokes about my appearance.

I knew how I looked and I knew what the cause was but they didn't.

One of the females said in front of me I don't know who's the ugliest Paul, Michael or Martin.

There was a patient there called Margot; I knew she hated my guts and I knew she thought I was very ugly.

I don't mean this in a bad way but she wasn't a million dollars herself if you know what I mean.

But I kept my mouth closed. She would come into the bedroom that I shared with Killian and Pat.

But Killian was mostly there with me.

She would give me the cold shoulder treatment as if it really mattered to me.

Where she would only be talking to Killian.

As I've said before I did not sleep a wink I was there.

Although according to my so-called medical records I slept like a baby. I really wish that were true. I probably wouldn't be writing this today.

As I've said before no nurse came in to check whether I was asleep or awake because I would have my eyes open for hours and never saw any nurses come in and to be honest they didn't give a damn.

Then the day I was being discharged Dr. Lorcan O'Driscoll Mulhern the so-called consultant psychiatrist said in front of me while present with some of the staff.

There is absolutely nothing wrong with him.

I kept my mouth shut again.

I didn't tell about my chronic insomnia or that my hair was falling out or that my eyes were paining or that I was totally exhausted or the sexual problems that I had.

But to be honest he didn't give a damn.

I remember leaving the hospital that day but my da would not come into the hospital to collect me so I sneaked out, not that they noticed I was gone.

Then I met my da at the entrance where he gave me a lift home.

So when I got home I was already starting to plan how I would run away from home and also I would get expelled from school.

This would be the total finale to my complete downfall where I would go into oblivion.

So I started getting more aggressive towards my sister.

It must have been around early March 1990.

When I got expelled from school.

I remember in the earlier months that this group of about three lads I think used to hang around near the drinking water tap; because of my illness I used to get very thirsty; my chronic insomnia and exhaustion had me worn out and tired so my mouth was always dry.

There were steps going up to the classrooms behind the drama stage near the water tap. When I went over to get some water these lads would make remarks or jokes each time I went over; it was to do with my appearance, how run down and worn out I was.

Then one day there was some young lad in the school yard who I thought was laughing at me so I punched him. I knew this would get me expelled as I had no illusions as to my fate.

Well I tried my best not to get spotted by him as he was with the school principal and both of them were waiting to see who had hit him.

After a short while I decided I had no choice but to go in. Then he pointed me out to the principal.

So they had me; I didn't deny it.

I remember seeing Mrs Muller, the same teacher who asked me what was wrong in November 1988. This time she had a look of disgust on her face and she had wiped her hands clean of me forever.

What I did to that young man was wrong and I do not condone such behaviour.

But Mrs Muller had no idea the hell I was going through and she should not have judged; but she did and this would not be the last time this would happen to me.

When I got expelled my ma and everyone else, at school especially, were making me out to be some sort of heartless cruel monster and maybe that's what I wanted them to think.

I wanted an excuse to run away from home, just as I'd been reading about a lot concerning the third Reich.

I wanted to be like a real Nazi.

As I said I was getting more abusive toward my sisters mostly with threats that I was going to hit her in these arguments my mother would come between us.

My mother told me recently that I actually hit my sister and maybe that is true but that was the exception rather than rule as it was mostly psychological but that does not make it right.

My ma said that I gave my sister a black eye that's a load of rubbish my sister never had a black eye well if she did it healed very fast because I saw no bruising whatsoever and she didn't use make up to cover it up.

I always came out far worse in the end and maybe I deserved it.

Then one day my ma could not take my abusive behaviour and she was going to go down Gorey to get away; then my da arrived; I kinda knew he might do something.

When he knocked at the door, I let him in knowing full well he was going to do something to me.

The moment I opened the door, without a chance for me to react, he punched me in the eye and twisted my arm behind my back.

I knew I had a bad black eye. I also knew it would never heal properly because of my poor health and that.

I remember my sister came in and was laughing at me after my da finished me off. I always came off far worse in everything that I did and have done since, whether I deserved it or not. Even later you'll read that when I would be minding my own business I would always be falsely accused of something that I never did.

I was so run down. I was exactly right however and to this day I have a big blue vein under my left eye which I'm very conscious about.

I would have to go into hospital to get cosmetic surgery, hopefully to get rid of it.

I remember around June 1991 my da was messing around with some optical equipment for his amateur camera hobby; when he looked through this lens he remarked: you have a big vein under your eye and laughed about it.

It did not seem to occur to him that it came from the black eye that he gave me the previous year.

I had thought to myself that maybe I was being too conscious about my appearance and that maybe it wasn't as bad as I thought.

But my da validated my concern.

When it happened I was 16.

I knew this would have consequences in later life trying to get a girl-friend and forming a relationship.

Till this day I never had a girlfriend or any relationship whatsoever and I know I never will as I'm a physical wreck, to add to my sense of total gloom and doom.

I would have loved to have gotten married and had children but I was never given the chance.

Till this very day it remains a very sad chapter in my life and I get jealous of other people of similar age or friends that I went to school with who are married with children.

I know I'm jealous but it really hurts me.

I know a lot of it is my fault but it happened when I was teenager and I was too young at the time to fully understand what would happen, especially in the years from 1988 to 1991, between 14 and a half years of age to my 17th birthday.

Those years were the most critical of my life. But, as you can see, the whole medical profession, doctors and nurses, failed me drastically; if they had done their job properly maybe things may have been different and, as you read more and more of this tale, it just gets worse.

From 1991 onwards I would try everything to get better but nobody would help or give a damn and only judge me but they know nothing about me or give a damn. I have been fighting all my life since to get help but to no avail and I never will.

Back to March 1990 when I decided to run away on the day I got beaten up by my da, which I deserved; so I climbed out the back window and ran away.

I got the bus into Dublin city centre but I stopped off at St. Gregory's Hospital to see if could get five pounds off Killian.

But I should have known it was a waste of time.

When I came into the ward that same rude nosey vindictive nurse was still there and her attitude was still the same.

I was trying to show Killian all the rubber stamps that I got from the An Oige youth hostels in 1985.

Every time I tried to show him, that nosey irritable nurse was there asking me to show what I had. I kept saying no and after several times she left us alone.

I was going to say to her: when I was a patient here you didn't seem to care much about me, why all the sudden interest? But I didn't.

Then I asked Killian could he give me five pounds as I was homeless and planning to go into Dublin city centre, which was all true.

He said he had no money but I knew he was probably lying; even if he had 50 pounds on him he wouldn't have given me a penny.

So that was the end of our so -called friendship.

I got the bus into Dublin city centre.

I remember I would walk around for miles mainly at night time.

I was too cold and frightened to lie on the pavement and anyway I still couldn't sleep.

Eventually I got into a hostel for teenage boys, a hostel near Ballsbridge in Dublin.

Although I used to lie on a mattress in the rooms upstairs, I still could not sleep a wink.

I must have had my black eye because some of the lads said they'd give me another shiner to add to that if I didn't shut up.

I remember there was a pool table which was the only thing I loved and enjoyed there.

There was a guy from Stillorgan there called Gary who shared the same interest as me in the Third Reich.

Most of the staff there were very lazy; most of them were paid by the EHB but gave the impression they were doing everything out of the goodness of their hearts and that we should all be grateful.

Most of the food we got was donated but one day I noticed all of the breakfast cereals were out of date by a considerable margin and so were many of the other foodstuffs; about the only thing that was fresh was the milk.

I remember me and a few other lads made a joke about Pakis robbing at the airport.

Then that ignorant old one that worked there started giving out about it in her narrow opinion.

She told me quite categorically that I was talking bullshit.

The only one that was talking bullshit was her.

I apologised, which I always regretted later.

She always brought her dog with her called Buttons.

I remember one of the lads who I didn't like got really cheeky and told me to get upstairs; I hit him a punch but he didn't even get a black eye, not that it makes it right.

Then I ran away again; I really just wanted to get out of that place.

Then of course I was homeless again but it was really my own fault.

I remember one evening I got talking to a man. I told him I was homeless.

He said you can stay in my place tonight. I said that's great. Thanks.

I remember he had a brother with a gammy leg. He was lying in a bed across the room.

I was sitting in a chair with a blanket over me.

That same man I was talking to was sitting beside me in another chair.

After a while he was trying to touch my private parts.

I said what are you doing? He said shush. Don't wake my brother.

He tried this several times during the night.

I managed to keep him at bay.

Early that morning I left and never saw him again.

I never asked his name and I do not remember what part of Dublin he lived in till this day.

I can remember what he looked like.

He had a greyish moustache and thick greying hair.

He must have been in his late fifties.

That was 25 years ago. If he's still alive, he must be in his mid-eighties.

I know I was stupid. But I was 16 and still naive at that age.

I of course would never do anything like that again.

As you try to learn from your mistakes most of the time.

Another day I was sitting on one of the benches on O'Connell.

Which I did quite often at the time. As there was nothing else to do.

I got talking to this boy.

Who told me he was homeless but only for a day or so.

So I told him I could get him a place in a hostel.

He told me he was 12 years of age. I was just four years older than him.

So when it got dark, I said we better get moving.

Somehow I got lost after walking for miles.

I asked these two young men: did they know a short cut to The Simon Community? As I was tired and lost.

They said they did. So the 12 year old boy and I started following them.

After a while I began to notice that these two young men had drink on them and were getting more aggressive.

I reckoned they were in their late teens or early twenties.

Then one of the young men started accusing me of taking advantage of that 12 year old boy.

I said what are talking about? I'm trying to get a place in a hostel and maybe myself.

Then he picked up a rock and threatened to kill me with it.

I got down on my knees and begged him not to do it.

He eventually put down the rock and we eventually made it. To The Simon Community.

When I got there, they took in the 12 year old boy.

But did not take me in because I gave them my real name because I'm always honest and stupid till this very day with everything I say.

They gave the two young men sandwiches and that was the end of that.

So after that I was still homeless. I nearly got killed and was accused of very serious allegations that were totally untrue.

But this was not the first and last time this would happen to me.

Strangely enough the next person I bumped into was one of the young men. Who falsely accused me of something I never did.

He was real friendly this time and just said hello.

That was the last I ever saw any of these young men.

I cannot remember what he looked like till this day and never will.

I remember another day when I was still homeless.

Somebody told me that you get money from the social welfare, if you were homeless, in a place called Charles Street.

Which was famous then but now is closed for many years. I think they opened a place on Gardiner Street instead.

I also remember that there were very few people with babies or prams or buggies in Dublin at this time, which I found quite odd.

But I did realise when the next census was done in April 1991.

That the birth rate had been falling since 1980.

I always thought when I was young that the birth rate remained constant throughout many decades and never changed.

But I was naive and stupid again. Now I know better.

Back to Charles Street.

I remember I had to sit down for many hours as there were so many people trying to get help.

Eventually I saw one of the welfare officers - I can't remember whether it was a man or a woman.

I told him or her my situation: that I had been homeless for a while. And

I was given a cheque for ten punts or pounds in the old money. Which was the custom then.

So I went to cash the cheque.

I remember going into this shop; there was a woman behind the counter and another talking to her; she was not a customer; they both worked in the shop.

I got the impression that the woman behind the counter was probably her own business.

I said to her and the other: could they cash this cheque for ten punts?

But both women ignored me as if I wasn't there.

I said several more times can I cash this cheque? They totally ignored me as if I wasn't there again.

Both women were extremely rude. I even got a large 0.5-litre can of 7UP.

But they still ignored me. So I gave up.

I was getting used to being treated like a leper.

I decided I had no choice but to cash the cheque in the bank.

I can't remember whether it was AIB or Bank of Ireland. It was one of the biggest banks in the country.

I think it was on Dame Street or near it.

I went into the bank and the manager came up to me. Can I help you sir? I said I'd got a cheque from the social welfare for ten punts with the name of this bank on it.

He said come with me sir.

So I went over and I got the cheque cashed and he said is there anything more sir? I said no thanks very much and left with the ten punts on me.

It was the only time I was ever treated well when I was homeless or in the whole of my life.

This was the only time I was not treated like a leper and I was shown compassion and decency.

I can't remember what the manager looked like.

He may be still alive. If he is and he reads about this.

Many thanks again for treating like a human being. God bless you. I will be eternally grateful now and forever.

I never went back to that shop again after the way I was treated.

I made sure to boycott it. But today I can't remember what street in Dublin it's in.

Maybe a night or two later I decided to make an attempt to stay in my auntie's in Deansgrange.

It was very late. I walked into Pearse Street Garda station.

I told the female Garda at the glass opening in the wall - I don't know the proper name for them.

That I was homeless and would it be possible to give a lift to my auntie's in Deansgrange?

She said they were not operating a taxi service; lie on the bench over there if you want to.

I was going to say thanks very much for the compassion and Christian charity but I kept my mouth shut as usual.

After lying on the bench for a few minutes I left.

I then got a taxi in Dublin city centre.

I told the driver to head to Deansgrange.

I think he charged six punts. It was early in the morning when I knocked at the door.

My auntie, cousin and uncle were in bed; my auntie looked through her bedroom window and saw me. She then came down and let me in.

I told her I was homeless. I knew she had a spare room.

So I stayed there for the night.

I still could not sleep a wink but at least I had shelter.

Although I was in the spare room all I did most nights was tossing and turning. But I never told my auntie that.

I remember being burnt out and exhausted. I hated having to go outside the house.

I remember when the sunlight came in the window, it would hurt my tired and weary eyes.

I also remember there were always shortages of food because my auntie never did much shopping, not because she was mean. But I think she might have been lazy or not to bothered to buy much shopping.

I remember sometimes there was no milk some mornings. So I had to go and buy some.

I did not like doing this because I felt absolutely terrible due to my bad health with all its problems.

Eventually I made my way up to Abbey Stores where my other auntie worked.

She barely said anything to me, as if I was just another customer.

I remember eating mostly Rice Crispies as this seemed to be the only breakfast cereal in the house.

The only house work I really did was the washing up. Mostly in the mornings. As my aunt, uncle and cousin were at work.

***

I remember every morning there was a huge pile of washing up as it was all from the previous night.

As nobody saw me doing this, my auntie got the impression that I did absolutely nothing in the house.

Mostly on the weekend my auntie would make dinner. Which I enjoyed as it was the only proper meal that I got.

I remember it was getting close to Easter.

One day my da called and we went out drinking. I think I remember drinking six pints of Guinness in an old pub in Dun Laoghaire with my da's friend Christy.

When I got back my auntie was unhappy. She said she thought something had happened to me.

I gave her all the Easter Eggs I had and went up to bed.

I can remember vividly that night. I could not sleep a wink again.

The drink in my stomach made me feel bloated and sick. I kept tossing and turning.

My da called the next morning to see did I want to go out again.

I said no way I feel terrible. I hadn't a hangover; it was just my chronic insomnia and the drink in my stomach that night that made me feel woeful.

I did not go out the door that day; I stayed in.

I began by now to realise that my auntie was getting fed up of me being there.

I remember one night my auntie's husband, my uncle, was drunk.

He called me an ugly bastard and an IRA supporter as he had been in the British Army when he was younger.

I tried to hold back the tears and not to let it get me too upset.

I know that when a person is drunk they will tell you with honesty how they think of you.

A month or two ago I was talking to my brother. He said the most honest people are drunks and children.

As they will tell you exactly what they think of you and I agree 100%.

I remember I told my auntie that I would try and get back into school.

So I went out to St. Brendan's CBS in Woodbrook Bray.

So I got talking to the Principal, Brother O'Mulligan. He said to me have you been making threats to that pupil you punched in the eye.

I said what are you talking about? I haven't been anywhere near this school since I got expelled.

Then the pupil was called down to his office with me there. He said one of the lads in school told me that I was going to come and beat him up.

I said that's a load of rubbish. I haven't being talking to anyone here in school. I left.

So then came Sean who I knew because he was in my class and was a bit of a miser.

He told Brother O'Mulligan that he had been making the threats against that pupil I had punched and that I had nothing to do with.

As usual again I was being blamed for something I had nothing to do with.

As I've said before many times it was not the first or the last time I would be falsely accused of something I never did.

Brother O'Mulligan believed me. Then he said if I take you back you won't embarrass me?

I said no.

After coming from St. Brendan's CBS I began to realise that I would never be able to come back.

As it dawned on me that my auntie would be getting rid of me soon and that I would homeless again.

I told her that the school would take me back and I could go to school from her place.

But she was dismissive and not impressed.

I forgot to mention my old friend Declan, a school friend of mine who introduced me to this service which was out in Bray, I think on Quinnsborough Road. I think it was a youth service.

It is long gone now. I remember Declan - I think he told me he was from Walkinstown.

I got talking one day and I told him I was homeless but living in my auntie's at the moment.

***

He told me that the EHB would pay auntie for keeping me there. I said that sounds good.

I said I'd tell my auntie about it. So I did and I told him where she lived and he told me what day he was calling out.

So I told my auntie everything and she said alright.

So the day Declan was calling I kept walking up and down St. Fintans

Park waiting for him to arrive with anticipation.

Eventually he came and I introduced him to my auntie.

He told her how the scheme worked and then he left.

After he left my auntie said she was not interested because she would be taxed too much.

So that was the end of that scheme for me.

I would say there was some truth in that but I also knew my auntie wanted to get rid as soon as possible.

I remember in the evenings when I was staying with my auntie, I would get very hungry as there was never enough food and also I still had a great appetite because I had a high metabolism rate at that age.

Some evenings I would buy sweets and bars of chocolate to feed my appetite.

I would walk around the Fintans housing estate but I made sure not to litter the place with my wrappings.

So I threw them in the bin in my auntie's.

It never occurred to me at the time that she would use this as another excuse to throw me out.

I could have hid the sweet wrappers at the bottom of the bin but I didn't think I needed to do that at the time as I had nothing to hide.

I remember once my mother came to visit me with my sister and maybe my baby bother.

My mother I think gave me about twenty punts or maybe more.

I knew I would need this shortly as I knew my auntie would throw me out anytime soon and I would be homeless in Dublin city centre.

I also tried to give the impression that I still hated my sister by threatening her again and it worked.

I remember my mother mentioning to me that my auntie told her best friend and others that I was some monster and didn't deserve any sympathy.

Her friend who lives in Shankill not too far from my mother said to my auntie I was just as bad as my father. The way he used to treat my mother.

My auntie's friend is in no way to judge anyone. She would want to look closer to home herself.

As the old saying goes those in green houses should not throw stones.

A day or two later my mother came back and this time my auntie threw me out which I had been expecting for a while.

Her excuses were that I had gotten from my ma and gave her none and that I had been buying sweets and not sharing with her and my uncle and cousin because she saw sweet wrappings in the bin.

A few months later I was talking to my ma about this.

I said she was just using those excuses to get rid of me.

I could feel tension in the house just after a week I was there and I knew my days were numbered.

I mentioned the sweets incident especially. It was like she was 10 year old schoolchild in the playground saying you got sweets and never shared them with me. So I'm not talking to you any more - extremely childish.

I know I could, but even I had my limits.

It must have been now mid or late April. I was still homeless and hadn't slept a wink now for nearly ten whole months.

I remember it must have been late April 1990. The weather was great; it had been an extremely dry winter and spring was dry and sunny.

I got on the diesel train in Bray to go to Gorey were my auntie Bridgit was on 1 Arklow Road; the house was demolished a few years ago and no longer exists.

I tried not to have to pay my train ticket to Gorey as I needed as much money as possible to get by.

I remember seeing two Irish Rail men checking for tickets. I kept going into the next train carriage to avoid them.

But eventually I began to run out of train carriages to go to. I was near the end of the train near where the driver's cabin was.

So I hid in the toilet hoping they would ignore me. But it didn't work for long.

They began knocking at the toilet door. I think I said I'll be out soon.

Hoping they would give up. But they didn't; eventually I had to get out of the toilet.

They asked me if I was alright since I was in there so long. I said I'm fine.

They did not know that I was pretending to be using the toilet in order to avoid them.

Then they asked me for my ticket. I pretended to be looking and then I said I can't find it. I must have lost it on the train.

So I said I'll try and look for it on the train. After going up and down the carriages I still could not find a ticket.

I said I just don't know where it is. They didn't believe me. Then one of the men said he'd have to call the Gards.

I thought they were bluffing. But they were serious. When the train stopped in Arklow.

The Gards were there. I told one of the Gards that I had lost my ticket and that I was going to Gorey.

I was told to pay for my ticket, which I reluctantly did and then I got back on and finished my journey.

I joked to one of the passengers about the delay at Arklow. I think he knew I was to blame and said nothing.

I know the ticket collectors do their job. But it was over the top. You'd think I had committed a major war crime or something. If I needed the Gards to help me, I know I would be waiting along time like when I was at Pearse Street Garda Station six weeks earlier when I was told by that lovely compassionate female Garda: we're not operating a taxi, who cares if you are homeless.

But I should have been used to that by now.

I stayed with my auntie the weekend. After about a day I began to notice that my auntie didn't really want me there.

Which was unusual for her as she was hospitable. I think she heard from my mother or someone that I had been causing trouble at home and that I was aggressive too.

The three days I stayed, I bought my auntie cigarettes as she was a heavy smoker.

I went down to the ambassador supermarket near the railway bridge that you enter going into Gorey from Dublin.

The bridge is still there. But the supermarket is long gone.

I bought my auntie sweets like cigarettes, which were her favourites and I bought myself SuperSplit icepops which were much better back then than they are now because you got much more vanilla ice cream than you do now.

I still remember tossing and turning every night I was there. I did not sleep a wink.

I remember my uncle Tommy from America had come the previous year to retire and bought the house beside my auntie at 2 Arklow Road Gorey Co. Wexford.

I already knew from rumours over the years that he was a miser and he lived up to my expectations.

As I said, the weather was very good this 1990. It was extremely dry and I remember my uncle remarking about the colour of the grass, that it was no longer green but white from lack of rain, and he was right.

I remember maybe that day walking up Gorey Town and he was looking at different bottles of wine and kept moaning about the price. I knew the way he was talking that he was tight with money and I was right.

After, I think I stayed at my auntie Bridgit's for three nights including the weekend; she wanted rid of me.

So I told her I wanted to make a phone call to Declan in Bray.

Without asking me, she asked my uncle Tommy: could Paul use your phone to make a call?

I knew nothing of this until he came into her house and then started giving me a lecture on economics; it must have gone on for about ten minutes or more. I just stood there taking it in and as usual I kept my mouth shut.

I told him that I would have paid him for the call first and I would have given much more money than what the call would cost in the first place. So he would have made a tidy profit - even in his economics - which would make perfect sense.

But forget about it; I'll go up and make a phone call in the public phone box, which shortly I did and told Declan I would meet him tomorrow.

So when I was heading for the train station I walked up with my auntie Gertie.

I think she knew I was homeless but said nothing. She could have said you can stay in my house for a while if you want until you get your feet back on the ground.

But she said nothing. I was waiting a long time for the train and she knew I was unhappy after the way I was treated by Tommy and everybody else.

I had purchased a return when I was stopped by the Gards at Arklow on the way down.

So I did not need to worry about ticket collectors this time.

So eventually I got on the train. But this time there wasn't a ticket collector in sight for the whole journey back to Bray - just typical of my situation.

I actually remember a lad mooning as we got near Bray. I had actually never seen this before although I had seen it on TV.

It must have been near the end of April 1990.

I remember the next day I was talking to Declan about my situation and as the weather was good we went for a walk and had an ice cream.

I suggested to him that I should head up way into the Wicklow Mountains and live in the wild.

I had always wanted to do this since I was a kid and still do till today.

He said you've been watching too much Grisly Adams and that it wasn't practical and to forget about it.

So I did. I think I was homeless the next couple of days in Shankill.

I spent most of my time walking around and trying to hide in wooded areas and in a field, which is no longer since houses were built on it.

Although the weather was great, the nights were still cold as the sky was totally clear all night without cloud cover.

The air was filled with heavy dew. If you were lying somewhere for long you could feel the dampness.

I remember trying to stay one night in an old Primary School St. Anne's as I knew they had a good bench to lie on.

How the tables are turned in such a short time. Only five years earlier in 1985 I was on top of the world.

I was in perfect health. Niamh was trying everything to go out with me and now I had lost everything.

I had no girlfriend to speak of. I was homeless. I had aged rapidly. I had not slept a wink for ten months and I was losing large amounts of hair and it was all my fault. I had no one else but to blame but myself.

I can remember thinking it to myself when I climbed off the railings into the schoolyard. How everything had gone so horribly wrong for me.

I remember thinking of Niamh. That she was sleeping in her bed. Totally unaware of my predicament and if she had have known, she would have gloated and said: now you got what you deserve. How the mighty have fallen and, you know what, she would have been right.

After lying on one or more benches, I was cold and damp from the heavy dew and I thought if I stay until morning I could get caught - how embarrassing that would be.

So I climbed over the railings and had to keep walking up and down till morning; at this time of the year it would get light at around 5am or maybe a little earlier. I was always dying of thirst.

I remember calling to my mother's around 5am in the morning.

I had to keep knocking at the door.

Eventually she opened the bedroom window. I said: can I get a drink of water. She told me to get lost.

I said: that's all I want. But she wasn't letting me in.

I was really hurt by this.

It appeared to me that nobody cared whether I lived or died.

The only good that came out my chronic health situation and homelessness was that nobody cared on my mother's side of the family or my father's side.

If I had never been homeless, I would never have known this.

Now I know what it's like for people who are homeless or sleeping rough; you're treated like a leper in society.

I mentioned this recently to my mother - we have both reconciled our differences since long ago.

My mother has a saying: your friend is your pocket and, you know what, she's right.

It's still exactly the same today as it ever was and always will be, unfortunately.

I remember another day in Shankill. I decided I was going to stay in St. Anne's Church just to get some shelter.

I hid behind one of the religious statues until the church was closing. I thought nobody saw but one of the men saw and told me to leave.

I was very disappointed with this as I had spent so much time previously praying for hours on end and trying to do my best for God and it seemed it had all been for nothing.

This was really the only time in my life that I felt abandoned by God and, maybe for several months after, I kinda lost my faith.

All I wanted to do was lie on one of the church benches for a night and then leave in the morning.

I had no intention of stealing or anything else.

I would never do that, then or now, because that is totally and utterly morally wrong.

But what can you do? Only carry on.

There was a new building site just starting in Shankill called Castle Farm.

It is there till this day.

I walked in one day and asked if there were any jobs going and the foreman, Jimmy I think, said there was.

I said great. When can I start? I think he said tomorrow. I said that's fine.

This was my first job and my first lucky break.

I rang Declan to tell him I'd got a job; he was amazed; he said that's brilliant, well done.

So I started my first job the next day at 8am as a nipper.

I told Jimmy Wexford - his nick name since he was from Wexford, just by coincidence near Gorey.

I told him I had no address since I was still homeless but I would go for a bedsit as quickly as possible - he said that's fine.

I think I was staying in a hostel on Lord Edward Street in Dublin for a week or so; thanks to Declan's diplomacy with my old teenage hostel, the EHB was paying for me stay there.

It was actually not so bad.

I remember sharing with one of the guys from the old hostel; he was from Finglas, a year or two older than I was.

I can't remember his name but he wore glasses.

Even though I was now lying in a comfortable bed in this hostel I could not still sleep a wink.

I would leave and go to work in Shankill early in the morning, mainly on the No. 45 bus.

Then I was moved to another room.

Where I met a man from the North. He told he worked as a fireman and when I got talking to him he said he was protestant.

But he was very kind and polite. I was very surprised by this.

Then he told me he was going to the pub for a few pints and he asked me did I want to go.

I told him I had no money. He said that doesn't matter, I'll buy you a few pints.

So I went and he kept his word and we talked and laughed. I never saw him after; the next day he must have gone back to the North.

But this guy was genuine and a gentleman. I wish all other protestants in the North were like him. There would be no troubles to begin with.

But unfortunately that wasn't to be the case.

I remember being moved up to the top floor of the hostel on Lord Edward Street.

I was in for a shock as each 4-bed couple was mixed. This was the first time in my life then and now.

I remember sharing a cubicle with American ladies and a guy from Sweden.

I felt uncomfortable with women not just for myself but also them.

As trying to take of your clothes getting into bed without being seen was difficult.

That evening when I was talking, one of the American ladies said to me you don't like us because we are American. I said no.

But she was right. This woman should have been a psychiatrist. She was better than the psychiatrists I've ever seen. But that wouldn't be difficult.

I remember the same lady talking about the other man in the room, saying he was Swedish and that he was good looking.

I could not sleep a wink that night either. But I pretended to be asleep because the women were sleeping across from me.

I got up early that morning for work without making a sound so I would not disturb them.

I made sure to be first in the dining room for breakfast.

I remember the man working there, coming into the kitchen and the derogative comments because of my scruffy appearance due to my bad health and also my clothes were dirty from work.

I said to myself I'll I have to try and get a bedsit as soon as possible as did not like this man's attitude.

I remember going to use the toilets which were mixed and I was shocked that it was full of female hygiene products; I had never seen anything like it before and I felt very uncomfortable.

It showed how quickly moral values were declining at this stage in history.

But I could do nothing about it as I was burnt out and exhausted from chronic insomnia and I had to hold down a job.

So I went that morning to work and that day I think I asked for a sub to put towards my deposit for a bedsit.

Jimmy Wexford said that's fine. I said I'll pay it back when I get paid.

So I went back to the hostel to ask if I could use the phones to make calls to see a bedsit.

They said alright so I bought the newspaper and started looking through.

Eventually I found a place in North summer Street. I did not know where this was at the time but one of the women that worked there knew exactly where it was.

She gave me directions to the place. What really struck me about her was that she was American and knew Dublin like the back of her hand and she was relatively young.

So I eventually got there; I was few hours early for my appointment with the landlord.

So I went for a short walk and came back and there was a man waiting there for the same bedsit. I was a little upset because he said he was first; I said I was already there before and I just went for a short walk.

But he insisted he was first and that was that.

So when the landlord came, your man got first look at the bedsit but to my delight he did not like it and said he wasn't interested.

I was willing to take anything just to have a roof over my head and a place to call home and to have my own independence.

I took the place straight away and gave the landlord the deposit. He asked what did I do? I said I worked on a building site; he was happy with that.

It was like a match box; you had a bad a little wardrobe a little grid cooker with ring plates and a tiny fridge.

But that's all I wanted. It was cosy as I would say and the rent was only 14 punts a week at the time.

I was working a 55-hour week and coming home with a 101 punts so I could afford it.

But as it was a long way from work I spent a lot on public transport, nearly more than my weekly rent at the time.

But I didn't care. I went back to the old teenage hostel and one of the men who I hated told me to go down to the Seven Eleven shop and ask for a cardboard box so he could give me my household items for new bedsit.

I did not want to tell him that I did not want to do this because I was very aware of my ghastly appearance and did not want to bother anyone in a shop even for a spare cardboard box.

When I was going down to the shop, I was hoping I might find a spare cardboard box in a skip and by chance I did and it was clean.

So I brought it back and said nothing.

He gave me some steel wool and plastic scrubbers and a few other things and I obviously moved into my own bachelor pad for the first time.

Now I had a place I could call home. I had a lot of commuting to work every morning.

Sometimes I would get the Dart to Shankill or the bus, mostly No. 45 Bus I think at Burgh Quay.

I think I mostly left my bedsit at 6.30am or a little earlier, sometimes at 6.15am.

I remember sometimes Connolly Dart station would be open when I walked down, sometimes I had to wait 10 or 15 minutes until it opened.

Also I was a long way from the Dart station and even further to the bus stop at Burgh Quay but the long walk did not bother me at the time as the weather was still great that summer of 1990; in fact it was the second hottest summer ever recorded in Ireland in the 20th Century.

I even knew this at the time because of how hot and dry that summer was.

I started work at 8am in the morning and finished at 6pm.

Sometimes I might be 10 or 15 minutes late but it was not my fault as the Dart could not get any faster to Shankill Dart station from Connolly as it was the first Dart in the morning.

Also even getting an early bus sometimes, you'd be about ten minutes because of traffic and stops along the way.

Sometimes on the bus on the way to Shankill I would see my auntie Ann waiting at the bus stop across the road in Deansgrange but she never saw me on the bus.

She worked in Middle Abbey Street at the time.

Years later I told her about this.

As I said I worked as a nipper on the building Site in Castle Farm in Shankill.

I did the same work as most of the men. At the lunch breaks I went around the building site with my notebook asking what they needed in the shops.

I mostly bought rolls with many different toppings like veg and meat.

I think these rolls cost a punt in the old money. I also got biscuits and bars of chocolate and other stuff as well.

I also put the boiler on before 10.30am and at lunch at 1pm so everybody had a nice hot cup of tea.

I collected a small sum of money to buy milk and tea bags once a week and I made my contribution too.

I remember some days coming with at least two bags of shopping.

I became well known in Shankill Village that summer and autumn and into winter.

As I was the biggest daily shopper in the village.

I actually knew one of the women who worked in one of the shops; I never actually knew her name.

But I used to see her walking in Shankill since I lived there since 1980.

She was very good looking but I never said anything I think she might have been two or three years older than me.

After I finished work at Christmas 1990, I never saw this woman again. I do not know where she went to till this day.

I assumed she must be well married by now. As I've said, she was good looking and would have no problem finding a handsome man.

They gave me the nickname Lenny.

I remember some of the men on the building site used to say to me: you must be raking it in. I said are you joking, if anything I'm making a loss which actually was true. I worked it out that I was losing 1.50 to 3 punts per week but this did not bother me as it was a small sum.

I still could not sleep a wink at that time either despite the fact that I was working hard.

I was burnt out and exhausted everyday but I carried on regardless.

I never told any of the men that I was a chronic insomniac.

Some of the men would say to me: Lenny you'll sleep well tonight I said I wish.

Despite my exhaustion I actually began to enjoy work.

My mother always said as long as you're in a job you'll sleep.

Well not in my case because I worked very hard and a 55-hour week and occasionally a 70-hour week and I still could not sleep a wink so that will give you an indication how serious my illness really was and still is till this day and will be until I die, which is not too far away now.

When coming back from work in the evenings I had a terrible habit of wasting a lot of spare time by waiting for buses and letting them go by, even if they stopped for other people, even though the bus could take me straight into the city centre. I can't really explain why I did this.

I was either inferior or subhuman to most as I was a wreck of a person and looked an old man of 90 even though I was only 16 years of age; of course nobody knew how ill I really was and nobody cared.

Eventually I would into the city at 8pm or later at 8.30pm.

Then I had a long walk up to my bedsit.

I would buy food in one of two shops, one not far from the Five Lamps. I would buy cheese and bread or maybe some corned beef to make sandwiches and chocolate. I know my diet wasn't great but that's how I lived in those days.

I remember once walking up to my bedsit when some young lads started calling me a knacker because of my scruffy appearance and that my clothes were covered in dust and dirt.

I just tried to ignore them as I was quite used to being treated like dirt in my life and still am till this day.

I remember there were, I think, four other bedsits in the same house as me on North summer Street.

I got talking to one of the men near me on the upstairs; he was Irish-American.

His name I think was Michael McDonnell, I'm not 100% sure, especially about his Christian name, as it's a little blurry.

He worked part-time in a public library in Dublin.

We became good friends at the time.

I remember him posting a postcard with a picture of Maxi on it from

RTE; we were in stitches laughing about the postcard he had.

I remember another time I was singing The Beatles' When I'm Sixty-Four; he joined in as he knew the lyrics too.

I remember he walked down most of the way with me when I was getting the bus.

I remember his bedsit was a lot bigger than mine and he had a black and white TV.

I asked him how much rent he was paying; he said 16 punts; I said that's not bad.

He got a lot more for his money as his place was much bigger than mine.

So eventually May turned into June. I remember the weather that June was warm and dry but mostly cloudy.

An archaeologist was brought on to the building site to check obviously archaeological remains which was the law and I think still is.

I got talking to him one day and asked had he found anything? He said there are remains from monks who were around about a thousand years ago.

I asked had he heard of German archaeologist Heinrich Schliemann? He said yes.

I got talking about WW2; he said he served in the Irish army during the Emergency. I asked him what sort of rifles he used; he said Lee Enfield. I was impressed as I know they were very good rifles.

Also in June the World Cup fever started. It was the first time Ireland had ever qualified for the World Cup.

So there was a lot of excitement. Everywhere they played loads of soccer songs brought out that year especially.

I can still remember them: Put em under Pressure, We're all part of Jackie's army, Ireland Ireland Never Never Say No.

I remember calling to my house in mid or late June to watch the football with da.

As if nothing happened the previous year. I of course remember the famous penalty shoot-out with Romania which we won and got Ireland into the quarter finals of the World Cup.

I remember waiting for the bus that evening and everybody blowing their car horns in celebration of that great victory.

I remember Ireland lost the quarter final, I think to Italy who were one of the favourites as it was in Italy.

Ireland lost and in that game Ireland kept getting bad decisions from the ref; the commentators on RTE were saying the same thing.

I asked my da why the ref was doing it and his typical smart remark, which he often said before, was: Why don't you ask him? Being really rude and cheeky as usual but that was my da.

I remember seeing the final of the World Cup between Germany and Argentina.

As you can guess by now I wanted Germany to win and they did.

I remember either Ruud Gullit or Marco van Basten spitting at Rudi Voller.

Rudi Voller complained to the ref and got a yellow card for nothing.

It must have been days later. When the Irish team came home to literally a Victory Celebration in Dublin.

I deliberately stayed away from it as I was burnt out and exhausted.

I had no TV in my bedsit. I just had a radio. That was really my only communication with the outside world.

But I just loved to listen to oldie pop music from the 60s, 70s and 80s mostly, and that I always hated ads and still do till this day.

I remember waiting at the bus stop and an old friend from primary school got talking to me.

He said you've got a beard; I told him I was working on the building site on Castle Farm.

He told me he was on his summer holidays from secondary school.

I also saw him in May when I stated my friend Sean O'Carolan would be waiting to go to school in St. Thomas I think.

We both talked less than five years later when we met again at St. Gregory's Hospital, Co. Dublin.

Also one day waiting for the bus going into the city centre, there was this beautiful young lady maybe the same age or a year or two older than me.

She was beautiful. I think she was wearing a horse riding rig with lovely long riding boots.

She was unaware how I felt about her and she had absolutely no interest as I looked terrible due to my poor health and I was filthy with dust and muck on my clothes.

I have to admit till this day that I love women dressed in horse riding gear, especially with those riding boots.

The women just seem to look great.

Now it was August. Around mid or late August I got into a little accident.

Jimmy Wexford was giving out to me to hurry and get to the shops. So I took a short cut across the field. There were large planks hidden in the long grass with big steel nails pointing out of them.

I did not see the nails and I stood on one which went up my left foot.

It bled for a while and then it stopped. I said to myself I'll be fine now.

But one of the men told me that I could end up with gangrene.

I started thinking about it and I was getting more and more worried.

I had this image in my mind of my leg being amputated.

So eventually I said to Jimmy Wexford I think I better head to the hospital for a tetanus shot.

He said I'll give you a lift. So he drove me to St. Sebastian's Hospital.

He told me when I arrived there that the civil engineering company I was now working for - Liffey Developments - had done all the ground on that hospital not so long ago.

I knew he was telling the truth as it had only been renovated recently in the last couple of years.

So I went into A&E and told the nurse that I had stood on a nail.

She asked had I a medical card I said no. So I paid her 12.50 punts.

I must have been waiting about two hours or more but I did not mind waiting. Other patients were complaining about having to wait so long.

Eventually my name was called. The nurse there said, gee your clothes and footwear are very dirty, have you nowhere to wash them?

This nurse was living in a different world as we never even had toilets never mind somewhere to wash.

I just told her I am working on a building site and we don't have those facilities.

She gave me a tetanus shot and cleaned the heel of my foot and then I got the bus home to The Silver Tassie Pub.

My boss never paid for my medical expenses and I still had to go into work the next day even though I was limping.

Which lasted for at least another week and I remember going up the stairs to my bedsit and how painful my foot was.

Then of course the lads at work were making jokes about getting a syringe in the bum but I ignored them.

This is probably the only time in my life that any hospital actually helped me; other than this, over the last 27 years they have done absolutely nothing for me except make me worse, if that's possible, and treat me worse than an animal and have absolutely no compassion whatsoever.

I just remember yesterday that I heard a nurse on the radio years ago complaining about pay or something or maybe working hours.

A nurse's job isn't a vocation she said and, you know what, she's right.

It's not even a job. As they are lazy, rude, ignorant, incompetent, arrogant and don't give a damn whether you live or die as long as they get paid in the end, plain and simple.

I remember in mid-August 1990 getting my summer holidays, without pay I think. But I had enough to get by at the time.

I think I got two weeks summer holidays which was the norm at the time for anybody in Ireland working on a building site.

It may have changed as that was nearly 25 years ago.

I don't remember too much as I was run down and I looked terrible due to my chronic insomnia and all the other health problems I had, and still do.

I just remember going down the road to the corner and buying bread, milk, cheese, biscuits, choc ices and occasionally the newspaper.

I remember reading about Saddam Hussein's invasion of Kuwait and also there was a photograph of the cast members of new film being made called The Commitments.

I also remember doing washing which I did once nearly every week when I was living there in my bedsit in North summer Street.

I had to boil the kettle maybe a few times as I had no running hot water.

There was a sink outside on the landing where I did my washing by using washing-up liquid.

Which did the job.

There was a small clothes-line in the backyard where I got my washing dry,

I also had a bath once a week. There was a gas boiler and you had to put 50p into it so you got running hot water for a bath.

I had never seen anything like it before or since.

I was actually impressed by the ingenuity and still am.

I had to wash my hair in the sink but there was no running hot water either.

So I had to bring a kettle of boiling water down the stairs with me.

I don't know till this day how I never scalded myself. As you had to be very careful when pouring out boiling water.

The sink would be full of hair which I washed down so nobody else would be complaining.

In late August I went back to work after my holidays.

It was the same old routine but I didn't mind it.

It might of a week or two later, the Irish-American lost his job in the library and could not pay his rent anymore.

I was going to pay for it myself and even buy him food and not look for anything in return as it is the Christian thing to do.

But I was planning to leave this bedsit and move to a better one and also nearer Shankill.

He did not know this as I wanted to keep it quiet in case anything went wrong.

I knew I would need money for a deposit and so I decided I would need every penny I had.

Even till this day I feel bad about it as I should have done more to help him.

But it's too late now. After I moved to Dun Laoghaire I never saw this man again but a few years later, when I was in a bedsit in Dun Laoghaire in the late summer of 1993 I saw a man the spitting image of him when I was out walking at the back of the Peoples Park in Dun Laoghaire. I was going to say are you Michael McDonnel who used to live in North summer in 1990?

But I said nothing as I did not want to look an eejit if I was wrong and it would be embarrassing.

He said nothing to me either so maybe it was just a man that looked like him.

He had a beard with kinda scarf or bandana on his head.

I'm terrible at remembering faces and still am till this day.

If there was a crime or a robbery and I got a look at the criminal and Gards asked me what he looked like?

My description would be terrible. The Garda asking would say you're not much help to me.

I'd reply you're right, I can't even tell what I look like or even close family members.

I've always been like that since I was a kid.

By late August a new foreman arrived on the building site.

He was young, about 28 years of age and from south Dublin. Which was very unusual as nearly everybody that worked on building sites in those days all came from the country.

I think his name was Michael. I can't be certain of that as he never told me his name and I never asked.

His surname was definitely Murphy but I'm not exactly sure of his Christian name.

He told me he lived on the North Strand and I told him I lived in North summer Street.

Which were in the same area.

I remember we both got the Dart to Connolly Station and we walked a little and made our separate ways.

I remember early September because of the very dry summer. Whirls of dust would get blown by the wind and the dry would irritate your throat.

I ended up with tonsillitis. I began taking Lemsips for it. Which gradually worked.

But after a while it still had not gone away.

So I went to my old GP Dr O'Dempsey O'Driscoll in Shankill Village above the old Quinns Pharmacy.

I told him I had no medical card. He said that's alright.

He examined my throat. I told him I'd been taking Lemsip for a few days.

He said they've done the trick; keep taking and you should get better and he was right.

He charged me five punts for my visit.

After a week or so my tonsillitis had cleared up.

My new boss Michael also got tonsillitis at the same time as me. I said did you get it from the dust; he said yeah. I said so did I.

Then he asked what doctor I went to.

I said Dr O'Dempsey O'Driscoll, he's just in the village above the pharmacy and I told him his practising hours.

So he also went to him about his tonsillitis.

Also in early September I decided to make an effort to get back home with my mother.

I remember calling to her one day. There had been a big change in the weather.

The first rains began to fall. There were actually thunder storms.

I tried for a few hours to convince my mother to take me back but it didn't work.

I left the house in torrential rain crying all the way to get the bus in Shankill Village.

When I was walking on the main Dublin Road into Shankill my old foreman Jimmy Wexford was driving his Toyota pickup truck.

He stopped and asked did I need a lift. I said yeah. He said do you want come out to Harold's Cross where I live and you can get the bus from there into the city centre. I said that's fine.

When I got to his house, he invited me in. He said would you like to stay for dinner? I said that'll great thanks.

There was a man there who stayed with him. He worked on the same building site as a JCB driver.

I knew he lived there with Jimmy as both men were from Co. Wexford near Gorey.

His name was Paddy; he always had a great sense of humour.

We were watching videos; I don't know what movies they were. I had never seen them before or since.

They only looked like they were made about a year or two before at the most.

As the picture quality was great and it just looked very modern.

Jimmy Wexford's wife cooked dinner.

She barely spoke; I said thanks for the dinner.

Then a while later when it was late and dark Paddy gave me a lift home in his VW Golf.

It was kinda half between a van and a car.

It had only two seats in the front.

I remember looking in the mirror that night in my bedsit and saying to myself: man you look terrible. But I could do nothing about it.

I remember a few days later, I was beginning to neglect work, hoping I still might get home.

Paddy gave out to me, Lenny do some work.

Later that day Jimmy Wexford was giving out to me and then said, Lenny you're an ugly bastard.

It had only been a few months since my Uncle Eamon had called me the same thing.

I knew I was an ugly bastard. I didn't need anyone to tell me that.

As I was very ill, burnt out with bags and dark circles under my eyes and my hair was greasy and dirty.

I looked dreadful and still do till this day and it's because I have been ill since I was 14 and it actually goes back to when I was 12.

But nobody knew how ill I really was and nobody cared.

After a few days I got my act together and started working hard again.

It was early to mid-September and I started looking for a new bedsit in one of the evening newspapers.

Then I found one in Dun Laoghaire.

I phoned the landlady in a public telephone box and I met her after work.

It was in a posh place called Windsor Terrace near Teddy's Ice Cream in Dun Laoghaire; everybody in south Dublin knows where Teddy's Ice Cream is.

The landlady asked what did I work at? I said on a building site. I think she was happy I had a full-time job.

I told her I'll take it and gave her the deposit.

This place was luxurious compared to where I had been before.

I had my own electric shower which was brilliant - instant hot water and you controlled the temperature better than most of the electric showers today.

I also had my own sink and toilet, all up a small flight of stairs in my own room.

I had a tiny two-plate cooker with my little kitchen sink and a bed that you could just lift and it folded back into the wall to give you extra space.

But I had plenty of room anyway.

I also had a brilliant view of Sandycove Strand and of the sea.

My rent was 28 punts per week. Which I left every Thursday or Friday for her daughter to collect when I was at work, beside the locker by my bed.

So that evening I paid my deposit and got my keys.

I went back to my old bedsit in North summer and packed all my belongings in a refuse bag and left; I might not have left a note to say to my old landlord that I was not coming back.

I just left my keys behind in the room for him.

I went to Connolly Station and got the Dart to Dun Laoghaire and moved into my new bedsit.

I remember a few nights there were more thunderstorms but I was snug in my new bedsit.

I remember in September the foreman Michael got himself a new place in Deansgrange.

He was from around that area of south Dublin.

I think it was called Springfield or something like that, nothing to do with The Simpsons.

He was delighted.

In late September I bought myself some Doc Martens. I think they were 40 punts. I bought them in a shoe shop in Dun Laoghaire; the lads at work were complimenting me on my new boots

Now in October it began to rain more often. So it was muddier and muddier.

I remember we set to work on a new building site in Clonskeagh, just off Bird Avenue.

I don't remember ever being in that part of Dublin before.

I would get the 46A to UCD and walk through the football pitches as there was this pathway with a short cut to Bird Avenue.

There was a man that came in to repair broken machinery.

I would talk to him sometimes. I think he was 40 years of age.

He told me he had a daughter and she was 16, the same age as me.

He said he would love to introduce his daughter. I was flattered.

Unfortunately nothing came of it. Even if I had have been introduced to his daughter, I would not have made a good impression on her as I was in bits from my illness and she could do a lot better.

I knew this, so I never brought the subject up with him anymore deliberately.

I remember another one of the women had an orchard and asked did any of the men on the building site want any apples.

I wasn't interested. She just wanted to get rid without them being wasted.

Then another day some lady came in looking for the foreman; she said to the driver of the excavator are you in charge? He said no.

Then when she'd left, he said I must look intelligent or dumb when she asked me that question.

I just burst out laughing. Paddy said, Lenny thinks it's very funny and I did. I think we worked there for two or three weeks.

One day Jimmy Wexford told us that there had been a tragic accident on the building site when everybody had gone home.

That a ten year old had been killed inside a large concrete pipe and that it had collapsed.

I was only six years older than him.

Then we returned in mid to late October back in Castle Farm in Shankill.

As I said the weather began to deteriorate as it was raining more and the building site was starting to get muddy.

That's why I had bought my Doc Martens because I knew the weather was going to change for the worst.

One day sometime in October I was going down to the local near The Peoples Park in Dun Laoghaire to buy food and get a few 50p pieces for my electricity meter in my bedsit.

I bumped into someone from Shankill; she worked in Mr Quinn's shop beside the Post Office which he ran as well.

I knew she knew me; some of her relatives live a few doors up from my mother's still today.

Her surname was Maguire; they were from New Vale in Shankill.

She was with her boyfriend at the time.

It was a Sunday and I was wearing my work trousers which were covered in dust and muck.

He said to me, why are you dressed like that on a Sunday? I pretended not to hear him and walked away.

I should have told him the truth: first of all I'm very ill and I don't have many changes at the moment because of my situation.

But I said to myself it wasn't worth bothering to try and explain as he would not understand.

It was either late October or early November when we got moved again to a different building site just off Booterstown Avenue.

Some of these houses were nearly finished. These houses were very posh.

Some of them might be four or five bedroom houses.

I often thought to myself that I could never afford to buy one of these houses despite the fact that I was working 55 hours a week; in fact it actually increased for two or three weeks. When I was working.

I think I worked seven days a week - maybe a 70 hour week - and still could never afford any of these houses in my wildest dreams.

But that went for most people who worked in building, not just myself.

There was a canteen on this building site for dinner, mostly fries, which I enjoyed, and there were a few portable loos which I had never seen before on a building site; this was luxury.

Then we went back to Castle Farm in Shankill in mid to late November 1990.

The weather had deteriorated further; the mud got deeper and deeper; even my boot laces fell apart due to wet conditions.

I had to use bricklayers' levelling string for bootlaces which were made of waterproof synthetic materials and they were very strong. But they did the job.

I almost forgot to mention I began gradually working more and more with a 19-year-old lad from Dublin called Kevin O'Dermot; his da was high up working with Liffey Developments.

We became friends. I remember he used to put Acros to support the beams on the upstairs floors of the houses so that the men put bricks and mortar without worrying about the beams collapsing due to the weight.

When we were putting up an Acro, Stephen would hammer two or three in to thick planks so the Acro would not slide off.

I remember one day at lunch when we were all eating, Paddy the comedian said to Kevin O'Dermot, what's your surname Mulhall, you mean fuckall?

We all laughed; that was Paddy - he usually told dirty jokes.

By now I had not slept a wink for one year and five months.

I was already exhausted in the morning before I even started work but I had to go on.

I almost forgot to mention the Irish Presidential election was in November 1990.

As I was just 16 I was not entitled to vote.

I remember some of the other workmen talking about it.

I think it was between Mary Robinson and the late Brian Lenihan Senior.

Anyway one day Paddy and one or two others said I hope Mary Robinson wins.

Another bricklayer related to Jimmy Wexford said that she was a communist as she was endorsed by the Labour party.

But I pretended to be totally independent which was a load of rubbish.

I had a feeling Mary Robinson would win it as there was a liberal trend starting around this time and it has been going ever since; in fact everybody these days seems to have this liberal agenda where anything goes.

Or they use the word 'equality' for everything and it sounds great if you're really gullible and stupid like most of the politicians and electorate are today.

Well what really won the election for Mary Robinson was a phone bugging scandal in 1982.

Which came conveniently at this time.

Brian Lenihan actually won more first preference votes than Mary Robinson; in most other countries Brian Lenihan would have been elected President.

But because proportional representation uses second preference votes for Mr Curry for Fine Gael, it gave Mary Robinson the Presidency.

I remember when she became President one of the first things she said was: Mna na heireann.

Her feminist agenda had already started. If a male elected President said fir na heireann there would be an outcry from most women feminists that he should apologise for that remark or stand as President.

But that's this stupid country and is till this day.

Then she said another thing, I'm in touch with the people of Ireland.

What a load of crap I said to myself and later to others; the only people she's in touch with is the rich people of Ireland.

Being a big fancy solicitor or barrister. Till this day she still gets her big pension from the state - it's over 100,000 Euros a year and she doesn't even need it.

I think she gave back a paltry 15,000 - how very nice of her.

I remember a few years ago about her boasting about how she got Irish families smaller over the years by getting easy access to contraception.

At the moment the birthrate is so low that more people die than are born and that's including the fact over 25% of births in this country are form foreign immigrants and that's a conservative estimate.

Nobody gives a damn; in any other country alarm bells would be ringing but not in this country and if you say anything, you're a racist.

People in this country keep comparing our birthrate to the UK; our so-called birthrate is slightly higher than the UK's per thousand births, but they don't compare the fact that the UK has a population of 62 million and we have a lousy three and a half million. Yeppee, we are going to take all over the world. Yes I'm being sarcastic.

I checked up the birthrate recently and one department of statistics said in the future we will have to bring in another over 600,000 foreign immigrants to make up the shortfall as the Irish birthrate continues to fall and people die off and age at the same time and again nobody in this country seems to give a damn; in fact they are actively encouraging it, which doesn't surprise.

You're probably saying to yourself, I don't see you doing much about it.

Well here's my answer. I have had chronic insomnia since the age of 15 and my eyes are paining me 24 hours a day and my lovely thick hair is nearly all gone and I have aged rapidly.

Thanks to the great health service in this country. Where the only people they are concerned about are foreigners. They want to wipe out the Irish race and they are doing a pretty damn good job.

They should get all the foreign immigrants in this country to pay their wages and salaries since they love them so much.

If I had been in good health I would have got married in my early twenties and had as many children as possible.

But I was never given that choice since nobody wanted to help in the last 27 years.

So I'm not a hypocrite. I can barely look after myself let alone find a woman or get married.

Thanks a lot to the great doctors of St. Bernard's Hospital, St. Sebastian's, Co. Dublin and how can I forget St. Gregory's, Co. Dublin.

The whole system is shambolic.

Later in this book, you might hear mention of the health of some of the patients.

Every patient is miles ahead of me.

Most would be married or have boyfriends or girlfriends; obviously there can't be too much wrong with them.

I'm not married with children or have a girlfriend, not by choice.

But because I've been seriously ill most of my adolescent and adult life and I have no chance of ever getting better.

Thanks a lot to the great doctors and nurses of Ireland for doing a bang up job.

I don't even know what these doctors or nurses get paid for as they're hopeless.

Back to late November 1990. After Mary Robinson got elected. I saw some young women singing the Simon and Garfunkel song Here's to you Mrs Robinson, Jesus loves you more than you will know.

Not only is that a blasphemy but an insult to God as Mrs Mary Robinson has more in common with the devil than God.

I remember in late November or early December 1990 the muddy soil had frozen solid from the hard frosts.

I was now beginning to put up scaffolding with another bloke called Murphy; he was from Greystones.

He was always rude to me. I remember once a huge brick fell from one of the houses and just missed me by inches; it was behind me and he saw it falling and said absolutely nothing; other workmen would have said, lookout you nearly got killed there, are you alright; but not him.

I just kept my mouth shut as usual.

I remember one day it was getting colder and when I was doing my nipper, buying rolls and stuff for the workmen's lunches, one of the two women that worked in that shop, who I began to know because I was a regular customer, said to someone, according to the weather forecast there's snow on the way and she was right.

A few days later working on the building site, it started to hail and later snow.

I had been through so many different weather conditions since I had begun work. As it had been extreme summer, which I got sunburn from, then thunder storms then wet weather and now frost, snow and cold.

But it never bothered me at the time.

Getting into December 1990. One evening I was told by my foreman Michael, from south Dublin like me, to find the yard brush.

So I searched every single house under construction inside and out and every nook and cranny.

You would think they would have more than one yard brush on a large building site as they are extremely cheap to purchase but as they were penny pinching, they did not.

But I still could not find it. I told the foreman this.

Then it got quickly dark as it was now December.

So Paddy who operated the JCB had the spotlights or whatever on so we could see what we were doing in the dark.

Then an argument started between Paddy and the foreman Michael.

Then Paddy picked up a sledge hammer he had in the JCB and threatened to hit the foreman Michael.

Eventually things calmed.

Then the foreman Michael gave out to me saying Lenny I asked you to get the yard brush and you said you couldn't find it.

Well I found it. I said I searched everywhere for it honestly but he didn't believe me.

The next day we all had a laugh about what happened the night before and the sledge hammer incident and all was forgotten.

At this time I had managed to persuade my mother to take me back home.

So I left my bedsit in Windsor Terrace Dun Laoghaire without even leaving a note to the landlady as I could not face her.

Mainly because of my drastic appearance. My da asked when I left my bedsit, did you leave a note for the landlady? I said no.

I remember one night in December when it was dark on the building site; it started to snow and there was thunder and lightning.

My foreman Michael said to me, Lenny it's freezing I think it's time we all headed home.

He used to always wear denim jeans and jacket.

I remember sometime later in December, one Saturday after everybody had gone home for the weekend.

A new general operative had only started working a few weeks earlier and worked as a landscape designer. We were given rolls of grass, which was a new thing which I had never seen before.

He told the boss before he left that he was experienced in this sort of work.

So I helped to dig the front and maybe garden for one of the first new houses to be finished in Castle Farm Shankill.

The man who had moved in seemed to have plenty of money. I think his wife might have been Chinese.

It must have taken a few hours to finish.

The new man who moved in gave me ten punts which I took and said thanks because I never got paid for doing that from Liffey Developments.

But he probably just wanted to say thanks for working out of normal.

I remember another big incident with a new worker.

Who told me that he had worked many years in the coal mines of Wales.

Which we all believed ad I knew he was telling the truth.

Well one day when Paddy was digging near a big water main, he hit it and there was a loud bang and an explosion as the water main got hit.

The new guy was soaked to the bone.

As there were no changing facilities or anything he had to wait a while until it was time to go home and got a lift from the men.

He must have only changed into clean clothes when he got home.

Well Christmas 1990 was now approaching.

I remember Paddy had been complaining his wages had been decreasing at an alarming rate and that it could not continue. I did not ask why this was happening to him as it really was none of my business.

By now I had not slept a wink for nearly one and a half years and it had taken its toll on me.

Although I had enjoyed working on the building site, my poor physical health was taking too much out of me.

So I decided that the day we were going to get our Christmas holidays I would give my notice.

I think we got our Christmas holidays on December 23rd 1990.

That day Paddy said he was going to have to look for a job somewhere else as he could not afford to go on.

I also announced that I was giving in my notice.

Paddy said, Lenny don't give up work just because I'm leaving.

I said it's got nothing to do with that.

Some of the others tried to persuade me to stay on. But I had made my mind up to do it for health reasons but they knew nothing of this.

Then as was the custom everybody was headed for a few drinks in Mikey Byrnes, the local pub.

They asked me, did I want to go; I said no I'd head straight home. Ah come on Lenny. No lads I'm fine.

I'm not sure but I think the company was paying for drinks.

But I did not want to go into the local pub as somebody might know me from the area and I wanted to keep a low profile because I had declined both physically and mentally and I never wanted to face anybody again.

My foreman Michael asked me, would I come back after the Christmas holidays to finish my notice but he knew deep down I wouldn't be coming back. I don't remember too much about Christmas 1990 back home with my mother.

But I remember a few days after Christmas my da was bringing up to my aunts and uncles and granda in Deansgrange with Christmas gifts and cards.

One card was for my auntie Patty. Before my mother took with her I slipped 20 punts, which was a lot of money then, for my auntie who had kept me for barely three weeks and in the end couldn't wait to get rid of me.

But now my belief in God had come back I was feeling Christian and now was full of charity to everyone.

My mother never put 20 punts in the card and my auntie never said and must have assumed my mother put that money in.

My auntie had no idea it was me.

I did not want to visit my relatives because of my ghastly appearance and wretched health so I stayed at home.

I remember watching The Simpsons for the first time.

At first I did not think much of it and thought it was all a load of hype and it would disappear and fade away.

But it didn't and it's become one of my favourite animated comedies. I find it a release from my bad health today.

When January 1991 came. I knew I needed medical attention for my chronic insomnia, painful and severe hair loss.

But there was nowhere to turn.

I worked it out in my head at the time. That I would have to wait until at least to January 1st 1994 until I could even try to get any help because the same evil, lazy, sinful, vindictive nurse would be there another three years in the same hospital St. Gregory's, Co. Dublin.

As most student nurses there did a four year tour of duty.

I knew she started more than likely on January 1st 1990 and would not be finished until December 31st 1993.

So I could not go back to that hospital and also Dr. Lorcan O'Driscoll Mulhern would still be there as he was the so-called consultant.

As I was a medical card patient or in the catchment area you would be always sent to that dump of a so-called hospital whether you liked it or not.

Whatever they call it, St. Gregory's, or St. Gregory's Hospital, unfortunately nothing has changed and never will. So I would have to go for another three years without a wink of sleep which would have dire consequences for me, then and now.

But it was already too late for me as all the damage had been done and I knew I would never get better and my life was over and had no prospect of getting married or having a family.

So in January 1991 I decided I'd better start exercising regularly in order that my health would not decline even further if that were possible.

So at dusk when it was getting dark I would go for my walks so as few people as possible would see me. I would go up to New Vale and then onto the back roads which were nearly always deserted. One day in early January 1991 when I was walking on the main Dublin Road, just about to turn up to New Vale, my old foreman Michael happened to be in a car, travelling home with a few other men.

I did not see them as I never made eye contact with cars or people because of my ghastly appearance.

He spotted me and the car stopped and he shouted, Lenny.

I said, how are you? He told me he had the rest of my wages that were due to me and they were in a small brown envelope

Which was always the way we got our pay packets then, back in the early 90s.

He said to me, I knew you wouldn't come back after Christmas and, as I said, he was right.

I have to admit it was very nice of him; he could have taken my wages for himself and I would have never known about it.

But he didn't and I have to give him credit for that and say a big thanks to Michael from south Dublin.

Many thanks again.

I now begin in January 1991. I call these next two and half years the doldrum years because I was stuck in limbo.

I still had chronic insomnia, now for one and a half years, so I still was burnt out and exhausted but I could do nothing and now I'm going to tell you why.

I worked it out that the same irritable nurse that was in St. Gregory's Hospital would still be there until at least December 31st 1993 because in those days nurses that were training to become a qualified nurse normally did a four year tour of duty not always in the same hospital.

But if a nurse was training to be a psychiatric nurse in a private hospital, they could be there if they really wanted I think for their full term.

I do not know if that has changed by now.

Also the bad apples, as I called them, have a nasty habit of sticking around for long time unfortunately.

Anyone who is reasonably good at their job usually disappears very fast just as you're getting used to them.

They either move on or leave the country or get promoted or even retire.

Also Dr. Lorcan O'Driscoll Mulhern would still be there. I definitely know this as a fact because he was there for many years later.

So I would have to stick it out for at least three years until I could try and get help.

I still say till this day you have two choices in what psychiatric hospital you go to in south east Dublin catchment area, either St. Gregory's or St. Gregory's Hospital.

If you have a medical card.

For example a few months ago I asked my GP Dr. Meadhbh O'Cullen could I go to St. Bernard's Hospital, Dublin, or another psychiatric hospital.

She said to me if you have private health insurance you may have a choice.

But it's not for you since you have a medical card.

As I said in January 1991 I would have to live with my chronic insomnia for at least another three years or in fact the rest of my miserable life.

All I did most days at home with my mother was watch television. I always liked military history and still do.

I also remember we had a couple of days of snow in January 1991.

I also remember hearing Pat Buchanan on American TV; it was one the

US television news networks, I'm not sure which one.

I had a lot in common with him and still do.

He spoke out against abortion and poor moral standards in society.

I think his sister's name is Sissy Buchanan, I'm not a 100% sure on her name.

Some TV news anchor said to him, some people call you a racist?

That's ridiculous, I'm Scottish, Irish and German descent. Which is true.

I still admire this great man till this day.

I had money saved up from when I worked on the building sites.

I gave my money each week for my stay.

I'm not exactly sure how much each week.

After a few months I'm not exactly sure, I had to cut my upkeep to my mother by half because my savings were beginning to decline.

After a few weeks of paying my way.

Somehow in conversation with my mother the subject of my weekly contribution came up. She was saying how much she was getting now from me.

She only mentioned what I had been giving for the last few weeks and never mentioned what I had previously given for several months, as if it never happened.

I was a little hurt by this. My mother does not remember any of this.

Even though I'm mentioning it now.

I tried to exercise regularly in order to try and maintain some sort of existence so my standard of health would not even follow further.

I mostly walked at dusk to avoid meeting people especially anyone I might know because I did not want to confront them and they might comment on my appearance and say what's happened to you?

You look terrible.

I know now that it was not a figment of my imagination because I met my old friend from primary school in St. Gregory's Hospital, Co. Dublin, in February 1995.

He said to me the lads from school would see me out walking and say, Paul is not the same as he used to be.

I don't know what's wrong with him.

I then told my old school friend that I had chronic insomnia since I was 15 years of age and my other health complaints.

Then he understood why I was the way I was.

I don't remember too much of early 1991.

I remember in April 1991 the national census forms came in the post.

At the time I thought nothing of it. I generally thought at that time the birthrate had basically remained constant and that there may be a small increase in population, maybe around 50,000 which isn't much - it would barely fit in the Aviva Stadium.

Since I was now just 17 years of age I was still stupid and naive and lived in a world of leprechauns and fairies with magic rainbows.

I really wish my country was like that.

So the national census forms were sent away and then maybe late August or September, the population statistics came out and birthrate and other figures.

I was in for a nasty shock.

The population had actually fallen and birthrate I know now had been in decline since 1980, rapidly.

I was shocked. I think it may have fallen by about at least 50,000 people.

That may not sound like much but in a country with a tiny population like Ireland that's significant.

I mentioned the results of the census to my father; he did not like it either.

But I now know he knew more than me.

I was upset and angry. That this had been allowed to happen because I now know all of the maternity hospitals would have seen a decline in the birthrate every successive year.

But did absolutely nothing; in fact, if anything, they encouraged it.

In fact they and others would boast about the fact the birthrate is rapidly declining and may it do so well into the future.

So that the Irish race will be extinct forever, like the dinosaurs.

I now wanted to have children more than never.

But because by now I was so ill and exhausted. I was burnt out so it was impossible for me to get a girlfriend and get married.

That's also one of my biggest grievances with the doctors and nurses in the health system.

As, if they had have done their job right in the beginning, I may have been married today with healthy children.

But I was never given that choice and so it really hurts to this day and always will.

I was trying to find why the population was declining and also the rapid decline in the birthrate.

I now heard of contraceptives and sterilisation and other forms of contraception.

I was still only 17 years old; I knew very little of these immoral things.

As I've said before everybody in maternity hospitals and feminists were really proud of this achievement; and may it long continue, they would say, until the Irish race is extinct forever.

And they are still at it till this day; in fact if everything they are even more fantastic.

None of them wants Irish women to have children but foreign women can have as many children as they like; in fact it's encouraged and it will never change unfortunately as they are all on the band wagon with this so-called liberal agenda where basically you can do whatever you like.

I think by 1988 the birthrate had already reached critical mass.

From then on replacements won't outstrip demand and not enough births are keeping up with replacements and it's even getting worse and nobody gives a damn, except me.

But I'm in no position to do anything because of my wretched health and in a few years when I pass away, a foreign immigrant will replace me immediately and everything will go on as before.

As I've said, many so-called Irish are really proud of this.

In any other country in the world with a far larger population, like the UK at the moment with a population of 64 million, alarm bells would ringing, saying we must do something about this serious situation.

At the moment many British politicians are fed up with the influx of foreign immigrants and want something done about it and they're right.

But here in Ireland everyone compares our country to Britain, saying how great it is.

Never mention any of these things.

The fact that cities in England alone have populations many times greater than Ireland's.

Such as London, Manchester and Birmingham.

If everyone here wants to be like Britain then why can't we have a population of 50 or 60 million of our own people and don't start bringing in 100s of thousands of more immigrants to replace and to slightly increase, giving the impression that we are doing a fine job.

It has become clear to me in the last few years that Irish women have no problem in having sex with a man married or not but as long as they don't get pregnant.

They want the best of both worlds to enjoy themselves and to have no responsibility in having to raise a child as it's too much effort and work.

Most of it is down basically to laziness and a bad attitude to life.

The feminists would like you to believe it's women's rights.

At the moment, despite the fact that over 26% of the nation is foreign-born immigrants and that's a conservative estimate as I believe it to be much higher if you take into account mixed marriages where the woman is Irish but the husband is foreign; and there's a lot they don't want you to know and also the fact many of the population are not racially pure, especially a lot of British, other foreign invaders who basically robbed our land and have no loyalty to our country.

I would put it at more like 50% of the population are non-Irish.

So it is even more alarming again and, as I've said before, it's going to get much worse, a lot worse, and there's not much I can do about it since I'm nearly dead and basically I'm impotent, not in the sexual sense but in my body.

Contraception, whether you want it or not, is shoved into you face everywhere you go, whether it's the local shop, supermarket, men's and ladies' toilets.

When I go to get my medication I have to face it again; you can buy them even in the Euro Shop.

I just read last night you can even get them free in student unions in Ireland.

You can take the contraceptive pill also, even on the medical.

Then there's morning after emergency contraception.

Even when I go down to Dun Laoghaire there's a big advertisement in the pharmacy window across the road in big writing saying Emergency Morning After Contraception Available Here.

I also remember when I was younger that the so-called Irish Family Planning Organisation had a clinic or office right beside St. Michael's Roman Catholic Church.

They did this deliberately in order to insult and humiliate and to rub it in your face.

We don't care what moral beliefs you have, here's what we think of you.

Now also they want to bring in abortion on demand.

At the moment they pass bills or legislation like the Protection of Life During Pregnancy Act; it sounds great.

But it really should be the called The Taking of Life Pregnancy Act.

It was a year or maybe more, I'm not exactly sure, I should have done my homework before I typed but you know what I mean.

They had a debate so we were led to believe everyone could express their opinion and be listened to.

But it was a forgone conclusion; their minds were already made up; it was nothing more than a talking shop.

Eventually what's going to happen?

When the next general election is held early next year in 2016, either April, May or June - I'm not sure at the moment.

Whatever government is formed after the election.

More than likely, especially The Labour Party or the abortionist Party as I call them, will say we will hold a referendum either next year 2017 or the following or definitely before 2021 before our term of government.

We will hold a referendum to amend the eighth amendment to the Constitution.

So once it's passed probably by a majority 70% or so to 30% or less it will be then passed and then as quickly as possible it will legalise abortion on demand once passed by the electorate; but if they can speed it up even faster, believe me they will do so.

I really do hope my predications don't come true. But I know they will.

The writing has been on the wall for a very long time.

How many abortions will be carried out every year? you ask.

I think it's between four to five thousand on average at the moment for so-called Irish women.

More than likely in the first year or two it shouldn't exceed this as many people in Ireland will be getting used to the idea.

It then probably will increase to six thousand and maybe even go higher again.

So not only will the birthrate go down but also the abortion rate will climb.

Everything in Irish society says: don't have children in any circumstances whether you want children or not because it's not a good lifestyle anymore and should be discouraged and discontinued as possible.

Only foreign women should have children and be encouraged to have them. While Irish women don't need to.

You can have a great time having sex with men as often as you like and not have the burden or responsibility of having to look after a child in your lifetime.

So within a couple of hundred years the Irish race will be extinct. The only people left will be foreigners.

Or as they now call them the new Irish people whose parents were foreign immigrants or descended from foreign immigrants; that's all that will be left in Ireland.

Congratulations to all the so-called patriotic Irish people. You just annihilated your own people and they will never ever come back.

Oliver Cromwell would be proud of you; even he could never do a better job.

And yet again our government and feminists and so-called equality organisations will be boasting about this around the world as if to say how great we really are.

After two or three abortions, will it then start to increase? As it becomes the fashion and norm in society, it will become something of pride among many women.

In fact in 10 or 20 years' time, if you're a woman in Ireland that hasn't had an abortion in your reproductive lifetime, there must be something seriously wrong with you.

Also this will be hailed as another great victory against the Catholic Church like everything else.

Many political parties, especially including the left and many women's organisations, will be very proud of this, saying now the Catholic Church is finished for good.

As if it was the only religion in the world. As if Muslims weren't against abortion; even other Christian denominations and many other religions throughout the world.

In the last several years France and Sweden, both countries worried about the decline in the birthrate, have encouraged more women to have children and it worked in both countries, which saw an increase in the birthrate.

Both countries are regarded as being very liberal, especially in sexual matters but found no problem with this and we should not.

If you even dared mention in public in Ireland that you wanted to increase the birthrate - it's been in a rapid decline for 35 years and there are not enough births to replace the dead and so on - there would be an uproar from nearly every political party and women's groups and liberals, abortionists and so on.

They would say, how dare you try and encourage Irish women to have children. I don't care how low the birthrate is, so what if more people die than are born?

We don't give a damn; we'll do whatever we want.

As some women would say, it's our bodies, we'll do whatever.

I don't give a damn if we all die, it's not my problem.

As I said, the national census took place in April 1991 I think.

I have already explained what the consequences for the country will be.

I really hope I'm proved wrong.

My da now had a new hobby, amateur photography.

These hobbies tended to last three to five years.

Anything he took his hands to, he could really pick it up fast and be quite good at it.

He even developed his own photos in the back shed.

I mentioned in 1990 when he gave me a black eye that never healed up properly.

In May or June 1991 he made a remark when he was looking either at a camera lens or his Schneider lens.

When he looked through the lens at my face which I was trying to hide because I knew I looked terrible.

He made a remark about the blue vein under my left eye, making a joke about it.

Saying you've got a big vein under your eye, haha very funny.

It did not occur to him that it was he who had caused it.

I said nothing as usual and kept my mouth shut.

I also remember I think it was the 1991 June bank holiday; my youngest brother was sitting at the table; he was four at the time.

My da said to him boasting about the fact the previous year how he had dealt with me and that if it hadn't been for him my da.

He basically said he had saved the day.

I thought to myself, the hypocrisy of him.

The very same man had done far worse than me over the years, putting a rock through the sitting room window in 1984 at night when I was in my pyjamas.

To get back at my mother at the time, I'm not exactly sure what for.

This is just a minor incident.

I cannot mention any of the others he did over the years as they are very serious and I do not want to cause trouble for my mother or my siblings so

I will not mention them in this true story.

I will try and stick to myself as it is about me.

I became a big fan of Zig and Zag and of course Dustin the Turkey.

These guys cheered up my whole life through this difficult period.

They became a household institution in Ireland.

I don't know why RTE cancelled their show many years ago.

They made a big mistake doing this. These guys were not only the best in Ireland for entertainment but in the entire world.

They will never be equalled again.

I was also impressed by Dustin's knowledge of Dublin.

One example: he was talking about is own political party The Poultry Party when he said, lads let's march from Bojangles in Shankill to SuperValu shopping centre.

I was really impressed by this because you literally have to be born and raised in Shankill to know this sort of information.

I know the man who plays the character Dustin is not in person from South Dublin.

I think he is from Stillorgan or Goats Town or that area.

I mean if you were to ask me somewhere in Stillorgan or Goats, how to get from A to B, I wouldn't have a clue even though I'm from South Dublin myself.

Maybe it's because I just don't get around much due to my severe illness or I don't have a car or I'm just stupid.

I remember in 1991, the Nissan Classic cycle race.

My hero Sean Kelly was in it again.

It took place every year at the end of September and finished on October 2nd to 4th depending in each calendar year on how the weekend Sunday fits into the calendar.

I remember Sean Kelly and Sean Yates got away from the pack early in the race.

I'm not exactly sure where it began; I think that stage finished in Cork.

The weather in the west had turned nasty; I think three inches of rain fell that day and I remember tree surgeons had to cut a fallen tree on the stage route before the cyclists arrived and they did.

Strangely the weather was not too bad; there was very little rain that day.

I remember Sean Kelly and Sean Yates cycling up St. Patrick's Hill in Cork; I cannot be 100% sure; you will have to look that up yourselves to confirm it.

As it's not stored in my memory banks and what I can remember.

The St. Patrick's Hill in Cork even for professionals is very tough especially after a long stage.

I can visualise both Sean Kelly and Sean Yates both climbing the Hill together and then Sean Yates won the stage less than a second ahead of Sean Kelly.

Sean Kelly became overall leader on general classification and went on to win that 1991 Nissan Classic of Ireland.

I also think that same year a few weeks later Sean Kelly won Milan-San Remo in Italy, another big scalp.

He also got away from the peloton and they never got a chance to catch him.

I was really impressed with Sean Kelly as he was in his twilight years.

Although he may not like me for saying that. Sorry Sean, I don't mean to cause offence.

I'm actually paying you a great compliment.

In early November the weather began to change; it started to get a lot colder.

There was snow on the mountains, especially in the west and the north of the country.

I think they were making the great Irish film Into the West because after the film came out several months later.

When the two young lads were going on their horse to the west of Ireland.

The weather was exactly how I remembered it. The snow on the hills and the rain and so on.

If you ever watch the film, you will know what I'm talking about.

I began calling down to my old friend Thomas, down in Clifton Park.

We normally talked about music. I remember one evening his mother gave us a bowl of custard and sponge cake I think.

I remember talking to his older brother one day who was a third level student in Donegal.

I asked him what the weather was like up there. I already knew the answer.

He said it never stopped raining, it was the worst weather he could remember.

As I always thought of myself as being an amateur meteorologist.

I told him why the north west of Ireland is one of the wettest places in Ireland especially in winter: as many Atlantic depressions hit Donegal straight in the face.

While Dublin is the driest place in Ireland and South County is the driest place in Dublin.

I call it the desert of Ireland. When I say this to people they give me strange looks even now.

As far as I'm aware the weather station at the quarry in Dalkey records the lowest average rainfall in Ireland. I could be wrong.

I do not remember much about Christmas 1991.

Although I remember my auntie Patty called a few days before for just a quick visit to my mother.

I just happened to be in the bath.

What worried me was if my auntie wanted to use the bathroom before she left; because I would have to get out of the bath and let her in to use it.

Thankfully she didn't need to use it. I was very lucky because I was trying to keep a low profile and got away with it.

In January 1992 I had now had chronic insomnia for two and a half years with no prospect of ever getting better.

My birthday was on February 12th 1992. I had turned 18 by now.

I did not want a fuss and I did not get it.

I remember very little.

I still tried to do walks, beginning at dusk through Dublin backroads where there was never much traffic.

I remember in February 1992 there was an RTE camera crew. I was taken totally by surprise.

The new motorway had just opened a few months ago - I think in October 1991.

All I remember was I was walking up Stonebridge Road when I saw what I believed to be a woman and a man looking over the new bridge at the new motorway, their car parked across the road.

I did not take much notice of this. I presumed they were either husband or wife or related to each other or just good friends just looking at the new motorway, and kept on walking.

Then they came across the road very fast and asked me, what do you think of the new motorway?

I saw the woman had a microphone in her hand and presumed they were from a local radio station.

I said it's great, most of the traffic through Shankill Village has dropped considerably. Just as I was finishing up I noticed a television camera on the man's shoulder.

Just as I was walking away it began to dawn on me what had just happened.

I said to myself, if they broadcast my interview on television, it would be very embarrassing for me.

As I was trying to keep the lowest profile possible.

The fewer the people knew of me the better.

I said to myself, I better go back and tell them not to show my interview on TV.

Just before they were beginning to leave, I said please don't broadcast on RTE Television.

They said they would not. I just had to take their word for it.

Till this day I do not know whether my interview was broadcast on television.

I just hope it wasn't. I tried for the next week or so to watch the evening news to see if I was on it.

I never saw myself on it but I never saw anything on the new motorway being mentioned, which I at least expected in some way but with another person being interviewed instead of me.

I just don't know till this day whether it was broadcast or not.

I remember TV in March 1992; it was on BBC 2 I think; it was a documentary about people working in Germany.

Then it mentioned about some nurses working in a hospital in Hamburg.

I noticed this after my appalling treatment by nurses in hospitals which would only get worse in the future.

There was this young Irish nurse complaining about the fact that one day an elderly patient called her, I think, a bloody Englander.

She said I'm not English, I'm Irish. I don't think the nurse really understood why this elderly patient woman in a Hamburg hospital would say something like this.

It of course goes back to WW2; the massive heavy bombing raids by the RAF and the USAAF were between July 25th to August 2nd. 1943. I might be a few days out with my statistics but I think in total there were either four or five bombing raids carried out in that one week alone.

Where at least at the very minimum 43,000 civilians were killed, I believe it to be much higher than this.

I think it was Operation Gomorrah. I know I've probably spelt that wrongly but any WW2 historians will know what I'm talking about.

After those huge raids that caused massive firestorms.

Many other bombings were carried out until the last days of the war.

That's why I'm saying the number of civilians killed is much higher than 43,000.

That young Irish nurse probably never even thought of WW2 as it was a long time ago. But the elderly female patient could still remember the horror that happened to her beautiful town and the massive death toll that her people had suffered, and she never forgot till her dying day.

The Irish nurse appeared to be in her late twenties. I think the BBC documentary had only been made a year or two earlier.

I'm trying to calculate what would be the Irish nurse's age now.

She must be in her early to mid-fifties by now at least. So she would probably be working as a senior staff nurse. Where now I do not know.

I remember in late March 1992 my mother started putting a lot of pressure on me to get a job.

I had cycled into Mountjoy Square Dublin to renew my old An Oige Youth Hostel Association membership. I'm not sure how much it cost, maybe a few punts.

I almost forgot in March that year as my mother was putting so much pressure on me to leave.

I decided to cycle down to Ashford in County Wicklow.

Where in the summer of 1985 I had stayed in in An Oige youth hostel and I thought I could do the same thing again and maybe start a new life for myself.

I actually remember I had this master plan that I would cycle all the way to Cork city and start a whole new life for myself and never have anything to do with my family.

But it did not quite work out like that unfortunately.

I seemed to go in circles for hours and hours. I thought I remembered exactly where the youth hostel was.

But I could not find it, no matter how hard I tried. There was absolutely nothing there, just a pathway and woods to nowhere.

I was also carrying a very heavy rucksack with all my belongings as I had no intention of coming back.

This rucksack was incredibly heavy so that my back was killing me.

I remember on the way through the Glen Of The Downs there was heavy sleet.

It was getting dark and I was still in Ashford Co. Wicklow. I had no choice but to head back.

I remember cycling back in the dark.

Eventually I got home. I just told my mother I'd been out cycling down near Wicklow and it had been snowing.

I asked, had it been snowing in Shankill? She said no.

I was totally and absolutely exhausted. For the first time in two years and nine months, I got my first night's sleep.

When I woke up next morning, my body felt very strange. I could feel the relief of tiredness from my body and my eyelids and eyes felt very strange.

But this was just a flash'n'pan. I never slept a wink until July 1994.

I think I got a job at the beginning of April 1992.

The only place I could think of. Was my old place Castle Farm Shankill.

So I went up and asked were there any jobs going. They still remembered me.

I got my old job back with exactly the same pay, 2.50 punts per hour.

After a few days my chronic insomnia was causing great difficulty for me.

I was totally burnt out and exhausted. Every day at around mid-afternoon around 2pm or 3pm I could hardly stand.

Even using a yard brush became a bid deal. I was so exhausted that even brushing light debris on the concrete floor of a house was like the hardest job in the world.

Every time I tried to brush as fast as possible, so I didn't look like I was lazy, was just too much for me.

I tried my best but I was burnt out. All I could do was try and hide in case anyone saw as they would say to me, you better get your act together.

One day my old boss foreman Michael spotted me and said, Lenny what the hell are you doing?

I can't exactly remember word for word what he said.

Basically any idiot could use a yard brush and he was right.

He gave out to me and I broke down crying.

Lenny, he said, you're very emotional. I said, sorry I'm trying my best.

I never told him what was really with me. I know he's still around some-where in Dublin, maybe not in the same job but maybe in a different one. I can't be 100% sure.

I was trying to calculate what age he would be today. I remember he told me he was 28 years of age in 1990 so he should by now 53 years of age.

So he should not be retired for at least ten years minimum.

After I finished work there that last time I never ever saw him again.

So that is nearly 23 years by now.

I knew I would not be in that job for long as there did not seem to be much work around.

So I started asking some of the brickies, was there any work going?

Most of them laughed at me.

I asked one of the O'Mulligan brothers was there any work? I climbed up the scaffold to talk to him.

He said, Lenny I can see you're very pale just standing here; I couldn't give you a job, you wouldn't be able; and he was right.

Although I was afraid of heights, that wasn't the problem. I was so burnt out and exhausted that I could hardly stand on the scaffolding; I was feeling faint and weak and dizzy.

I remember coming home in the evenings from work.

I was so exhausted I just fell into the chair in the sitting room and couldn't move for hours as I was so exhausted.

I tried at two or three to lie on my bed but I could not fall asleep no matter how exhausted I was.

I was totally finished and I had no prospect of getting medical help and I never will.

Eventually I was laid off after about four weeks.

To be honest there was just no work left on that site for Liffey Developments.

So I was told that the workers who had longest service with Liffey Developments would be kept on and the others with the shortest service would be let go.

I knew immediately that meant me and I was let go that very same day.

I'm not bitter or angry with Liffey Developments as they were perfectly right in what they had to do at the time and those who had been the loyalist employees were kept and those that weren't were let go and that included me.

The only problem was. When I told my mother what had happened she did not believe me.

I can perfectly understand why you just got the job four weeks ago and now you're telling me they let you go?

Yeah that's right ma just bad timing on my part.

Yeah really, my ma said, do you expect me to believe that?

There was no point in me arguing with my ma because her mind was already made up yet again.

I think in May 1992 my parents put me under pressure to try and sign on the dole in Dun Laoghaire Labour Exchange.

My da told me even the next door neighbour is on it. He passed away in 1999 I think.

So I went down. I had an interview with a young woman. I can't remember what she was like.

I told her I had been working on a building site in Shankill. Obviously she checked up and knew I was telling the truth.

She told me to come back, I'm not sure when.

It must have been a week or two later.

So I received my first dole payment. I'm not exactly sure how much, maybe between 40 and 50 punts. I could be wrong.

When I first got my dole payment, I thought I was a millionaire.

I must have paid at least half if not more to my mother each week.

I remember buying the new Gillette Razor. I think it had two blades together, which was cutting edge at the time. Sorry for the pun.

Now razors have up to five blades together.

I remember shaving with this new razor. Although I had facial hair growing since the age of 14.

I was still very poor at shaving. Because I was so exhausted I could not shave regularly.

I needed plenty of practice, trial and error.

Now that I had a regular income the pressure from ma had been taken off for the time being.

I think the summer of 1992 was very wet. I could be wrong.

I remember in June I would cycle up the fields near Woodbrook Golf Course and hide my bicycle in a small wooded area and then go on walks around the fields.

I remember the big ditches were saturated with water and when I went walking around footways of the fields they were also saturated.

I tried my best not to get my feet wet. But it was impossible.

I have never seen so much water covering that area in my life. What

124

was so unusual was that it was the middle of summer which is of course the driest time of the year.

Even in the wettest winters I had never seen so much water in these fields.

Sometimes I would cycle to Carrickmines and then to Enniskerry and down the big hill to the dual carriageway and towards Shankill.

I can still remember the surface water on the roads - any sort of incline water would run down; of course my feet would get wet again.

I remember one day that summer in 1992 I decided to go down the old path near a very small old cemetery.

As I had first been there in June 1983 with my school class from St. Anne's Primary school with my teacher Miss Murphy.

I wanted to bring back the good fond memories of my earlier childhood, a kind of nostalgia.

So I cycled up one day; as I was making my way into the lane way, some posh woman basically started interrogating me.

Do you know there have been break-ins or robberies around here recently?

I know nothing about it, I said. Which I didn't. But this woman wouldn't give up.

As if I had something to do with it. I said, I'm only up here cycling. Which I was.

As like everything in my miserable life, I always happened to be at the wrong place at the wrong time.

I said to myself forget about this. This woman has already made her mind up.

So I think I cycled on to Carrickmines and Enniskerry.

I remember I found this tranquil place on the road down from Enniskerry.

Where the River Dargle flows, it was like a mini waterfall or similar but it was beautiful and peaceful.

I started stopping off here every time I cycled down.

As all my troubles vanished for a short while. It was like being in heaven.

I still had not slept a wink for three years. But as I said, I had nowhere to go for help. So I just had to hang in there.

Like I have been doing for most of my life.

The summer went by very quickly.

I don't remember too much about the autumn of 1992. I think the Nissan Classic bicycle race may have been on in late September, early October 1992.

I don't remember who won it. As I was beginning to lose interest in most things since I was becoming even more ill and just wanted to keep a low profile and hope for a miracle.

That somehow I would get better. But I never would.

I've called these the doldrum years since I could not go anywhere for help.

That's why I don't have as much to say right now. But it will get more interesting later - bear with me.

I remember Christmas 1992. I bought myself my first music album, Huey Lewis and the News Greatest Hits on cassette.

I thought it was great.

I also bought myself two or three Caffreys Snowball Boxes.

Pure greed again. I thought I could eat them easily. I remember I could feel the sugar grinding my teeth when I closed my jaw.

It was my own fault.

Then January 1993.

Around January the weather of course had gotten colder; I could see the snow on the Wicklow mountains. So I decided to cycle there. It was much further than I thought.

It took quite a while to get up there and it was more inland than I anticipated.

When I got to the top of one of the mountains, the terrain was very difficult. There were big pools of water covered in ice. But when I stood on them my feet would go through and they would get wet.

Also I remember seeing red deer; I think every time I tried to catch up with them, they would run away in herds at incredible speeds. I gave up trying to catch up.

Then on exposed hills heavy snow showers got driven in and they turned into minor snowstorms with gale force 8 winds.

Even though I had a good coat on me, I could still feel the bitter biting cold.

It seemed to take forever to navigate my way down and to get my bicycle to get home.

Eventually I made it and managed to cycle home before it got dark.

I never mentioned it to my mother. She just thought I'd been out cycling for the day.

I had to leave my bicycle way down one of the mountains because of terrain.

My next Birthday was February 12th 1993. I was 19 years of age.

I remember going to FAS in Loughlinstown around the time of my 19th birthday.

I went in and asked were there any courses going at the moment?

The lady said that all the computers had crashed caused by the Michelangelo virus.

Just my luck again as usual.

I think my mother had put pressure on me to get a course. But I failed again, to her disappointment.

My mother began to start putting more and more pressure on me.

I knew she no longer wanted me around.

As in her eyes I was just a dosser. She didn't seem to realise how ill I really was.

One day I remember she said, you can't go around wrapped in wool.

By May of 1993 I knew my days were numbered. I was getting plenty of hints to move out of the house by my mother.

I calculated at the most I had no more than two months before I was gone and I wasn't far out.

By late June 1993 I was looking for bedsits in the evening newspapers.

Eventually I found a place in Clarinda Park, Dun Laoghaire.

Although it was a dump, I took it.

It wasn't cheap either - beggars can't be choosers.

I moved in early July 1993. I had managed to save some money over the last year or so.

I tried to calculate how long I could stay there before my money ran out.

I worked it out about two months and yet again I wasn't far out.

Yet again I would have a nasty experience.

When the landlady came to collect the rent on my first week there.

Being dumb and naive and stupid as I usually was.

I said to her, would you like to come and I will give you your rent.

Then when she came in, I just closed the door behind so she would have some privacy when I was handing her the cash.

Then she totally over-reacted; she caught the impression that I was trying to take advantage of her and opened the door and went off, kinda unsettled.

I myself was upset over this as I was just trying to be friendly. I considered that bedsit and the entire three-storey house as hers and so presumed that bedsit was her sole property and that I was upset and it was my duty to be gracious even if that meant her coming into my bedsit and taking the rent in cash from me.

But she got the wrong idea totally, the complete opposite to what I was doing.

Now here I go again, having to try and explain myself. I shouldn't have to.

I had absolutely no interest in this woman sexually or otherwise. I was not in the remotest bit attracted to her in any way.

I don't even like this woman; she was not even good looking.

Even if she was the most beautiful woman in the world and she was not. My intentions would still be the same.

I would never try and take advantage of a lady in any way till this day. As I'm a gentlemen and still behave that way.

Have I made myself clear? Thank you.

***

Then shortly later her husband came accusing me of trying to take advantage of his wife.

I again kept my mouth shut as usual and said nothing.

He said from now on I will be collecting the rent from you.

I said that's fine.

After he left I broke down crying, not entirely sure of this serious false allegation.

I thought about the fact that my mother threw me out. I was extremely young and could not get any help. I was still only 19 years of age. But I was like an old man and the social welfare cut me completely so once my savings ran out I would be homeless yet again.

I thought to myself how had my life gone so horribly wrong since the age of 12 till now in just over seven years?

From a handsome 12-year-old boy without a care in the world, and I could have any girlfriend, I went to a decrepit old chronic insomniac burnt out and exhausted with no money or prospects, no chance of ever getting any medical help, never in my life having a girlfriend or going to a disco or night club.

Till this day I've never enjoyed life. As I've said before, death can only come as a release for me. How had it all gone so horribly wrong?

I was in that bedsit in Clarinda Park in the summer of 1993 from early July to early September.

As I just said, I had savings but I worked out that paying rent and food I would run out of money in about two months and yet again my prediction was accurate.

I remember I robbed my da's pocket radio. This is the best pocket radio I've ever come across.

You could pick up foreign radio stations as well and the sound quality was great.

I remember the pop songs at the time were mostly The Water Boys 'Glastonbury', one of the greatest pop songs ever written.

'Yellow' from U2 and Freddie Mercury's 'something…Being Alone' which was a number one I think that year; also 'The Crying Game' by Boy George.

There were also some other great songs that summer but I can't remember them at the moment.

I remember going down to Dunne's Stores grocery shop which is now gone.

I used to buy mushroom and chicken in an aluminium foil box laminated which I boiled in a pot.

This was usually my dinner; I really enjoyed it. They don't sell them anymore.

I used to buy a lot of corn beef slices for making sandwiches, and cheese.

I also used to go down to the local corner shop where I bought King Crisps and Finches Fizzy Orange.

That corner shop is still there.

I would go for walks at the back of the Dart line where you had more privacy.

Also late at night I would walk on Dun Laoghaire Pier. I did this at night so nobody could see my drastic appearance.

One day I thought I recognised my old friend from 1990 North Summer Street.

He looked the spitting image of him. The same beard and build.

I was going to say hello but I said nothing to avoid embarrassment in case of mistaken identity; he said nothing back to me.

So I assumed he wasn't the guy. But I could be wrong.

I also remember one day I was walking on a narrow footbath past Teddy's Ice Cream towards Dun Laoghaire Centre.

I stepped off the path to allow the lady to continue and to my astonishment she said, thanks.

I tried to get social welfare as I was not working and my savings would not last forever.

So one day I walked all the way to Dalkey to see the welfare officer.

I tried to explain my predicament. She said to me how could a mother want to throw out a handsome young man like you?

I said, look I just want to get some money to pay the rent and food.

She then told me I would have to get a letter from my mother stating that she had made me leave the house in writing before I could even think of getting anything.

So I went to my mothers and my da wrote a letter saying why I was made to leave home.

So a day or two later I brought the letter back to the welfare officer and she said it wasn't good enough.

Your mother did not put her address and something else. I said it's all there but it made no difference.

I literally gave up. As usual in my great world everything in my life so far has worked against me: my severe illness, no money being homeless and nobody gives a damn.

By now I had literally not slept a wink for over four years.

So into August 1990 I decided one evening to go into Dublin city centre. I was going to see if I could survive on my own sleeping rough but in my case not sleeping at all.

I remember walking down the Quays at night. I remember seeing the Santa Maria used by Christopher Columbus; it had been used to celebrate in the previous year, 500 years since the discovery of the Americas.

Of course it wasn't the exact real boat. That had sailed to the Americas but an exact replica boat was in dock in Dublin that very night.

Eventually I found an unused piece of land with some grass verges on it.

There was no one around. I think I had a sleeping blanket. I lay on some pieces of cardboard but I never slept a wink.

I got the first 46A from Fleet Street; I think it was 5am or 6am.

I was totally and utterly burnt out.

Eventually I got back to Dun Laoghaire. When I arrived at the building where my bedsit was I realised I'd forgotten my keys for the front door of the building.

I had to wait for someone to come out so that I could go back in.

Eventually after half an hour to an hour some man I'd never seen before came out. I said to him I'd forgotten my keys and I walked in and got back into my bedsit.

***

It must have been about 7.30am to 8.00am.

The moment I rested on the bed I fell asleep. I must have woken several hours later.

It was the only night's sleep I had there in the entire two months or in my case, an afternoon's sleep.

I was literally dead from exhaustion.

In late August I was trying to raise the sash window; it was huge and extremely heavy I had a small board to hold it up.

But then there was this almighty crash. The board moved and the sash window came crashing.

There was a huge crack in the window and some of the broken glass was protruding out.

I was really worried in case the landlord would kill me.

When I got down to the entrance of the building, to my astonishment you could not see the broken window because of the height of the building.

As I was on the top floor.

I knew I had less than two weeks of money to stay in the bedsit.

After the first week in September my money was all gone.

So the day my rent was due I left early that morning before 8am because I had no money to give the landlord and also I'd left the broken window.

I had to try to scribble a message on a piece of paper to explain I had left but I had not even got a cheap pen for 10p as I had absolutely no money left.

I had to use a burnt matchstick for a pen.

The only luck I had was my old bicycle although the tyres were thread bare.

It was my only means of transport. As I had no money for bus or train fare.

Also by good luck back in March or a year earlier I had bought myself a set of wets for bad weather.

And the weather had changed for the worse. The night before I left, the wind came up and it started to rain heavily.

It would remain like that for the next one to two weeks.

This was unusual as Septembers were always dry except on very rare occasions.

This was one of the wettest Septembers in many years.

But fortunately I was lucky I had bought my wets.

So I cycled back to my mother's and told her I was homeless and had absolutely no money left and I had nowhere else to go.

My mother does not remember this. Only a few years ago I told her what had happened.

My auntie Madge just happened to be there. My mother told my auntie about my situation; my auntie was just as cold as my mother.

You're old enough and ugly enough to look after yourself my mother said; my auntie totally agreed with her.

After my auntie left I got down on my knees and begged my mother, could I stay for a couple of nights. I think I might have even cried.

A few nights that's all, she said.

The next day I cycled all the way out to Tallaght in the rain. I knew there was a lot of building going on.

I must have gone to six or seven different building sites. I said at each different building site, I'll do any work – nipper, anything; I'll even work for one punt an hour or less. But nobody wanted to give me a job and to be honest I couldn't blame them.

I looked dreadful; I was totally burnt out and finished; I couldn't hold down a job, even for a day, I would have gotten the sack.

So I decided my last hope was Jacobs Biscuits on the Begard Road in Tallaght.

I pretended to the security guard that I knew a lad there.

He said what's his name? I said Mick. Mick who? Then I admitted I was just looking for a job.

Can I go in and ask is there anything going round? He said, you can't do that; you need a CV.

I said, I don't have a CV. Well, he said, you need one.

So that evening I headed home. I knew the game was up.

I knew I'd be lucky if I had two nights left at home before my mother kicked me out.

The next day I thought seriously of robbing a bank or building society.

How I was going to carry it out and get away with it.

I remember being in Bray, Co. Wicklow. I'm need to be sure about the events that unfolded.

I have never told anyone till this day.

Somehow I bought a toy gun for one punt. What really puzzles me is even where I got the one punt in the first place, not the rest of it, because as far as I can remember I had absolutely no money; maybe I stole the toy gun in one of the toy shops; that's all I can think of.

Well anyway I had to try and make the toy gun look as real as possible so I changed little bits here and there to make it look real.

I made my adjustments sitting on a bench on the banks of the River Dargle.

I made a balaclava out of a white plastic bag, putting holes in it for the eyes.

Then I picked a Building Society near the River Dargle in Bray which is now long gone.

It took a while to work up the courage to do this and my nerves were in tatters.

I went into the Building Society with my toy gun and plastic bag with holes.

But there was nobody at the desk. They must have seen me come in and scattered. I did not hang around for long and got away empty handed, still not a penny to my name.

I thought the Gards would arrest me soon but to my surprise I got away with it.

Well I'd actually not done much to begin with. But that was still a serious arrestable offence.

So finally, after about three nights at home in my mother's, she said you have to go.

I said I've nowhere else to go, I've no money, I'm homeless. I don't care get out.

I said to my mother when I was leaving, you'll never see me again and I really meant it.

I want nothing to do with you or anybody else.

I know you often see children or adults fighting with their parents and saying the same but after or a few days they come back.

But not me; this time I meant every word I said. I had no money, I was extremely ill, homeless and with not a friend in the world.

And till this day it's always been me against the world and always will be.

I actually had tears in my eyes cycling into Dublin City Centre hoping to find a hostel to stay in.

I went around to several hostels in Dublin City; I think most were full.

Then I got to The Iveagh Hostel in Bride Street, Dublin 2 I think.

The man there told me that there were a few vacant rooms in the hostel. I told him I had no money; he told me to go to Charles Street and ask for money to stay in the hostel.

So I went down to Charles Street where there were a lot of people, maybe 20 or more, looking for money from the social welfare.

Eventually I got to see a welfare officer. I can't remember whether they were male or female.

The person there either gave a cheque or a small sum of money; it probably was a cheque.

So I went back to the Iveagh Hostel and gave it to Karl O'Higgins; I might have cashed the cheque before I went. I can't remember.

No, I probably gave him the cheque as they were used to dealing with Charles Street and were used to receiving social welfare cheques.

So I now became a resident of The Iveagh until July 1994.

Also in this hostel all your meals were included in your stay there, which was brilliant.

The next day I must have gone down to Thomas Street Labour Exchange to claim dole.

I might have had to get a birth certificate on Lombard Street to prove my identity. I'm not exactly sure.

After I got my birth certificate I went back to the Labour Exchange on Thomas Street and I was entitled to my dole money every week.

So I started to settle in The Iveagh Hostel.

I still could not sleep a wink.

I remember the bedrooms were very cold that September as they had not turned on the heating yet.

I wasn't the only one complaining about this.

As two elderly gentlemen were also complaining of the cold.

Both of these men must have been in there early eighties; I could be wrong.

I remember overhearing one saying, I had to wear all of my clothes and coat in bed as I was freezing.

I remember one smoked heavily as well.

These gentlemen were true dubs born and raised. I had a lot of respect for them.

I got the impression that both men were single and had no close family.

After a week or two I never saw them again. I would say now that they both have passed away.

God Bless them.

I began to make friends with a guy called Johnny; he must have been in his late fifties; he was one of the old timers and he had spent most of his life in hostels.

He told me he was originally from Stradbally, Port Laois.

He was harmless and he was the type of guy who really couldn't look after himself properly.

He was just a simple bachelor all of his life.

Don't get me wrong, he wasn't stupid; in fact he knew a lot more than me he was street wise.

As he had seen it all for many years in different hostels.

Which I would slowly learn.

Every week after getting my dole I would go back to The Iveagh Hostel and book myself in for the whole of the next week so I would not go homeless again.

Because we also got our meals included in our stay, nearly all of your dole money was spent.

So every week all residents would queue to get an additional supplement from a welfare officer who would be there in the hostel just one day a week.

I think her name was Sally O'Brien; now I could be wrong with that as it sounds like a famous Irish name.

She had a northern accent so I assumed she was from Donegal or Derry.

She must have been in her thirties; I could be wrong but if I'm correct, she must be in her early fifties now.

She was not bad looking. I remember she had lovely blue eyes and I think she was a brunette.

Don't worry. I had no romantic intentions as this lady I think might have been already spoken for or if not she had absolutely no interest in me or any of the other men.

Eventually the heating was turned on. In fact it was a little too warm.

But I found a way of controlling temperature by leaving the window open to late at night when I had to go to bed, even though I couldn't sleep anyway.

In late October or maybe November 1993 a few rooms had been broken into and some items had been stolen.

It must have been some time in November. I had about 70 punts saved up and I left it in a wardrobe. I also left my window open facing the toilets.

One evening I actually saw one of the young men; he went out through the toilet window and straight into my room.

He never knew I saw him. I could have opened the door and caught him but I was too frightened to do it in case he threatened to kill me if I told anyone.

I had often seen him in the TV room; you'd think butter wouldn't melt in his mouth, he rarely even spoke; he must have been in his early to mid-twenties, three or four years older than me.

I knew I was no match for him. As by now I was a physical wreck from my illness and he looked in great health.

He would have beaten the crap out of me. I was very frightened. I went to the desk where the man in charge was Karl O'Higgins and told him that money had been stolen from my room.

The guy who robbed me just happened to pass by. I said to Karl O'Higgins, that's the man who stole my money.

Can I get a room upstairs? He said okay, that's no problem.

So I went upstairs and got my new room.

It was very spacious; I had sockets for plugging electrical stuff in. I had my own sink with both running hot and cold water.

But the only problem was the cold. The heating was not great as the radiator needed bleeding. I did not want to bother anyone about this problem as I wanted to keep a low profile.

Even if the radiator had've been working fully, I think I still would have been cold.

I had to wear my clothes in bed including my good coat and still I was freezing.

I suppose it didn't make much of a difference as I couldn't sleep any way.

I remember around this time. I think I might have got a medical card and visited a GP on the South Circular road.

His name is Dr O'Cain; he's on the South Circular Road; to my surprise I think he's still there now, because when I checked on my computer and put in Dr O'Cain and it came up with the same name and address; he must still be practising; I thought he would have retired but maybe not.

There was a comment page for patients of Dr O'Cain and I gave my comments which were highly critical of him and now I'm going to tell you why.

I went down and there were a large number of patients waiting; there must have been about 10 to 15 patients, including a nun.

After waiting a long time I eventually saw him.

I was trying to tell him I had chronic insomnia and other things but he was not interested; all he kept asking me was, how long are you in this hostel? How long do you think you will be there? And so.

He just kept asking questions about where I was staying. He wasn't the slightest bit interested in my health.

He gave me Dalmane 30mg and Mellaril. He said, if they don't work you're on your own.

His exact words. As I've said before about the medical profession in Ireland, it's terrible.

I should have been well used to this by now and it would only get worse, not better.

I saw a TV programme on RTE 2 about Camden Street in Dublin about the night life around there.

It was recorded around St. Valentine's this year, 2015.

So that's only a few months ago.

What really shocked me was the lack of morals and the condoning of such behaviour.

What really shocked was the HSE was giving out free contraceptives to anyone in that area, young or old, promoting promiscuous behaviour.

The HSE is funded by the tax payer; these people who are out enjoying themselves are obviously very healthy having fun and sex.

Maybe I'm wrong. Are their priorities not wrong? I've been ill for nearly 30 years, I can't get proper medical treatment and never will.

I've written at least 20 letters of complaint to different Ministers of Health, also hospitals, and nobody gives a damn whether I live or die.

I just don't know what the hell is going on in this country; their priorities are totally and utterly wrong.

People who have absolutely nothing wrong with them physically or mentally and have no morals at all are given better medical treatment than I'll ever get, but that wouldn't be difficult.

Can anybody see my point of view? If I had not seen this true life story of what people do in this area I would not have known about it.

Although I already had an idea this sort of thing had been going on for a long time and was condoned.

Through the years as both a patient in hospitals and going to my GP, I've noticed that people with very little wrong with them are treated far better than me and that's not going to change anytime soon.

I have even fought just to get sedatives which barely work at all.

Every time I've been in hospitals I've been treated worse than an animal

I've been humiliated, rundown, made fun of, insulted, laughed at and told basically to get lost.

I now know that not only am I the only man in Ireland with my condition but in the world and would you think anybody would interested? NO.

I just got a reply from St. Bernard's Hospital, Dublin.

Saying basically the matter about my treatment in St. Ludwig's Ward in the summer of 1994 has been dealt with or finished.

I might send a last letter asking for the dozenth or more times. Why I could not get a second opinion. Why I could not see a male doctor and also less important because they don't have to do it why I could not see a dermatologist.

As far as I know in any public hospital in Ireland if you ask for a second opinion, you're entitled to one and if you ask to see a male doctor you're entitled to one, whatever any other maltreatment I received.

But Dr. Caitlin O'Larkin Devlin said no to all these requests quite categorically and has never been held accountable and never will.

That's justice for you in this country. My GP Dr. Meadhbh O'Cullen who I made a complaint about to the medical council over a month ago last Thursday 09/04/2015. When I had to get my prescription she asked me about it again saying she would have to give personal medical information of mine to the medical council, just to let me know.

Which was actually good of her because normally you would be kept in the dark.

By just a bad coincidence a medical report from Naomh Theodores, Co. Dublin arrived on her desk just the day before Wednesday 08/04/2015 to help back her story up; how very convenient.

She asked, did I want to change my mind about my complaint? I was actually seriously thinking of changing my mind.

But I said, if you had not have mentioned this to me about giving very private and medical information about me to the medical board and if I'd have found out I might have lost my temper and came down to your office and gave out to you.

Then she said I would have called the police. I then said nothing and left. I then decided to not rescind my complaint after all as her attitude has not changed one bit.

I had to ask Dr. Eoghan Rogan Friday 03/04/2015 to ask Dr. Meadhbh O'Cullen so that I can get a three monthly prescription from now on as I want less and less to do with any of the medical profession as I'm distancing myself away as much as possible from now on.

In fact if they just sent my prescriptions in the post and I never had to see a so-called doctor again till the day I die shortly it couldn't be better.

I will hopefully change my GP for the last time and it give one more shot and if that doesn't work.

I will await my fate, which is not long. Whenever I get this book finished.

There is a local GP who deals in men's health. I looked him up on the internet; he basically is my last hope.

I will not get my hopes up but give one final go and when that fails I'll spend the last one or two years of my life as best I can and arrange funeral details.

I did look him up last night; he only takes private patients so that ends that.

Also I was studying his procedures in carrying out his medical treatments and by now it would not benefit me whatsoever.

I also last checked all of Dublin's GPs and hospitals on men's health and it's a load of rubbish.

Either it's reproductive help or sterilisation or as they call them these days STIs which are all there for young men and women.

My chronic illness is nothing whatsoever to do with these immoral things and the other thing is only for homosexuals, of which I'm not one.

So that puts an end to me ever getting any proper medical treatment in this country but that's been like that since I was 14 years of age and I'm now 41 years of age.

Sorry I keep changing the subject when I'm angry.

Back to November 1993. I became friends with a man there. I cannot remember his name.

But I remember he told me he was a lorry driver. He said he'd been around the world.

I remember him mentioning Mexico; he told me that other Mexican road users were very rude; I knew this already because if you are a white I think the Mexicans call you Gringo.

They tend to be racist towards white men. As you can guess, it goes back to wars with the USA and former colonial powers.

He said he would give the finger to rude road users in Mexico.

He told me when he was staying in a hotel or guest room he felt a rat nibbling his feet.

I knew he was a good sleeper and I'm going to tell you why I know this.

The weather that late November and December 1993 was very wet.

During the days we would play chess.

I had not played chess since I was kid so I'd forgotten how to play it. So he taught me.

Once I learned the rules. We started playing many games every day. I really enjoyed this.

Chess really is a great game of manoeuvre and strategy; to the outsider it's terribly boring.

But when you're playing chess it is exciting and time flies by; minutes become hours.

I never won a single game of chess against him until finally one day I actually did.

As the old saying goes, the student becomes the master.

I remember once he bought fish and chips from the famous Burdock's in Dublin which was around the corner.

One day we got talking; I mentioned that I wanted to find a bedsit or a flat of my own.

He told me he was thinking the same thing himself.

Then we both suggested why don't we join forces and get a better place for ourselves; I would deeply regret ever doing this.

So we went down focus point where all the bedsits and flats that were advertised in the local and evening newspapers were all printed out on a single or a couple of sheets of paper, making it easy to look for a place and it was also free.

I remember there was a young woman about my age who I was fond of.

I had seen her before there, I think when I was first looking for a hostel to stay in a few months previously but I only remembered now.

She said something to me. Have you not found a place of you own? You're not still in a hostel? I said yes I am.

She was actually concerned about me; I was touched. I have never seen her since.

But I've fond memories of her. I barely remember what she looked like; I remember she had freckles.

But sometimes I like that in an Irish woman. As it proves her Celtic origins.

In the morning after I had my breakfast and when the lorry driver and I were going out flat hunting I would have to go to his bedroom door and knock loudly many times as he was fast asleep; he was murmuring.

I was of course envious of him as I still could not sleep a wink and he was the total opposite.

Back to flat hunting. I remember in December 1994 that truck driver and myself walked all the way out to Glasnevin; he knew the directions. I hadn't a clue.

We went into Glasnevin Cemetery; it was my first time there.

We marvelled at the different gravestones and tombs and crypts.

I remember looking at where all the archbishops of Dublin and maybe bishops were; I was impressed.

I knew he was anti-Catholic from talking to him in the hostel.

He remarked how posh their burial graves were. I defended myself by saying you've got to remember after Catholic emancipation in 1829 there was an explosion of Catholic faith throughout Ireland and that's why everything religious was given preference because of centuries of persecution from Britain.

But at that time in 1993 there was a huge anti-Catholic feeling in Ireland and still is till this day.

They blame the Catholic Church for everything; if the weather is bad it's the Catholic Church's fault. As the old saying goes, if you had diarrhoea it would be the church's fault; apparently it's the only religion in Ireland.

Well he looked at a few flats in Glasnevin but said they were not good and said let's go. I remember in different parts of Dublin looking at flats; he did the looking as I kept a low profile due to my bad health.

Then a few days before Christmas 1993 we went to look at a two-bedroomed house near the East Link not far from The Point Depot.

He went to see the house. I kept a low profile. Then he came back and told me somebody famous owned the place; he said she was an Irish actress on RTE; I think it was Glenroe.

I have not seen this Irish actress for many years; maybe she's retired now, I don't know.

He then told me he was taking the place. I now began to get cold feet.

I began to think that people might get the wrong impression that we might be homosexuals or something and I began to think of my illness again.

The next day he started to put pressure on me to cough up the money.

I said I don't want to go ahead with it. He turned aggressive towards me; I was scared and broke down crying.

He just said to me you're not mentally well are you? Because of my illness being burnt out and exhausted I was in a severely weakened state.

So if I got into a fight with another much healthier man than me I did not stand a chance.

I told him I had some money saved up in my mother's in Shankill. I could give him this.

I told him I had about 90 to 95 punts and I would give him all of my savings.

He then suggested we should take a trip on the Dart.

So we did. I paid for both our tickets.

When I got to Shankill he followed me down to my mother's but stayed up at the top of the road.

I went down to my mother's and she let me in. I said nothing about what was happening.

I went back up the road and gave him all of my savings being the idiot I am.

Then he said he wanted more money off me. But would wait until after Christmas to get it.

I said I will be in The Iveagh Hostel in January 1994 and will give you more money; he said that's fine.

I spent Christmas 1993 in my mother's. But I made sure to book my room in The Iveagh Hostel.

During Christmas I got speaking to my ma and da and started to tell them what had happened to me; they were shocked.

My da said if he saw him he would kill him. My relationship with my da started to change by now; he wasn't as rude as he used to be and became a little more understanding - don't get me wrong we were never close.

But from now our relationship became more cordial; he became a little bit more understanding.

I think he was beginning to realise I was not well. Because in the following years he would make remarks about the psychiatrists and doctors, about how bad they really were.

I don't remember much else about Christmas 1993.

I went back to The Iveagh Hostel in January 1994. I used to watch TV in the TV room obviously.

I was expecting that lorry driver fella to appear any day looking for more money and indeed he came one evening down to the TV lounge and came over to me looking for more money.

I said I have none; I was shaking. I said again I have none and he left.

But for the next few weeks any time I left the hostel to go to the labour exchange on Thomas Street I was always on the lookout in case he was watching or following me.

But thank God I never saw him again.

I remember there was snow one day in January 1994. One of the lads called Richard made a joke about snow to one of the female cleaning ladies.

I think there were three or four cleaning ladies working in the hostel; I remember two of them, Dympna and Joan.

Dympna must have been in her early 60s but Joan was much younger, maybe in her 30s.

Joan was good looking.

Once a week our rooms would be mopped by one of the cleaners, mostly Dympna on the basement floor.

Where I was. There was this young man, maybe in his early twenties. When Dympna would start cleaning the rooms in the morning once a week.

As I never slept a wink it didn't bother me. But this young man, who was far healthier, enjoyed his late mornings.

When he had to get out of the room just once a week. The amount of moaning he did, giving out about not having a lie-in.

He would use foul language that went on for ages; he was also paranoid. He used to think I was watching him just because I would walk around the perimeter of the corridors in the basement to get exercise so I would not have to go outside.

There was also another man in his 30s with the same problem as him being paranoid and very rude too.

I had far more important things to be doing than watching people coming and going out of their bedrooms.

Although most nights me and Johnny would hang around together near the dining room which was closed at night.

But we would see people coming and going mostly on a Friday or weekend night. When they would be going to night clubs or pubs.

There was a man there; I don't remember his name now but he had a great sense of humour.

One day he said to Johnny and me, if youse keep walking up and down the corridor you'll have the floor tiles worn out.

I remember I said one night to the man in the room beside, Peader O'Mulligan, keep an eye on my room.

He said I'll put a glass eye in it for you.

There was another man called Carlow, obviously because he was from Carlow.

He told us once at dinner that he had been in a pub and had free drink all day.

He said it was Brush Shield's birthday; I think he was 50 so this year he should be 71 years of age.

Peader O'Mulligan was an alcoholic; he would often not come out of his room for two or three days after a drinking spell.

One night he badly cut himself and needed stitches; he was left with a large scar on his nose.

I think there was a nurse called nurse Mor; I might be wrong.

I told her one day what was wrong with me. She said you better go to a doctor.

Thanks for the great advice. I remember Oisin O'Dermot calling her a lesbian since she was no help to him either.

I think she only concentrated on the elderly patients. A new man came in called Joe; he said the roof of his house had been blown off in the winter storms.

I remember he smoked a lot and he suffered from respiratory problems.

One evening, things got so bad that an ambulance had to be called for him as things had gotten so bad.

When he got back a few days later he was complaining about the staff in the hospital. I did not take much notice at the time.

But I should have. As I would find out many months later to my horror.

He also had a wicked tongue when he was in a bad mood.

I think I ripped up my medical card as it was useless to me. As I could not get any medical help.

A month or two after that I decided I would need medical treatment as my health was in serious trouble.

So one day I got talking to my da. He suggested there was doctor working for Dublin Corporation in a deal with the trade unions. If you were related to an employee, you could be seen for free. So I decided to give it a go.

I'm not exactly sure where it was it was, either Mountjoy Square of Parnell Square, somewhere in the north inner city.

So I went and there was a huge crowd in the waiting room; it could have been more than 20 people.

After waiting a considerable amount of time, I eventually saw him.

I began for the first time to tell somebody what was really wrong with me.

This doctor was brilliant. After I told him everything, he said I'm going to give you a letter of referral to St. Bernard's Hospital, Dublin.

He even told me what Dart station to get off at – Booterstown, he said. Well I actually later found out that it was Sydney Parade Dart station which is the closest to St. Bernard's Hospital.

I also had to go for blood tests to St. Sebastian's Hospital, Co. Dublin.

I read the letter of referral and what I remember is it stated I had psycho-sexual problems. This was not far from the mark.

It remains the best diagnosis I've ever got till this day.

I also asked him that I would just see a male doctor as I was embarrassed as it was a male problem.

He said that's fine, I'll arrange that.

So it must have been around May 1994. I went one day to St. Sebastian's Hospital.

This would mark the beginning when things would start to go distinctly wrong for me.

So I went to the hospital. I showed them my referral letter and went to wait where my bloods were supposed to be taken.

I met my old school friend Uiseann O'Higgins who I knew from primary school; he was there for the same thing as me.

So after waiting about two hours two nurses arrived. When my turn came.

They said my letter of referral was for private patients; I said I did not know this.

Then they started making fun of me but not in a nice kind of way.

They were running me down making derogatory comments, insulting and laughing at me.

As I've said before I should have been used to this by now.

I was obviously hurt by this. I left the hospital crying. Not only had I an extreme illness to deal with but also the heap of insults to go with it.

I knew my appearance hadn't helped my cause. I knew it was one of the reasons they were insulting me.

It did not appear to them that I may actually be very ill even though it was supposed to be their so-called job.

But as you well know by now neither the doctors nor nursing staff have a clue what they're doing and never will as they're too ignorant, negligent and stupid.

The only thing at the end of the day is their salaries or wages.

After that fiasco I was still in the Iveagh Hostel. The weather began to improve.

I remember walking down the Quays near St. Jame's Gate and I saw for the first time in my life the old wooden quays in the River Liffey.

The tide had gone out. I was really amazed at this site as the old quays must have dated from the early 1700s.

It was either late May or early June 1994 when I went in to Professor Liam O'Mullen Davis with my letter of referral. I gave it to him.

He looked at it but said nothing. Then he said when a bed becomes available we will let you know.

I said that's fine. I now began to get my hopes up. I thought now that this would be a real chance to get better and that I would give everything I had.

I thought since he was a Professor that he could perform miracles.

I just thought of Albert Einstein and imagined him doing everything to get me better.

But I would be quickly brought down to earth very fast.

In June 1994 I was preparing for my medical treatment in hospital and began to imagine everything like it was in the good old days, not a care in the world.

I don't remember how I got contacted; it must have been by post, either in my mother's house or in the Iveagh Hostel.

I remember a week or so before I went into hospital I put all of my sayings in the church.

I walked down Thomas Street and went into the beautiful church at John Lane.

When I was putting the money in one of the places for donations in a wall of the church, one of the lay men accused me of trying to steal from the church.

This was preposterous. I had actually put in about 70 punts of my own money which was a lot of money at the time.

I said nothing again as usual and kept my mouth shut.

Yet again I had been totally and falsely accused of something very serious and the complete opposite to what I was doing.

As by now you can see this is becoming a habit either being in the wrong place at the wrong time.

Or having people jumping to massively wrong conclusions and making very serious allegations against me.

On maybe my last dole day before I had to go into hospital I decided to open a Post Office account.

I forgot to mention in the last few months before I went into hospital, we all started to collect our dole from for Kevin Street Post Office.

There was a long queue at the Post Office. Eventually my turn came.

When I asked to open a Post Office savings account, the post mistress there was not happy because it was very busy that day and she had not got the time for me to open a Post Office savings but I went ahead with it.

I could hear her grumbling and moaning and also the bad attitude. But eventually I got my new account opened.

I never got to use that new Post Office Book with my savings as they were posted to The Iveagh Hostel which I never returned to, to get it. As I was too ill.

I arranged the day before I left The Iveagh Hostel for good that Johnny would mind my personal items until I was discharged from hospital. I had most of my stuff in a big black refuse bag.

But I would never see any of my personal items again because I was too ill to collect them.

But he said he would keep them in his bedroom until I got back.

I think I took the 45 bus from Dublin city centre and I stopped outside St. Bernard's Hospital.

I told Johnny what hospital I was in and how to get there if he wanted to visit me.

I remember it was raining when I was waiting for the bus and of course getting off at the hospital.

I went to the admissions desk and told them I was been admitted into the hospital. I asked them to check for my name and they said which ward I had to go to.

It was St. Ludwig's Ward, the ward of horror as I would later remember.

I came into the ward, walked up to the nurses' station and asked, was my name down for admissions? The staff nurse said yes. I think it might have been Sorcha Bangahan. I actually remembered her from my first time in a psychiatric hospital in November 1988 at 14 years of age in St. Gregory's Hospital, Co. Dublin.

Within the next week or so, I started to remember most of the staff nurses from 1988.

What really amazed me was that none of them had aged and what great health they were in compared to me back then.

I had aged a lot since November 1988 when I had lovely thick sandy hair, clear complexion, big clear bright eyes and I could still get a night's sleep; but that would change very quickly on June 39th to 1st of July 1989; from then I had not slept a wink, literally by now for five years.

I had bags and dark circles under my eyes; most of my lovely thick sandy hair was gone forever and I was a physical wreck and I was just 20 years of age.

I was amazed at how these women had kept themselves so well and had not aged a bit.

While I was the complete opposite. I had totally forgotten about any of these staff nurses as it seemed a long period in time.

I began to remember their names when they introduced themselves in the first couple of days.

Sorcha Bangahan, Dervil, Jackie Clare, Slaine McCarthy, some of the others but I still don't know some their names till this day but I knew at least three or four from my memory in 1988.

It brought back a touch of nostalgia for me. Briefly, as they would all let me down except for Dervil.

One of the student nurses came down with me. She said I had to get my details on a computer. This was all very hi-tech for me at the time.

I think her name was nurse O'McDermot. I don't remember her Christian name.

She was in her early twenties. That day when I was brought into my room with two other beds I waited to see my new male doctor.

After a few hours my new doctor arrived but she wasn't male. I was already disappointed.

It was the infamous Dr. Caitlin O'Larkin Devlin. I was willing to give her the benefit of the doubt which I would deeply regret forever.

So for the first few days nothing too much happened as I was been put on a new drug called Risperidone.

It had to be ordered in. So that's why I had to wait. Now and again Dr. Caitlin O'Larkin Devlin would interrogate me in her private room downstairs.

I'm not sure if she read the later of referral from Dr. OBannon; if she did she showed no reaction whatsoever.

She kept asking me privately, are you a homosexual, she said. I said no.

Then another day she asked me the same question, are you a homosexual? I said no yet again.

Then one day I told her I had been a patient of Dr. Lorcan O'Driscoll Mulhern in St. Gregory's Hospital, Co. Dublin.

She then asked me for my medical records from St. Gregory's Hospital. I agreed, getting the impression she was going to really help me.

I now deeply regret allowing her access to my private medical records.

As she just wanted to know all about my private life and had no intention of doing any good for me whatsoever.

Looking back with hindsight I wish I had done things differently.

Then, maybe the same day or another, she boasted that this was one of the best if not the best psychiatric wards in the country.

I was going to say to her if this is one of the best in the country I wouldn't like to see the worst.

If the place was so great why the hell am I am writing this true horrific story of mine?

By now I should be married with 10 or 15 children, enjoying life to the full.

Instead my life is a total nightmare; death will come as a release to me.

I just want to get this damn book written before I'm dead.

So I can tell everyone my harrowing story.

I remember two student nurses would come to talk to me during the first few days I was there.

These two young ladies were very well mannered and polite.

I remember both - their Christian names were Dervil and Bronach.

In fact the first day or second day after I had been admitted, I heard a young lady's voice; my back was turned to her as I was sitting on the bed facing the window.

Dervil said to me, you must be from Dublin?

Well I'm really a county Dub more than a real Dub.

You have to be born and reared between the two canals. It's not good trying to be something you're not.

She kinda agreed with me.

Well I'm from county Dublin as well.

I said, where? She said Booterstown. That's just down the road, I said.

The other young lady was from Lucan. These young ladies looked great; they obviously were in much better health than me.

I don't think they really knew how ill I really was because I never mentioned anything about my illness as it never arose in conversation.

The student nurse Dervil had a great sense of humour. She asked, how many brothers and sisters do you have?

I said two brothers and a sister. I would usually always reply with same question.

How many brothers and sisters do you have? I think she said six. I could be wrong.

She also asked me, what age are you? I said I'm 20. Then I replied with the same question.

What age are you? She said 21 years of age. Then I asked what month was she born? May 1973.

You're nine months older than me I said. I later found student nurse Bronach was 22 years of age.

I remember maybe a week or two later. When I was sitting in a chair in the TV lounge.

Student nurse Dervil said to me, you look very mature for your age.

I was going to snap at her, wouldn't you if you hadn't slept a wink practically for five years?

She would have said, I never knew that. Now you know don't you?

When a lady about the same age as you.Says you look very mature for your age.

You know that's not a good sign. Basically you look old.

At least the only thing I can say about student nurse Dervil is that she was honest. Not like the other spineless weaklings who would fill your head with a load of rubbish.

I could use much stronger language. I also remember student nurse Dervil did a night of the graveyard shift; by that morning she was burnt out and exhausted and could barely stand.

At least she could go to bed that morning. I kinda took my anger a little bit out on the student nurse without her realising it.

I said to myself, I've been doing this now over five years, tossing and turning night after night with no sleep in the daytime either and nobody gives a damn about me. So why should I care about her?

She also made that comment about how old I looked, not realising that it was down to a very serious illness which I still have and always will.

It's still happening today. The nurses may make a remark about your appearance without realising you could be seriously ill even though you're in a hospital.

The same place where they are meant to be looking after you. But they can't even do that.

In fact they're totally useless.

After waiting three or four days my new wonder drug arrived. YePeeh!! Risperidone.

I can't exactly remember whether it was the day before I was being put on that new drug or a few days afterwards.

I had actually got talking to staff nurse Fiona Mcbride O'Hanlin in private in a small office.

I was trying my best not to be explicit; after about 10 minutes she began to understand.

You get easily aroused. I said, that's right.

But the rest was just too hard to explain to her. I told her not to mention this to any of the other nurses as they would be laughing at me.

So a day or two later. When I was talking to Dr. Caitlin O'Larkin Devlin at the nurses station, when there was no-one else there except Fiona Mcbride O'Hanlin, who was just across at her office with door opened, she told me to tell Dr.Caitlin O'Larkin Devlin what I had told her a day or two previously.

I tried my best to explain to her what was really wrong all these years, but it was all in vain.

All I can remember her saying: 90% of men have that problem.

As far as she was concerned, the matter was now closed.

She judged me. She made me out to be some sort of pervert looking for attention.

Yes, I was looking for attention, medical attention, not the type she was thinking of.

I never got medical attention, nor have till this day.

I have no doubt in my mind I was discriminated against on gender or sex, whatever you like to call it, or both.

When I explain later you will totally understand my argument.

I only found out in my medical records after the freedom of information.

That Fiona Mcbride O'Hanlin put the word masturbation in my medical records. I had no knowledge at the time.

Although I had told Fiona Mcbride O'Hanlin not to mention it to any of the nurses. Although technically she didn't.

It was there in writing for all the other nurses to see. But I was totally unaware at the time.

None of the other nurses mentioned it to me even if they knew.

I'm not angry with Fiona Mcbride O'Hanlin as her intentions were good. Even I could see that.

I tried to explain to Dr. Caitlin O'Larkin Devlin what was really wrong with me all these years since the age of 12.

Dr. Caitlin O'Larkin Devlin assured me everything was going to be alright.

Within a very short space of time the side effects began to kick in with a vengeance.

I thought I was going to die. No, really I did. I'm not exaggerating. It's hard to describe how I felt; it was like I was going to drop dead or have a heart attack.

I told her how bad I really felt. This is basically the only time she kinda listened to me.

I'll give you five milligrams of Valium to calm me down. The 5mg of Valium actually helped only as so far as not feeling the fact that you were going to drop dead or have a heart attack.

But the rest of the side effects were unbelievable.

I had severe nausea, so severe that even if I looked at food I would want to vomit, even though my stomach was empty.

Then I had near blackouts, dizziness, headaches.

I tried my best to walk straight down the corridor to my bedroom. I actually thought I did a great job at this.

Until one of the patients, a day patient at the time, his name is Derek Moriaty from Goatstown, told me one day I was going from side to side in the corridor.

I hope he does not mind me using his name; he was 21 years of age at the time. So he must be 42 years of age by now.

You would think one of the staff nurses would have said something to me about my poor balance in the corridor as I passed the nurses' station.

But yet again not a murmur from any of the nursing staff; thanks for looking after me, I really appreciate it. In case you can't tell, I'm being sarcastic.

Also it would take me about an hour to dress myself in the morning. I would get up around 6.30am, not that I could sleep anyway. I could have got up at 3am in the morning if I'd wanted but I would have been bored out of my mind.

As I said, it would take me about an hour to dress because I kept getting blackouts, dizziness and headaches trying to put my trousers on and my socks and runners.

Sometimes the staff nurse would walk in and out of the room when I was trying to get dressed and said absolutely nothing as if it was the most natural thing in the world.

I remembered this nurse when I was 14 years of age in St. Gregory's Hospital and I knew she remembered me.

Also at this time I could not sleep although this medication was meant to make me sleep; it did help me relax at night in bed. But I still could not sleep a wink.

Actually the first two nights in hospital I actually slept a bit.

About five hours the first and about five hours the second but after those two nights for the entire six weeks I spent there I did not sleep a wink.

The reason I slept the first night for about five hours was how comfortable the bed was compared to the one in The Iveagh Hostel, where the mattress was like concrete.

The reason why I slept the second night, for about five hours again: staff nurse Slaine McCarthy gave me a sleeping tablet. I don't remember the name of it.

After around five hours of sleep that night my eyes in the morning were drowsy and heavy.

Staff nurse Slaine McCarthy thought I was still asleep. I said, no I wasn't. Yes you were, she said. No I wasn't, again I said. But I gave up arguing with her; it was useless.

Now I'll tell you what really happened that morning after taking the sleeping tablet. As I've already said it made me drowsy and my eyelids were heavy but I was still awake.

As I could see staff nurse Slaine McCarthy come and hear what was going on in my surroundings.

Despite all her years of experience, and I worked it out she must have been in her mid to late fifties by then so she had about 35 to 38 or 39 years of so-called experience behind her, but she still got it wrong.

I know I've heard of patients being awake during operations and being totally paralysed, unable to do anything about it as the doctors are totally unaware of this.

Until the operation is over and when the patient gets their faculties and tells the doctor what really happened, they would never know, and now I know why.

I know that's a lot more serious than my case but I'm just pointing out to you just to show how they can still get it wrong.

Even if patients are drowsy or their eyelids are heavy, as in my case, if a staff nurse comes in she will assume that the patient is asleep.

Only the patient will know the truth.

Back to where I left off. I did not sleep a wink for the next six weeks in St. Bernard's Hospital.

Each night I could see the staff nurse come in about four times a night; they're really meant to check every hour.

But get lazy and feel once every second hour is sufficient and are also sure if the patients are asleep, how will they know anyway.

But I did because I was awake every night but my eyelids were half closed, according to them, or in my case half opened.

This is where they're totally incompetent again. They just assume you're asleep because they're not really bothered to be sure.

The only staff nurse that came in hourly was Dervil as she was not as lazy as the rest.

Approximately 1am, 2am 3am, 4am, 5am, 6am, 7am and finish her shift at 8.30am I think.

As I've said, these are appropriate times, hourly give or take 5 or 10 minutes to get around to the three bed-roomed rooms of the 21 bedroom ward.

Now you're going to ask: why did you not tell them you were awake every night you were there?

Now I'm going to try and explain if I can.

First I was very shy because the nurses are very beautiful and it's hard to work up the courage to speak to them and also because of my rundown and ghastly appearance and I felt as if I knew most of the staff from 1988.

When I would try to explain anything, in their minds, it would be: he looks terrible.

How did he age so rapidly and what the hell happened since I last saw him less than six years ago?

So I decided not to want to bother any nurse as little as possible.

But one morning I did try and tell one of the staff nurses who I knew from 1988.

She was rude and arrogant; I was not in her league as I was poorly educated and very ill.

I told her one morning I did not sleep a wink last night; yes you did, she said.

There was no point in arguing with her. Her mind was already made up; she did not want to listen to me.

I was going to say to her, I saw you come in four times last night and four times the night before and the night before.

Then she would have said, how do you know this? Because I was awake all night.

I also remember she asked what age I was? I said I'm 20 years of age.

I knew by her questioning that this was more than just curiosity because she remembered who I was from 1988 in St. Gregory's Hospital, Co. Dublin.

She must have thought to herself, my God he's aged a lot since I last saw him.

She looked exactly the same since I saw her in 1988 but that went for all the staff nurses that I could remember from 1988.

How great they all looked and how much I had aged and looked terrible even though I was much younger than them.

It never really occurred to them. That I may actually be very ill even though I was supposed to be in a hospital.

Also I could not shower properly as I was having blackouts and dizziness in the shower.

When I told Dr. Caitlin O'Larkin Devlin this, she said get yourself a chair and sit in it when you're having a shower.

It was the way she said it. Like I don't give a damn. That's compassion for you.

You would never think I was in an actual hospital. More like a concentration camp.

I tried my best to stay on that damn drug Risperidone but after seven nights on it my body would still not get used to it; in fact if anything it got even got worse.

That night when staff nurse Dervil was giving out medication, I told her I couldn't take that medication anymore; it was killing.

She said okay and after she had given all medication to the other patients, she brought me into a small private room.

I said, Dervil I'm sorry. It's killing me. I'm not able for...I'm sorry for letting you down.

Then I broke uncontrollably down, crying; it must have been more than ten minutes.

She put her arm around me. This remains the only time in my whole life as a patient in any hospital that I was shown compassion.

I have never forgotten till this day and never will.

I forgot to mention after being in the hospital little more than a week, Dr. Caitlin O'Larkin Devlin was already trying to get rid of me because I remember being still on the Risperidone.

My mother had no phone back then as only rich people had phones back then.

I told Dr. Caitlin O'Larkin Devlin that my mother had not got a phone. So I could not get in contact with her.

So she suggested me writing a letter to my mother. How very nice of her.

As she was just trying to get rid of me.

I was too ill to go to the shop to get a stamp across the very busy road at the hospital.

The side effects of the Risperidone were killing me.

So one day staff nurse Fiona Mcbride O'Hanlin accompanied me over to the shop to get a postage stamp.

But when I got the footpath to cross the road, I couldn't do it.

My legs were like either jelly or incredibly heavy; also I was very unstable on my feet and I had dizziness and blackouts.

I was extremely frightened I would get killed crossing the road. I would not make it across alive.

So I said to Fiona Mcbride O'Hanlin, I can't do it. So we both turned back.

As I said I'm trying to work out in my head roughly how long I was in hospital before I was already getting kicked out by Dr. Caitlin O'Larkin Devlin it must have been no more than 10 days after I was admitted.

Dr. Caitlin O'Larkin Devlin was arrogant, rude, vindictive and didn't give a damn about me.

When I asked her for a second opinion she said No.

When I asked her, could I see a male doctor she said No.

When I asked her could I see a dermatologist about my scalp, she said no yet again.

Dr. Caitlin O'Larkin Devlin decided to put me on an injection. I think it's a called a 'depox'.

It's called a depox. I'll have to try and find it in my medical records.

Every time when she told me what the side effects were, they were the complete opposite to what she said to me.

For example she told me that the medication that I was put on would make me stiff getting out of bed and it would make me slow.

Instead it was the complete opposite.

Instead I was completely restless for nearly 12 days.

I had to keep walking up and down the long main corridor in the main hospital and I could not sit to eat without my legs shaking up and down vigorously.

I would try my best to sit down for as long as possible. I would try and count up to 10 seconds in my head. But then I would have to get back up again for a few seconds and then try and sit down again and count up to 10 seconds and get back up again and again and again. I think you get the message.

I couldn't do anything about the injection because it stayed in my system for 12 days.

After that she put me on different medication again.

When she put me on the new medication I asked her what does it do? She raised her voice: you know what it does. She looked her eyes up to heaven.

When she put me on different medication again about a week again I asked her what does it do? She raised her voice yet again: you know what it does. She looked her eyes up to heaven yet again.

These drugs did none of the things she said.

Except for terrible side effects. That's about the only thing I got out of them.

She looked her eyes up to heaven alright. But if she believed in heaven is another story.

I reported Dr. Caitlin O'Larkin Devlin to the Medical Council several times.

A total waste of time as usual.

I also made over a dozen complaints to St. Bernard's Hospital – another total waste of time.

I remember one day I was trying to tell Dr. Caitlin O'Larkin Devlin about the side effects of the medication she put me on.

When I started to tell her what they were, just as I was getting going, she turned around straight in front of me as if I wasn't there and walked down the corridor in St. Ludwig's Ward.

This will give you an example how rude this so-called doctor is.

I almost forget one day Slaine McCarthy started asking me many personal questions.

It wasn't done out of compassion or kindness.

But being extremely nosy.

She started with how many brothers and sisters do you have, what ages are they, what are their names, it just went on and on.

Do you have a girlfriend? Do you like women?

I said to her, I'm not answering any more of these personal questions.

So the next day Dr. Caitlin O'Larkin Devlin asked me to come down with her to an empty bedroom so she could talk to me in private.

I then knew in my head she was going to give out to me about my conversation with staff nurse Slaine McCarthy.

I was yet again correct. So Dr. Caitlin O'Larkin Devlin gave out to me.

I tried to tell what really happened but it was useless.

I was totally in the wrong and that was the end of that.

The hypocrisy! Dr. Caitlin O'Larkin Devlin giving out to me. It should have been the other way round.

After the way she had been treating me, worse than an animal.

Also one day earlier, when in conversation with staff nurse Slaine McCarthy, I told her I buried some personal effects of mine in the woods.

I should have not told her this. Because a day or two before I got discharged or kicked out.

I told Dr. Caitlin O'Larkin Devlin I had no money as she was so kind and understanding in case you can't tell, I'm being sarcastic.

She said, haven't you got stuff buried in the woods? I said to her, I don't have any money buried in the woods or any valuable items.

They're just of sentimental value. But she didn't give a damn whether I lived or died.

As if I would keep large sums of money buried in the local woods. I'm stupid but not that stupid.

I got discharged or kicked out around mid-August 1994. Staff nurse Dervil said goodbye to me.

I was going to say to her, I'm not even better, in fact if anything I'm even worse than when I came in.

Not only had I got my chronic insomnia and my eyes were paining me 24 hours a day, 365 days a year, and my scalp was itchy, greasy and dirty and also my hair was falling out in large amounts. But I also had to deal with the awful side effects that did not wear off for several weeks.

I've said before they kicked me when I was down and gave me the final boot when I was leaving.

The staff nurse Dervil said, come back and visit us sometime. I don't think she realised how seriously ill I really was.

Even if I wanted to come back in to visit the nursing staff, I was so ill at the time, that it was virtually impossible for me to do this. As I was totally burnt out and exhausted

I almost forgot to mention the Respiradone was still in my system for nearly the next two months.

I thought I had gone sterile from it.I'm going to be a liitle explicite my semen for the nearly the next two months was none existent.I had nobody to talk about this and had to live with it or deal with it myself at the time since as it was so embarrassing.

The day I got back home to my mother's from hospital I was in a state of shock.

What had happened to me? I had tried my best to get better. I tried to tell them very private and personal details in order to try and get better. But I had failed miserably.

I was literally in a state of shock for about a year after being kicked out of St. Bernard's Hospital.

It would not be till around May or June 1995 that I would start making complaints to St. Bernard's Hospital.

What had happened to me there.

When I made my first complaint, I was told that patients had only six months after the incident to make that complaint.

I tried to explain to them that I did not know of this because nobody ever told me this before.

If I'd have known this I would have made my complaint much sooner.

I tried to tell them I was in a state of shock at what had happened to me and that is why I was so slow in making my complaint in the first place.

But it did not wash with them.

Also Dr. Caitlin O'Larkin Devlin bailed the country and had headed off to England to a new job.

Which got me totally by surprise as I still expected her to be working somewhere in Dublin or even another part of the country.

Because I wanted to meet her face to face. But I never got that opportunity either.

In case I haven't mentioned it, I briefly met Dr. Ciara Murphy, either from Donegal or Derry because she had a northern accent.

She was as cold as ice. She was prescribing me, I think, 5mg of Valium for the severe side effects of the Risperidone.

I would meet her again in September 1995.

So back in late August 1994 my mother would be giving out to me. To do the washing up.

I could not do this simple task; not because I was lazy. But because of the side effects of the medication. My legs could not support me. So I could not stand at the kitchen sink in order to do this simple task.

I got upset and started crying but my mother never knew. She kept on giving out every day.

She did not understand how seriously ill I was.

I forgot to mention: when I was in St. Bernard's, after getting dressed in the early morning I would go down to the TV lounge. I would have to sit facing away from the window because the sunlight would hurt my eyes because my eyes were real tired from sleep deprivation.

I had this problem since I was 15 years of age. Since July 1st 1989 and it was now slightly more than five years later.

With the exact same problem.

Back again at home. The side effects began to wear off. So I had to go up to the EHB clinic to get some money from the welfare officer.

There was always a huge crowd there, waiting for different payments mostly.

I actually saw Mrs O'Higgins there. I had not seen her since May 1990.

When I was homeless. I just might have said hello to her. Both of us were embarrassed to be there.

I got money from the welfare officer. But after a few weeks he said to me, you nearly have enough stamps to claim something - I can't remember now.

Then he told me I'd have to sign on in the Labour Exchange in Dun Laoghaire as he could not keep giving me money every week.

I also bumped into one of the female patients. That was in St. Bernard's Hospital.

Her name was Aoife, from Foxes Grove, Shankill, Co. Dublin.

I just talked to her for a couple of minutes. It's a small world we live in.

In September 1994 my eyes started to pain me far worse. I don't understand exactly what brought this on so fast.

I know it's from sleep deprivation because my eyes were always paining me.

But now the pain got far worse.

I calculated that if this kept going on veins would start appearing in the whites of my eyes.

I calculated it would take no longer than two months and I was correct yet again.

By November 1994 veins began to appear in the whites of my eyes and have been there ever since.

As I've already said, three weeks exactly ago I had to go to the eye and ear hospital.

Where there was a large red blood clot on my left eye. There the great doctors could not find anything wrong and told me there was nothing to worry about.

That very same evening blood came out of my left eye. These doctors are great. In case you can't tell, I'm being sarcastic.

The doctor told me it was one of three things. I think they were severe coughing and vomiting and then she said maybe from lifting heavy objects all the time.

That's not from any of those explanations you threw up. It's from severe sleep deprivation.

I was here in 1995 with the same problem and I nearly got killed after leaving this hospital.

Back to September 1994. I decided to go up and get my personal items I had buried in the woods not too far from my mother's. The nickname for the place is Vietnam.

I went there after all the school children were at school so I could keep a low profile and not get disturbed.

So I eventually dug up my buried belongings and put them in a black refuse bag.

As I was leaving I slipped on the mound which was damp and hit my back.

I was totally winded; I could barely move for several minutes or even longer.

I thought I was going to die. There was nobody around to help me as usual.

It wasn't just the fact that I got badly winded. It was my weakened physical state. Because I was so burnt out and exhausted I could barely cope with this physical blow to my body.

In late September 1994 my GP Oisin O'Devlin asked me, would I go and get my medical records from St. Bernard's Hospital.

He gave me his business card with his details on it.

His qualifications his name and address.

As I've said before, because of my weakened state even getting to Dart to go to St. Bernard's Hospital was like a trip to the moon.

Because I was so burnt out and exhausted. I had to go on my best day. When I had as much energy as possible.

So eventually I made my way in. I met staff nurse Fiona Mcbride O'Hanlin. I asked her, could she get in contact with Dr. Caitlin O'Larkin Devlin so I could get my medical records?

So I went into the office and Fiona Mcbride O'Hanlin phoned Dr. Caitlin O'Larkin Devlin. I gave staff nurse Fiona Mcbride O'Hanlin, Dr. Oisin

O'Devlin's business card.

When staff nurse Fiona Mcbride O'Hanlin was talking to Dr. Caitlin O'Larkin Devlin her attitude had not changed; I could hear her on the phone; I can't exactly remember now what was said but I do remember the attitude of Dr. Caitlin O'Larkin Devlin and it had not changed one bit. She was still as vindictive as ever.

Eventually I was told no. I wouldn't be getting my medical records. Although it was my GP Dr. Oisin O'Devlin who would be seeing them, not me.

You'd think I had gone in to get Dr. Caitlin O'Larkin Devlin's medical records, not mine.

Obviously she had something to hide. As I would begin to find out many years later.

I went back a few days later to my GP Oisin O'Devlin; he asked, did you get your medical records? I said no.

I tried my best but Dr. Caitlin O'Larkin Devlin said no and that was the end of that.

I almost forgot, I'm going to send away for my medical records in St. Bernard's Hospital.

As I mislaid my original records. There could be much more incriminating information in them.

But I will have to wait at least four to six weeks before I get them.

So maybe in six weeks' time. I may have to put serious information in this manuscript of mine.

All I can remember in them is Paul Byrne has delusions of hair loss.

I really wish these delusions were true because I would not be nearly bald and also I would not have bags and dark circles under my eyes and my eyes would not be paining me 24 hours a day, 365 days a year for nearly 26 years by now.

Here is a letter dated 22 August 1994

Dr. Caitlin O'Larkin Devlin.
Psychiatric Department
St. Bernard's Hospital
Dublin

He believes that his hair is falling out because he is playing with himself sexually but has only told one or two members of our team about this and as such it may be unwise to mention it.

***

Many thanks for facilitating an early appointment.

Yours Sincerely,

Dr. Caitlin O'Larkin Devlin, MB, MRCPsych,
Registrar to Professor Liam O'Mullen Davis

I have only had this from my medical records from St. Gregory's Hospital.

As this was a correspondence between I think Dr. Caitlin O'Larkin Devlin and Naomh Theodores, Co. Dublin, with Dr. O'Plunkett. I could be wrong about Dr. O'Plunkett's name.

Her real signature is on the letter signed by her.

It's only dawned on me today that I actually had a team. It's the first I've heard of it. When I'd been talking to any of the staff nurses they never mentioned the word team to me at any time.

The only other person I told about this was staff nurse Fiona Mcbride O'Hanlin; as I mentioned, she put in my medical records 'masturbation'.

Then that infamous day. When I was trying to tell Dr. Caitlin O'Larkin Devlin what was really wrong, she didn't want to know.

She came to her own conclusions without mentioning them to me. If I hadn't have got my medical records from The Freedom of Information Act, I would have never known.

It's not a belief, it's a fact. As I've already told before. I'm going to have to be explicit here.

If I have to masturbate, my scalp becomes hot and itchy and greasy and my hair darkens in colour and my hair falls out.

This started when I was 15 years of age, beginning on the night of June 30th to July 1st 1989 and still continues till this day.

But the amount of hair I lose now is much less because most of my thick hair is now gone forever.

Also I have a better method of washing my hair and scalp, no thanks to Dr. Caitlin O'Larkin Devlin or Dr. Lorcan O'Driscoll Mulhern or Dr. Ciara Murphy or Dr. O'Plunkett or any of those other quacks out there.

Many thanks to all the great doctors and nursing staff out there for doing such a great job.

What would I have done without you?

I'm being sarcastic again. If the doctors and nursing staff would only just listen to the patients, maybe they would learn something.

But they never will because they're too arrogant. Full stop.

Back to October 1994. I still could not sleep a wink and the pain in my eyes became far worse.

By November the first veins started to appear in the whites of my eyes and have got worse ever since and still are; as I just said, three weeks ago a big red blood patch appeared in the white of my left eye.

It has kinda cleared up but now there are another bunch of permanent veins in my eye and they will be there forever.

Thanks to the great medical health service in this country. Also many thanks to the great Sight and Vision hospital.

In case you can't tell, I'm being sarcastic.

I don't remember much of Christmas 1994; only I was still extremely ill like most of the previous Christmases.

January 1995, another miserable year. I remember it snowed on the Dublin mountains.

I went up one morning and when I got to the rugged pathway to The Smelting Tower it was covered in a sheet of ice.

I had never seen this before. What must have happened is it had rained earlier in the night and then when it got colder the rain water running down the hill turned into ice.

I had to walk on grass verge edges in order not to slip or fall.

My 21st birthday February 12th 1995; I was in bits. I was totally burnt out and exhausted.

I wanted no fuss.

I had no birthday cake or anything else. I might have got a few birthday cards from close family and relatives.

That was about it.

Like my 16th birthday and 18th birthday, I don't even remember. I had no birthday cakes or parties as I was too ill and totally burnt out and exhausted.

What a great life!

I waited till my 21st birthday had passed because if I was in hospital, you would get a birthday cake and every one would be wishing you happy birthday and I would be embarrassed and feel awful due to my severe illness as I was totally burnt out and exhausted.

I must have gone to my GP Oisin O'Devlin the very same day or next day to ask, could I get admitted to St. Gregory's Hospital.

Not that I wanted to go to that dump. It's just you don't have a choice because I'm in the Catchment Area unfortunately.

I think I got admitted on the 15th or 16th of February 1995 into St. Gregory's Hospital.

That's actually extremely fast to be admitted to that so-called hospital.

When I got admitted staff nurse Coll saw my date of birth and asked me, did I have great 21st birthday party?

I said no! I didn't even have a party. I'm too ill for any of that.

I don't remember too much about my treatment there; like the other times, even my medical records are sketchy.

Although, wait there.

I remember I met my old St. Anne's primary school friend Sean O'Carolan. I was down in the basement going to have a cup of tea.

When I heard a young man's voice saying, how are you Paul? Hay wait a minute, don't I know you. You wouldn't be Sean O'Carolan? I haven't seen you for years.

What are you doing here? Then he asked me the same question.

I told him I had been ill for years now. He said, the lads would talk about you when they saw you out walking near New Vale, Shankill, Co. Dublin.

They would say, Paul isn't the same any more. He acts strange. He doesn't talk to anyone.

He looks dreadful. We don't know what's wrong with him.

I told him I had chronic insomnia since I was 15 years of age. I was totally burnt out and exhausted.

Then I asked him. What was wrong with him? He told me he tried to commit suicide.

They were putting his body into a body bag and found a pulse.

He was taken to St. Sebastian's Hospital, Co. Dublin and his stomach was pumped out, with charcoal I think.

Then Dr. O'Plunkett arrived and asked him, what happened? He then told her.

Then he was taken to St. Gregory's Hospital.

Where I met him then.

Then one day I asked him. Why did he try and commit suicide? Then he told me and I was shocked.

I can't tell you for the sake of his privacy.

I think I actually got the an odd night of sleep.

I think it was for three reasons: the medication I was put on and a new bed and also the powerful central heating that was on all night and day.

I remember one day in March 1995, Dr. O'Plunkett asked me, did I want to go to Naomh Theodores?

I asked her what would happen? She told me I would be seeing a group of psychiatrists.

I thought this would be great as maybe they would be able to do something for me.

But yet again I would quickly realise it was a load of rubbish as usual.

I said, yes of course, getting my hopes up as usual. But I would be quickly brought to reality.

So Dr. O'Plunkett took me in her car. We arrived at Naomh Theodores. I went up a few levels of stairs and was told to wait in a room with some book shelves in it. I remember seeing some books on Sigmund Freud.

Then Dr. O'Plunkett took me into a room full of women. There must have been at least six to eight women there.

I noticed that these women were very young, mostly around 21 years of age to 25 years of age - I could be slightly wrong.

Then I was asked to tell them what was wrong with me.

I told them everything. I then told them I was losing my hair and it was dirty and greasy. No! No! They said you have beautiful hair. Then I told them about the bags and dark circles under my eyes.

No! No! Yet again. You look great.

The compliments kept flowing. According to these young women, I could do no wrong.

Not only was I the most handsome man in the world, I also possessed other great qualities.

I could do no wrong. I was perfect in every way.

According to them. I was already guaranteed a place in heaven. Obviously they had direct contact with God.

I'm not mocking God. I'm just telling you what they told me.

I'm like no other man. I have no problem with women showering me with compliments.

But when it's a load of crap. Then I have a problem.

Just after I left the room. It occurred to me I should have asked one of them out on a date.

I should have said to one of the trainee doctors, can I go on a date with you?

She probably would have said, no. Well why not? I would have said.

You were just saying how unbelievably handsome I was and that I was the most perfect man in the world.

What's the problem then?

Well I can't date you. Why not? There could be a conflict of interests as I am training to be a psychiatrist.

There isn't a conflict of interests; first of all you are not a fully qualified psychiatrist and you are not treating me as a patient.

So there is no conflict of interest. So you weren't really paying me compliments.

It was a basically a load of rubbish to make me feel better. Is that right? How did you know that? Because I didn't come down in the last shower.

It's what psychiatrists would call positive psychiatry; if you're paid enough compliments it might actually work.

But unfortunately for them. I was so severely ill that not all the compliments in the world would make an ounce of difference.

What really amazes me is that in about six months' time, Dr. Ciara Murphy would insult me to such a level, like I was the lowest form of life on the planet.

From one extreme to another in the same service. How very extraordinary, don't you think?

I will mention this later.

I was getting about one or two nights of sleep a week there in St. Gregory's Hospital.

I think I got discharged at the end of March 1995.

I remember going to Eva Hall, Co. Dublin. The most boring place on earth.

The main room was where everybody sat down. Most of the patients smoked like troopers.

There would be a huge cloud of cigarette smoke hovering in the room. Even though there were fans in the ceiling.

After a few days there the effects of smoke on your respiratory system would begin to have an effect on your health on top of your illness to go with it.

I think I paid a visit to St. Gregory's Hospital.

One of the female student nurses there, I'm trying to think of her name.

I can't remember it. But she told me she was from Tuam in Galway.

She asked me how I was. I said, I feel terrible. They did absolutely nothing for me.

She just looked on with astonishment.

One of the other patients there, who I still recognised, said to me, I told my doctor I still wasn't well and they took me back straightaway. Well not me, I said.

Although she must have been in her early 40s, she looked far better than me.

Although that wouldn't be difficult. She didn't have bags and dark circles under her eyes and she had lovely thick clean hair even though she was about twice my age.

How very strange.

I remember going to Eva Hall for no more than a couple of weeks, from my mother's by Dart to Blackrock Co. Dublin and the bus to Sandyford. I think it might have been the No. 114 - now I could be wrong.

***

I soon got fed up of this place and had enough.

Apart from the few nights sleep I had from mid-February to end of March 1995.

My chronic insomnia continued at home. Now I decided to begin writing letters of complaint.

I think it might have been the then Minister of Health.

This was around May or June 1995.

I wrote them by hand as I had no computer back then. So everything had to be done the old-fashioned way.

I tried my best to write neatly. I got no responses at first; then I wrote a second letter and heard back saying, I'll be looking into it.

I've been hearing that now for nearly 20 years and nothing changed.

I also began writing to St. Bernard's Hospital, Dublin.

I was complaining about Dr. Caitlin O'Larkin Devlin.

They then told me that a complaint had to be made within six months.

Which I absolutely knew nothing about back then because, when it happened, less than 12 months later, I was only 20 years of age.

But that counted for nothing. As I've learned, these guys are utterly ruthless.

And then I found out that Dr. Caitlin O'Larkin Devlin was no longer in the country and was now working in England.

I had wanted to meet her face to face but I never got that choice either.

I never thought that she would not be still in the country. I said to myself before I started writing letters of complaint.

That at the worse she would just be working in a different hospital, more than likely in another part of the country.

But she was gone. Just my bad luck yet again as usual.

P.S.
I'm too burnt out and exhausted to go for a walk today. Even though the weather is beautiful.

Back in May and June 1995, although I had gotten a couple of nights sleep in St. Gregory's Hospital.

My chronic insomnia had returned with a vengeance.

The pain in my eyes was incredible and my whole body ached from head to toe.

I'm not exaggerating; the pain was incredible, even when lying on my bed I was still in extreme pain.

I sent a letter of complaint to Prof. Liam O'Mullen Davis in St. Ludwig's Ward at St. Bernard's Hospital about Dr. Caitlin O'Larkin Devlin.

After waiting a couple of days I got impatient. So I called on the telephone by making a call from a public telephone box as my mother did not have a telephone back then.

I got talking to Prof. Liam O'Mullen Davis's secretary Helen O'Kelly. I still remember the name.

I said, is Prof. Liam O'Mullen Davis there, I would like to speak to him.

She then started to get cheeky. Yes he is here. Do you want to speak, yes or no? As I've said before the attitude I got from Grainne O'Mulligan. Well yeah, I said. Well no you can't speak right now, he's too busy, and that was the end of that.

So the next day I got the Dart to Sydney Parade. I walked to St. Bernard's and went into St. Ludwig's Ward.

I think staff nurse Sorcha Bangahan was there.

I asked her is Prof. Liam O'Mullen Davis in his office? Yes he is, she said. That's fine, I said.

So I went in. I complained about what happened to me.

When I was a patient there last summer under Dr. Caitlin O'Larkin Devlin.

But I was wasting my time. He didn't seem to care whatsoever.

So I left, yet again very disappointed.

I almost forgot. When I was a patient in the summer of 1994.

The nurses were always concerned more about foreigners than their own.

For example. One of the staff nurses who I remember from 1988.

Started talking about her work in Africa as a volunteer nurse there.

I know it's her business where she wants to work and that's up to her.

She was more concerned about foreigners than her own people.

I know I'm feeling sorry for myself.

But when I was a patient there I was going through hell and not once did she ask me how I was or are you okay and she often passed me in the corridor in St. Ludwig's Ward and I could barely stand at the time and when I would be walking, as I've mentioned before, I would be going side to side in the corridor.

She would just walk past, like I wasn't there. Also when it would take over an hour to dress myself in the morning.

I'm not a 100% sure, it was either her or another nurse who I also knew from 1988.

It could have been the same because they looked identical; she was a brunette.

As I said she would walk into the room as I was taking over an hour to dress myself and walk out casually like it was the most natural thing in the world.

As I've said before not only am I the only man in Ireland with this severe illness but also in the world.

There is no man in Africa with my illness and if there was he would get better medical attention than me.

That wouldn't be difficult. A doctor or nurse would just have to ask, how you are?

I would be shocked if that ever happened to me. Somebody actually asking me how I am.

I've never heard that before. That's a new one.

Also I remember staff nurse Sorcha Bangahan talking about the soccer world cup 1994.

I hope an African country wins it. I know she's entitled to her opinion like anyone else.

But because they're African countries, they should get preferential treatment.

The summer of 1995 was an absolute nightmare for me. The pain was unimaginable.

My whole body, my eyes, everything.

I wrote letters to most European embassies looking for help.

I wrote letters to Bono, Paul McCartney, other famous people that I can't remember.

I even wrote one to the Vatican.

I wrote a letter to W.H.O., Amnesty International and other world international organisations about my severe illness. I only heard from two people.

The Dutch embassy and Windmill Lane Studios in Dublin docks, U2's recording studio.

It just got knocked down recently.

But I heard from no-one else that I can remember.

I also asked my GP Oisin O'Devlin, could I be admitted back into St. Gregory's Hospital, Co. Dublin.

I think I asked him this in June 1995. But I was told I would have to wait until a bed became available; as it turned out, that would not be till September 1995.

Three whole months I would have to wait.

I must have written to at least a dozen sleep labs in the USA asking if I could give myself as a Guinea Pig.

But I heard from none.

What really amazes me is how I got the addresses of these places, especially the sleep labs in the USA.

As there was no internet back then and I did not even have a telephone.

Any phone calls I made were in a public telephone boxes.

I think I even wrote a letter to Australian Prime Minister Paul Keating. I might have his Christian name wrong. I know the surname is Keating.

But I never heard from him either.

I almost forgot, in that summer of 1995 I tried to get in contact with the Mother Superior of the Nunnery in St. Bernard's Hospital, Dublin.

I got to the entrance desk in St. Bernard's Hospital. I asked the man there, could I get in contact with the Mother Superior?

After he made a few phone calls, he got me in touch with her. I don't know her name.

I got talking to her. I told her about the way I was treated by Dr. Caitlin O'Larkin Devlin and how ill I am.

Then she asked me, what age are you? I said, 21 years of age.

Then she said, will you donate 35 punts to St. Bernard's Hospital?

I said after the way I was treated, worse than an animal, are you mad?

She seemed more interested in money rather than my serious bad health and my complaint about the so-called carers in the hospital.

I'm going to write a letter to the Mother Superior about this, to The St. Bernard's Hospital.

You seem more interested in money than people's health. Somehow you lost your way.

Most hospitals in this country are founded on the principles of looking after the sick and poor.

I'm one of those. But so far I've experienced none of these principles.

As I've said before, I've been treated worse than an animal and that's putting it mildly.

I would have had no problem in donating 35 punts at the time even though that was a lot of money back then.

If I had have been treated with respect and dignity or even a little compassion. But I never got any of these and I never will.

I also remember another incident, whether it was around that summer of 1995 or a year or two later.

I wanted to speak to the Mother Superior in person in St. Bernard's Hospital.

So when I would see one of the nuns walking in the corridor.

I would ask, could I please talk to the Mother Superior? Before I was even finished with the sentence.

The nun would turn around and literally disappear, whether it was through a concealed entrance or door.

This happened several times with different nuns. I eventually gave up and went home very disappointed yet again.

By early September 1995 I was getting ready to be admitted into St. Gregory's Hospital.

A few days before I was admitted I was making yet another phone call in a public phone box across from Sandycove & Glasthule Dart station.

I was on the phone talking to some local health organisation.

When this young lady started banging on the door of the phone box, shouting at me, being very rude and telling me to get out as she wanted to make a call.

So I got out, having to cut short my conversation short in order to accommodate her.

I should have been getting used to this sort of treatment by now.

I got admitted sometime after the first week in September 1995.

I was put in St. Pius ward; it's like a prison; you're locked in 24 hours a day.

I remember some of the patients: Maggie O'Dempsey, a pharmacist from Glenageary who I would meet again in 1997.

There was Mhuire O'Lonegan. I can't remember the names of other patients at the moment.

I remember a man in his late 50s or early 60s. He told me he fell into the canal and got admitted into a different hospital before he was admitted into St. Gregory's.

One day I was talking to him about a trip taken by Harvey Firestone, Thomas Edison, Calvin Coolidge and Henry Ford.

One day all four men were out on a Sunday drive When there was a squeaking noise coming from the car.

So they pulled into a garage. They told the young mechanic about the squeaking noise.

The mechanic said, maybe it's the engine? No I'm Henry Ford and it's not the engine.

Okay the mechanic said, maybe it's the electrics? No I'm Thomas Edison and it's not the electrics.

Okay the mechanic said, maybe it's the tyres? No I'm Harvey Firestone and it's not the tyres.

Right, said the mechanic, so you're Harvey Firestone and the other two guys are Thomas Edison and Henry Ford. I suppose the other guy in the car is Calvin Coolidge, US President?

And it was but he did not believe them and just made a joke about it.

I also started talking about the Kaiser.

When your man who had been taken out of the canal said to me, you must be a very religious person and old-fashioned.

How did you know that? I said but I got no reply.

As I said, I still had my chronic insomnia. One evening on St. Pius ward as the night shift staff were starting their shift.

I told the male staff nurse about my chronic insomnia and if it was alright to keep him informed.

He basically said, don't be bothering me I'm not interested and I don't give a damn.

There was also a student nurse, I only remember her Christian name Peig; I was nearly the same age as her; she was only a year or two older than me.

Before I start, student nurses in St. Gregory's Hospital have tremendous powers.

They seem to be even more powerful than the staff nurses. I think it is because it's a private hospital and also to cut down on staff numbers in this so-called hospital.

So one night I said to myself I better tell one of the nurses I can't sleep - it was either 2am or 3am in the morning.

I had learned from previous mistakes like in St. Bernard's Hospital.

If I was awake all night to make sure to let the nurses know I can't sleep.

So I got up and went over to tell nurse Peig that I couldn't sleep.

I was just telling her and then she pushed me with both of her hands two or three times through the nurses station's door and slammed the door in my face.

Yes you heard right: in my face. This really happened to me.

As I've said before, you're damned if you do and you're damned if you don't.

So for the next several days, until I got moved to St. Pius' Ward I did not bother any of the nurses at night in case they would take a bite out of me.

I actually saw this same nurse Peig over a year later in the same hospital.

I recognised her immediately. You'd think butter wouldn't melt in her mouth.

I reckon if I saw her today I could point her out to you.

As I can remember her face very well still. Which is unusual for me. As I'm terrible at remembering faces.

***

So I was moved to St. Pius' Ward. One day I decided to head in to the EHB headquarters in Dr. Henry's Hospital in Dublin.

To get information on certain health matters I had been talking to Brigitte O'Hara as she worked in the call centre there.

I might have left after lunch in St. Pius' Ward. I thought I could make it back by tea time without anybody noticing I was gone.

So I got the 46A bus into Dublin city centre. I had to walk down the Quays towards St. James Gate and on further to Dr. Henry's Hospital.

I actually passed an old friend of mine from The Iveagh Hostel. I can't remember his name now.

He was drinking cans of alcohol and he noticed me. I said hello. He then said hello back.

I had not seen him since I left the previous year in early July 1994 so it was over one year and two months since I'd last seen him.

I eventually got to Dr. Henry's Hospital and after a while I briefly spoke to Brigitte O'Hara.

I said to her I never got my helpful advice documents from you. That you promised to send to me in the post weeks ago.

She said I'm sorry about that. I wasted my time going there as usual.

So I got the 46A bus back to St. Gregory's Hospital.

I must have just missed tea.

Then staff nurse Riona O'Comiskey asked me where I was? I said I was downstairs in the Snooker Room. No you were not, she said. I said I also went out for a walk around the pitch and putt.

No you weren't, she said, because I checked. I said, then we must have just missed each other around the grounds.

No you weren't, she said. So then I told her where I really was. I went into the EHB to Dr. Henry's Hospital to try and get medical help because none of you are doing anything for me.

She said to me, don't you raise your voice to me.

I said you have no idea what I'm going through; then I broke down crying.

Then I also told her about student nurse Peig on St. Pius ward. What she had done to me a few nights before.

How she physically pushed me at least twice or three times out of the nurses' station and slammed the door in my face.

***

I have checked my medical records in the last week and staff nurse Riona O'Comiskey never mentioned once my complaint against student nurse Peig although she mentioned most of the other stuff that I've just told you.

Even when you make a complaint, it's not even mentioned let alone anything done about it.

How convenient again.

Also Riona O'Comiskey had my wardrobe door opened and went through all of my personal belongings including correspondence with Bono and a few other famous individuals.

That I can't remember now and she asked me about them.

I said I'm desperate for help.

Later that evening I was in the TV lounge and staff nurse Riona O'Comiskey came in and gave me. Some Yoplait yogurts and a banana and a spoon.

She had gotten them from the kitchen, which was next door.

I was really touched by this act of charity. As I had not even asked for anything even though I had not eaten since lunch and had missed my tea.

Riona O'Comiskey remains the best nurse I ever came across in St. Gregory's Hospital, Co. Dublin.

Although that would not be saying much.

She was the only nurse there to show some compassion. I have never forgotten that.

Although, maybe a day or two later, I was put on a drug that made me restless again.

I could not stop walking up and down the St. Pius' Ward.

I had only complained a few days ago that I could not walk properly because of the pain I was in.

Staff nurse Riona O'Comiskey said to me, well you're walking fast enough now.

I was going to tell her. Why I was walking so fast because of the side effects of the medication.

But I said to myself, what's the point?

If she was any good at her job she should have copped onto this.

But she didn't. But that goes for every nurse I've encountered in my whole life so far and I don't thinks it's going to change.

I was disappointed as staff nurse Riona O'Comiskey left that ward and hospital. At the time I thought she was just on holidays.

But I've never seen her again since then. I have no idea where she maybe is.

Any good nurses disappear forever. While the bad eggs stay forever.

***

A day or two later I met the infamous Dr. Ciara Murphy

Who I'd briefly met over a year earlier in St. Bernard's Hospital.

She was as cold as ice. Nothing had changed. I said to her not to put me on the same medication that was been dished out to nearly all the other patients as if everybody had the same condition.

I said to her I have chronic insomnia, my eyes are in extreme pain, so is my body.

My scalp and hair is itchy, dirty and greasy. But she still gave the same medication as everyone else despite the fact that I told her it would not work for me.

Later that evening I think, or maybe the next evening.

She asked me to come into one of the spare rooms between St. Pius' Ward and the corridor leading to St. Pius ward.

She became very nasty to me. She began to insult me and degrade me and run me into the ground like I was the lowest form of life on the planet.

Do you think you're special or something? It was the way she said it, like I've just explained.

I said no. A few hours later I asked to be discharged from that so-called hospital.

I had had enough of being insulted and treated worse than an animal and I did not want to be in the evil Dr. Ciara Murphy's care, if you can call it that.

So the staff nurse got the doctor on call. I told him, I want to go home, I've had enough.

He said, can you not wait till the morning? I said, no I want to go home.

Okay, he said. I got my carrier bag and signed my discharge papers.

Then I had to call for a taxi. I waited a while, then one came. But the front entrance was locked.

He was tapping at the window. I tried to tell him to wait until I got someone to open the door.

He waited and eventually one of the security staff opened the door and I left.

Where to? he asked. Shankill, I said.

While he was bringing me home, I told him how bad I had just been treated and that is why I called for a taxi - I had just signed myself out.

He was shocked at what I had just told him.

Eventually I got to my mother's in Shankill. But I had not got the proper amount to pay for the taxi.

So I went into my mother's and asked her for change. She had none. Then I asked my father - I'm not sure whether he had change or not.

But eventually I paid the taxi driver and he went on his way.

Then I told my mother and father what had happened to me in St. Gregory's Hospital.

They were shocked but not surprised.

A few days later I went up to my old GP Oisin O'Devlin. I told him what had happened to me.

Then he suggested I try a drug called Anafranil.

I did not expect anything wonderful.

But to my amazement, I slept that night for the first time properly since I was 15 years of age back in March or April 1989 before my serious and crippling illness kicked in.

It was literally like a miracle. I did not want to get my hopes up but the next night I slept again.

This is amazing, I said to myself, I just hope this keeps up; and I slept a third night. I could not believe it.

Also now the pain in my eyes began to diminish and also in my body. It's a miracle, I said again.

My quality of life began to improve dramatically. After a week or two the world seemed a beautiful place.

I remember one evening my da was driving us home through Monkstown, Co. Dublin, when I saw my old friend Seamus Hanley walking home in the dark I had worked with him on Castle Farm building site Shankill Co, Dublin.

He told me he lived in Mounttown Flats Monkstown.

So it really was him and he was heading home. But he never noticed me in my da's car passing him by.

That was the last time I ever saw him. So it will be 20 years next September since I last saw him.

When I went back to my old GP Oisin O'Devlin and told him about my amazing improvements from the new drug he had put me on.

How I had managed to get sleep and the pain in my eyes had gone and also in my body.

He said to me, you have risen like a phoenix from the ashes.

I had chronic insomnia for nearly six years and three months and in all of that time.

Not one psychiatrist or other physician or any nursing staff had done anything to help me whatsoever.

That will show you what a very poor effort they had made in trying to get me better.

Despite the fact they were supposed to be experts and they are on huge sums of money and also getting large sums of money from big pharmaceutical companies.

I could not type yesterday because I am so ill.

I'm trying to make funeral arrangements.

So I got my sleep back in late September 1995.

It was literally a miracle.
But all of the damage had been done. My eyes are damaged forever; the bags and dark circles are under my eyes forever.
I'm now nearly bald. All of my lovely thick hair is gone forever.

My great uncle Eamon Walsh passed away in late September 1995.
He was the kindest man in the world. He would never say a bad word about anybody.
He would never judge in any way.
He was very religious. Going to Mass at least every Sunday. I would not be surprised if it was much more often.
He always loved praying.

I was talking one day to neighbour Melissa. I asked her who was painting her house - it was an uncle or something.
I asked her where he was from. Monkstown Farm she said. I said I've got relatives from Monkstown Farm.
What's his name? Sean Heinz she said. I've got great auntie and her maiden name is Heinz.
Then I got talking to her uncle by marriage and I asked him, did he know Eamon and Maureen Walsh and he said yes.
I said they're related to me. I said they were very religious people.
He told me one day, when he was young, he was with them. When he had to kneel down and say prayers with them.
He thought it was funny at the time.
In late September or early October 1995 the Divorce Referendum was on.
I was not registered because I was too ill at the time.
I called up to my old friend Ronan. He had only recently got back from the USA.
He had gone over in June 1995 with my best friend Peter.
He told me both of them had been working, mainly removing lead paint from old houses.
He said he had to wear a protective mask and suit.
I was watching TV with Ronan in his house. When the mention of the Divorce Referendum came up.
He told me he was in favour of voting yes for it.
I said to him that it was wrong and when I explained to him.
He said I never would have thought of it that way.
I said I was not registered to vote.

After being on Anafranil for a few weeks I started putting on weight.

I did not take much notice of it at the time until about three or four weeks later.

I bumped into my old friend form St. Anne's Primary School.

Who I had just met in St. Gregory's Hospital.

Sean O'Carolan said to me, you've put on a lot of weight since I last saw you?

Have I really? I had noticed my clothes getting tighter.

I must have been putting on a stone each month in weight. But because I was getting my sleep back I did not care at the time.

I had weighed no more than about nine stone before I stared taking the Anafranil.

Within several months I was over 15 and half stones in weight.

Yes, you are hearing right.

Although I had gotten my sleep back, I now felt like a beached whale.

My confidence began to take a blow. I now began to feel depressed because I was so fat.

One day late in 1995 my brother made a remark, you'll need a bra shortly. Because I had male breasts from all the weight I had put on.

One thing I can say about my brother. He is not afraid to hurt your feelings by being brutally honest with you.

I also began to perspire or sweat a lot since I had put on the weight.

I had never had this problem before in my life.

I don't remember much of Christmas 1995.

I don't remember much of my 22nd birthday on the 12th of February 1996.

I'm sorry I can't find my admission records in St. Gregory's Hospital.

I think in March 1996. There seems to be very little about it in my medical records.

As over the last few months I have found very little about this admission to St. Gregory's Hospital.

I think I stayed between less than a week so I must have been discharged in late March 1996 I think.

I don't remember much of the summer of 1996 at the moment because I'm so tired.

I tried to get admitted back into St. Gregory's Hospital in late August 1996.

I was waiting to get a bed in hospital and began to get impatient.

So one day I went up the EHB, Co. Dublin, I think - I could be wrong.

I was complaining but I got nowhere. I also think I had several letters previously complaining of my illness.

I left and decided to break a few small windows. So I picked up a few small rocks.

I made sure nobody got hurt because the windows in the part where I was throwing the small rocks had virtually no one in it at any given time.

So I broke a couple of small windows and walked down from the EHB, Co. Dublin, to get the Dart home. I did not realise somebody was following me in a car and had called Dun Laoghaire Garda station.

I just managed to pass St. Michael's Church when a Garda car stopped. I knew then I was in trouble.

I ran for it but some Gardas put me to the ground and handcuffed me.

They brought me into the Garda station.

They noticed I was sweating a lot and took off the handcuffs. They did not know that my profuse sweating was from the medication I was on.

I was then put into a cell. I can't remember but I explained I was very ill and that is why I broke the windows.

They then began to understand the reasons for my actions.

I got a surprise at lunchtime when I got a bunburger and chips. They were delicious.

They got them from The Miami Cafe.

One of the Garda then told me that he had asked a doctor to assess me.

After a while I said I just want to go home.

The Garda then told me that a doctor was on his way and it cost I think 80 punts for his callout fee.

So he said to me, can you wait till the doctor comes?

I said okay then.

Then later the doctor came. This doctor was arrogant and rude.

I said to him, can I get admitted to St. Bernard's Hospital, Dublin or St. Rupert's Hospital, Dublin?

No, he said, you'll go St. Gregory's Hospital or none at all.

There was no point arguing with this ignorant and arrogant man.

You'd think he was doing all of this out of the goodness of his heart.

Like he was not paid or something.

I can't remember exactly whether it was the next day or a little later.

I went with my mother and sister and brother to Naomh Theodores, Co. Dublin.

I was told I would be admitted that day if I made my way up to St. Gregory's Hospital.

I had my shoulder bag which was very heavy to carry.

Myself and my mother and brother and sister. We walked all the way to that hospital.

It seemed to take forever. But we got there in the there.

***

The doctor who was admitting me was American his name I think was Dr. O'Higgins or something like that.In St Gregory's Hospital Co. Dublin.

He kept asking me about the broken window panes at The ESB, Co. Dublin.

As usual the doctor was less interested in my health and concerned with other matters.

I think I got admitted on the 6th September 1996 or 9th of September 1996.

Into St. Gregory's Hospital.

This would be the longest period I would spend in a hospital.

I must have been on St. Pius' Ward for a few weeks. I remember staff nurse Sasha Doherty; she had very long red hair.

I also remember staff nurse Aine O'Scully who I had known since 1995 the previous year.

I can still remember some of the patients: Gerry, Lorraine, Michelle, Vincent, Sean, and also Eamonn who I would have a terrible falling out with over two and half months later.

I remember the weather in late September started to change; I remember the thunderstorms. I walked through the tunnel with thick plexiglass and I could hear and see the heavy rain beating off it.

I made friends with some people. There was this woman around her late 40s, probably the same age as my ma now.

She was from the northside of Dublin. I used to talk to her a lot and I also helped her to learn how to play snooker.

There was an 8ft by 4ft snooker table on the ground floor. Which no longer exists.

Nearly everybody enjoyed playing snooker as it helped to pass away time.

This is really the only thing I enjoyed in that hospital.

I also did occupational therapy. I would do woodwork - it was on either once or twice a week.

I also enjoyed doing baking. I think that was on only once or twice a week too.

Sasha Doherty asked me to keep a diary of my daily life or how I felt.

Gerry told me later he was asked to do the same thing.

I punctually kept writing in my diary every day.

But I remember Gerry wasn't as punctual as me because one evening he had to start filling in everything that had happened over at least a week or two because he told me so.

My sleep pattern at this time was not great but not too bad either.

Some nights I would get a good night's sleep, other nights I would not.

I'm not exactly sure what medication I was on; it might have been 60mg of Dalmane, Anafranil and one or two other drugs, without I would not have slept a wink.

Eventually in October 1996 I was moved to St. Joseph's ward I think.

But our base was St. Ludwig's Ward - now that name could be wrong.

I just can't remember exactly 100% its name. So please forgive me if I'm wrong.

I remember in October I was sent to St. Rupert's Hospital; they were going to check my sleep pattern.

At that time I think I was on Olanzapine, Tofranil and Dalmane.

I actually was getting good sleep at that time. As the beds also on St. Joseph's were extremely comfortable.

Even my da commentated on them. How comfortable they were and if he says they're comfortable they must be.

As I've said all the drugs in my system and the very comfortable bed helped me get the best night's sleep since I was 15 years of age, before my catastrophe.

I got taken by taxi to St. Rupert's Psychiatric Hospital, Dublin.

This doctor or someone put all these electrodes to my head using something like glue so they would not fall off and I had a device like the old-fashioned Walkman.

It seemed to take me forever to find my way out of the hospital because I just kept walking around in circles; the place was so big.

Eventually I found my way out and got a hackney taxi back.

The car windscreen had a very large crack through it. I was astonished that this vehicle was allowed to be driven on the roads.

I asked the taxi driver what had happened but I can't remember what he told me caused it.

That night I slept well, with the monitor device connected to my head.
So the next day I went back to St. Rupert's Hospital.
And the doctor there took the electrodes from my head.
Then I got a taxi back.

I remember for the next several weeks there was what I called 'glue' in my hair.

I remember Michelle O'Kennedy, one of the patients; she was always very generous with her money.
She was claiming the dole at the time the same as myself.

When we all would be in the coffee shop, she would buy us all tea and sometimes something else.
She told me she lived with her mother in Fitzgerald Park, Monkstown, Dun Laoghaire, Co. Dublin.
We became good friends. Before we both got discharged in early December 1996.
I asked would it be okay if I called to visit her? She reacted strangely saying, no you can't do that.
So I left it at that and said no more.
It wasn't like I was going to run away with her or anything I'm not like that.
I just wanted to visit as a friend.

Myself and Gerry would often play snooker in the hospital. He was the best snooker player I came across there.

There was a staff nurse called Peig - she must have been in her mid to late forties then.
She may be retired by now.
I can't remember exactly when. But one day when I did not want to go to Eva Hall, Co. Dublin.
She did not like it. The reason for this is the fewer patients on the ward, the less work she has to do.
So basically she just wants to get rid us for most of the day so she will have as little work as possible to do.

***

So she pretends that it is all in your good interests to go there.

That day I refused to go Eva Hall.

About half an hour later I asked if I could go downstairs and play snooker.

She said, no since you wouldn't go to Eva Hall. I'm not letting you play snooker.

It was like she was a 10-year-old spoilt girl in the playground.

Since you wouldn't give any of your sweets you're getting none of mine.

This is how childish some of these nurses really are. I'm not kidding.

This is a fully grown woman I'm talking about.

I went down to the end of the corridor and sat down with some of the other patients and told them what had happened and they just laughed about how childish this was.

Also I overheard staff nurse Peig saying to some of the other nurses there in the office, this is a short cut or easy way of doing things that I picked up when I was a nurse in England.

This was not the first time I overheard talk like this. Where you could openly hear them admitting how lazy they really were.

I also remember staff nurse Muireann O'Mulligan from Co. Wexford openly admitting how lazy she really was.

A few weeks earlier in St. Pius' Ward. I heard her say to some female patients that she had trained as a general nurse but the work is harder so she became a psychiatric nurse since the work load is so much less.

Staff nurse Muireann O'Mulligan often would be in the office on St. Ludwig's Ward.

She was incredibly lazy; she never budged from that desk. I don't know what exactly she was doing.

I often said hello to her. But she was so rude. She totally ignored me like I wasn't even there.

After a week or two of this I eventually gave up trying to be friendly because she pretended she didn't even see me.

Like I wasn't there. So I no longer tried even talking to her as it was a waste of time.

As I've already said, she never budged from that desk except for her lunch or if she used the bathroom.

I had seen this since I was 15 years of age from many different nurses so I should have been used to it by now.

I remember a little bit about Halloween 1996 because the staff nurse that bank holiday weekend told me I could have gone home that weekend.

How very nice of her concern for me.

The real reason she had mentioned this to me was not because she was worried about me.

But to get rid for the bank holiday so she would have less work to do with fewer patients on the ward.

Her only concern was her work load.

In November 1996 things slowly went down hill. There was a patient called, I think, Niall O'Colla; for some reason this guy took a personal dislike towards me.

He hated my guts; eventually I would feel the same way about him.

One example was I had left the Billiards Room and let him use the snooker cue and balls to play snooker.

When you normally finished you brought all your snooker equipment back up to the office.

So if anyone else needed to use them they would just ask one of the nurses in the office and they would give you them to you and you would go down and play snooker until you were finished and then leave them back in the office again.

So after tea was over I went down to the snooker room but there was nobody there.

So I went back up to the office and asked, could I get the snooker equipment to go down and play snooker?

I was told that they did not have them. I said Niall O'Colla was the last person I saw with them.

So I went looking for him and eventually found him in the coffee shop having a laugh with some of the other patients.

I politely asked him, do you know where the snooker equipment is? As it's not in the office.

He did not like this. His attitude I had received many times before from him.

He got annoyed that I was asking him this question and became angry so I left.

A few weeks later when I was going to Eva Hall; he was also going that day.

I noticed he seemed pretty popular with the other patients.

All of them were wishing him good luck.

One even gave him a bar of chocolate. I noticed Shirley O'Bannon seemed to think he was great smiling at him and I think she may have given him a bar of chocolate.

So he was popular with the ladies. Maybe you're saying I'm jealous.

Well not no really. If they want him. They can have him. I wish them all the luck in the world.

I think at this time the nursing staff were taking blood samples from me regularly for several days to see would I be compatible for a new wonder drug called Clozapine.

Most of these staff nurses were very rough taking blood with a syringe.

My arms were always badly bruised.

One day when I was playing snooker on my own.

Some visitor from outside the hospital thought I was a junkie because of all the bruising on my arm.

I said, no it's from getting my blood taken, that's what's causing the bruising.

I either had not enough white blood cell count or too much.

So I was not compatible and I was not put on Clozapine to my relief as I would have to get an injection once a month and after what happened to me in 1994 in St. Bernard's Hospital, I never wanted that to happen to me ever again.

November 1996 and I remember the weather really changed; one night there was very heavy rain that turned to hail and storm force winds.

I was in my bed that night in a room I was sharing with another man; I can't remember his name but he was very quiet and kept to himself.

He seemed to sleep a lot or was just in bed all day. But on the rare occasions he was up I remember he had an electric guitar with an amp. I was impressed by his guitar player's fingers sliding up and down the scales and frets like a guitar hero.

He might have had depression.

I also forgot I had been sharing my room with a guy who was like an eating machine. I remember him in the middle of the night eating all sorts of chocolate bars from Twixes to Skittles.

The amazing thing was he hadn't an ounce of weight on him.

One night he offered me a bar of chocolate. I said no thanks.

I remember the guy who stayed in bed all day and night. The staff nurse would bring him is medication.

This would come back to haunt me later.

I also got to know a guy called Vincent on the same ward as me.

We both had one thing in common: music.

We both would talk about The Beatles; he also played the guitar.

I remember he told me, there are three chords in Paul McCartney's & Denny Laine's song Mull of Kintyre.

Vincent was from Co. Dublin but passed away a few months later.

I will mention that later in this book.

I remember Vincent was talking to a young woman. I asked him what her name was; Lorrane he said.

That was the first time I had heard of that name before.

There was another big character Josey from Co. Offaly; he had a great sense of humour and also loved singing old songs; he was very popular with the young ladies.

Even though he must have been in his 60s at least.

He used to wear a tracksuit that I remember.

I used to call him the outlaw Josey Wales.

***

The weather in November 1996 started to get colder and patches of ice were on the footpath of the entrance to St. Gregory's Hospital.

I remember a middle aged man had his wrist in plaster. He told me he slipped on ice and fractured his wrist.

I was playing snooker on my own and he asked me for a game. I duly obliged.

Then Eamon O'Kennedy walked into the snooker room and said I was taking advantage of his unfortunate situation with his broken wrist. I said nothing.

I remember while I was away at home during the weekend and got back to St. Gregory's Hospital, Eamon Kennedy had taken ill - it was from the side effects of his medication.

I knew exactly what he was going through since it had happened to me a number of times.

But especially in the summer of 1994 in St. Bernard's Hospital.

When the Risperidone nearly killed me.

He had been taken by ambulance to St. Bernard's Hospital.

When he got back I asked him what had happened.

He told me he'd been taken to hospital and when he got there I think one of the staff nurses wasn't too happy because all she had to go by was what medication he was taking.

I said you should have been accompanied by a nurse to St. Bernard's Hospital; that's normal protocol.

But he wasn't and the staff nurse was not too pleased. She was giving out about it.

None of this seems unusual to me. As I've said before, I've been dealing with this sort of incompetence all of my life with hospitals in this country.

I remember I think news broadcaster Eugene O'Sulliebhan's son was also a patient there.

He had this fancy and expensive keyboard which I just got a glimpse of in his bedroom.

He would make threatening remarks to me. But I think it was from his mental illness.

Gerry Land would tell him to shut up.

Sometime in November 1996 one evening I used to call Eamonn O'Dermot 'Fergal Sharkey' as a kinda joke; it was really a compliment as I think he was great in The Undertones.

I actually said to Eamonn O'Dermot, it's only schoolboy humour.

It must have been late November 1996 one evening. There was a phone call in the corridor.

He said it might be for me. I said I think it's for Feargal Sharkey as a harmless joke.

But he did not see it that way. We happened to be sitting beside each other in the corridor; he then hit me with his arm against my abdomen and chest.

I got a fright and I was pretty shook up by this.

It took me a while to get out of the chair.

A short while later I told the nursing staff exactly what had happened.

My side of the story and also his side of the story, including me making jokes about his name being Feargal Sharkey.

Then I think late that night he was talking to the staff nurse Winifrid.

I needed to get my medication to go to bed. I got fed up waiting so I went up to bed.

After a while the evil staff nurse came up to my bedroom.

I said I wanted to get my medication, but you were talking to someone.

She said she was busy. Somewhere in the conversation, she said Eamonn O'Dermot had been provoked by me and what he had done was basically in self-defence.

I was going to say if it were the other way round I would be the one being accused of assault whether I was provoked or not, as I had experienced throughout my whole life, at school or teenage boys hostels or men's hostels. Double standards yet again.

But I kept my mouth shut yet again and said nothing.

I was trying to be as polite as possible.

I was now in bed. So I asked the evil and lazy staff nurse Winifrid, would it be okay if she were to bring up my medication which was kept in a small brown envelope.

Then she went ballistic.

She tore straight into me. I cannot put it into words until this day, as it's nearly impossible to describe.

She berated me, was extremely rude, vindictive, nasty, bitter and made me out to be the lowest form of scum on this earth.

I have never forgotten this till this day. It will remain with me till my short life ends.

As I've said before, I have been homeless in hostels; I've met alcoholics, junkies, paranoid maniacs and other mad people.

But so far this is the worst anyone has ever spoken to me in my life so far.

This so-called, supposed-to-be a nurse.

Maybe I'm wrong here? Are nurses meant to compassionate, understanding, caring?

As you have learned by now, this is an absolute load of rubbish.

These people are nothing more than a bunch of monsters.

The only thing they're interested in is their money and nothing else.

The welfare of the patient is the last thing on their mind.

For the next few nights I would try my best to avoid this evil nurse.

I would meet her again nearly 10 years later.

I think she might be still in St. Gregory's Hospital.

As I've already said before, she is the rudest and laziest person in the world.

Wasn't I provoked by her that night?

However I didn't assault her.

Double standards and hyprocrisy yet again within a matter of hours.

The next few days I kept asking to be discharged from hospital as I was very unhappy there yet again.

I got discharged in early December 1996.

I would not be admitted into hospital again until the summer of 2006, nearly 10 years later.

I was now on Olanzapine - I'm not sure how much - and maybe one or two other drugs including Dalmane.

I slept reasonably okay from now on for a while.

So I didn't need to go any more to hospital.

Thank God.

I do not remember much of Christmas 1996.

My 23rd birthday was on February 12th 1997.

The social worker Shauna O'Mulligan told me about a new place in Co. Wicklow.

It must have taken over half an hour to find this place when I got off the bus.

Eventually I found it.

There was woodwork, one or two ancient computers to use, a kitchen for all our meals together each day as we took turns, and sewing and maybe a few other little things.

After a few days I became disillusioned.

The staff that worked there were very lazy, especially the lady in charge.

I really mean it. They just didn't do anything.

One day when I was doing sewing which I had to teach myself.

As the woman who was supposed to be teaching me was too busy talking to one of the other women there who was far more experienced at sewing than me.

I had got some of the sewing patterns wrong. Since nobody was teaching me.

I tried to show the lady teacher that I had not sewed the patterns properly.

But she really wasn't interested.

So I got fed up of that.

The computer class was even worse. The two computers were ancient and nobody showed me how to use them.

As I had never used a computer before.

So I get fed up of that.

The woodwork class was not much better.

So I got fed up of that as well.

I also noticed all the relatively new cars the staff were driving, especially the lady in charge.

Who's car seemed to look brand new. But she never did any work as far as I know.

I decided I had enough and one late afternoon.

When we were finished I said to the lady in charge. That I decided I would not be coming back.

She accepted my resignation or whatever you like to call it.

I never went back there again.

I'm not sure if the place is still open or not.

As I've said, the 'Last SunSet' for me there for good.

I think some time in March 1997.

I started going to Eva Hall, Co. Dublin.

I can actually remember hearing about two women who had been murdered and viciously stabbed to death.

In a house owned by St. Brendan's, Grangegorman, Dublin.

By coincidence the man found guilty of their murders was I think convicted of their murders last week.

It took nearly 18 years to convict him.

I remember getting the Dart to Blackrock Dart station and then getting the No. 114 bus I think to Eva Hall.

I paid for both Dart and bus fare separately until one day.

I can't remember some young man his name told me that the one ticket paid for the entire journey as they were connected to each other.

I told him I was just a simple peasant and I didn't know of these things; he just laughed.

I remember we ate sandwiches which we had to pay for. However they were very cheap.

I would hang around with James who was originally from Co. Wexford.

However he lived in Dalkey with his brother.

Both of us would get the same bus and Dart home every day.

As I got more friendly; I said to him maybe I can call into your house on the way back on the Dart?

He said quite categorically, no you can't. So that was the end of that.

The main Sitting Room was full of heavy smokers including James.

There was always a huge cloud of smoke in that room even though there were ceiling fans.

Which made no difference.

I began to feel the effects of this on my physical health.

Especially my respiratory system.

***

This place was doing me more harm than good.

Just before last Christmas 2014 Dr. Liam O'Mullen Dempsey asked me, did I want to attend there again, in front of my mother.

I said no. He was just trying to get me out of the way and to keep me quiet.

My mother knew exactly the same thing.

Back to 1997.

Once a week we went on the mini bus up to Johnny Foxes Pub for a coffee just to get away from Eva Hall.

I noticed something in my medical record a week or so ago.

Mick who worked there said I had poor personal hygiene.

That may be in fact true. The reason for this was my very poor health.

Although it never occurred to Mick.

I told him my hair and scalp were itchy and I had dandruff.

He checked my shoulders and said you don't have any dandruff.

That's because every few hours I would make sure I brushed all the dandruff off my shoulders.

It never occurred to Mick that, although I was stupid, I was smart enough to try and look respectable.

I remember James and I always just missed the South Bound Dart and had to wait well over half an hour to 40 minutes for the next Dart home.

As the diesel train to Wexford always came at that time every bloody day.

There was a young woman from Blackrock; both of us hated each other.

I don't think we even spoke once to each other.

It was just a personality clash, nothing personal.

I think the last time I may of seen her was in 1998.

I don't know exactly how long I attended Eva Hall.

However I must have stopped going some time in early summer 1997.

I think there was a general election on in 1997. I could be wrong.

The weather that summer was wet as far as I can remember.

I went to visit my old friend from St. Gregory's Hospital.

Whom I had last seen in late November 1996.

It was now August 1997. I still had his address written down on paper. Which I no longer have.

It still took me a while to find his house in Co. Dublin.

I called to the door. His father answered. I said, is Vincent here?

He passed away a while ago, he said. I'm sorry about that, I didn't know.

And then he shut the door.

I knew then what had happened. It took me a while to take it in.

I then went down to San Siro Chipper and bought a batter burger and chips and got the bus home - I think it was the no. 45A bus.

By the time I got home my batter burger and chips were cold.

By about October 1997 I was getting very restless at home.

For some bizarre reason I wanted to leave home.

Yes you heard right. This restless period lasted about six months; then I settled until I got my bachelor pad in June 2007.

I know it was usually the other way round; my mother was always throwing me out.

***

But this time I wanted to leave.

My mother kept telling not to go.

I decided to try and go back to St. Gregory's Hospital for some bizarre reason; also I had wanted to leave home.

I went into St. Gregory's Hospital in November 1997.

I had to wait several hours to see a doctor.

Her name was Dr. O'Salmon I think. She was as cold as ice.

I tried my best to persuade her to admit me.

I even told her I'd go to St. Ludwig's Ward if there was nowhere else for me.

No, she said. I didn't ask you to wait here. You Know? I can ask reception to order you a taxi home.

How very kind of you, I thought to myself.

Thanks for being compassionate and understanding.

That would be the last time I would be in St. Gregory's Hospital until the summer of 2006.

I remember the song Barbie Girl by Aqua was on the TV and radio all the time that November 1997.

I don't remember much of Christmas 1997.

I can't remember much of my 24th birthday, February 1998.

I must have put myself on Dun Laoghaire Rathdown Council housing list.

Because I remember now I was on that list for about nine and a half years because in June 2007 I got my first house.

Where I now live.

However I tried to leave home again.

I thought somehow I could get back to The Iveagh Hostel, Bride Street Dublin 1 or 2.

It was definitely March 1998 because when I was looking for directions I noticed a lot of foreign tourists.

It may have been the day before St. Patrick's Day; I had completely forgotten.

How stupid of me. The busiest time of the year for hostels to fill up with foreign visitors; my timing could not have been worse.

I went down to The Simon Community; the lady working there wasn't too bothered whether I got a place or not.

She told me The Simon Community Hostel was completely full up.

I know she was telling the truth.

I asked her, was Peader O'Mulligan a resident in the hostel? She said, yes he is.

The previous year Johnny had given me this information.

When I last met him in The Iveagh Hostel. So he was telling the truth.

I asked the lady in The Simon Community, could I leave my heavy shoulder bag?

As it was too heavy to carry around. She said okay.

So I went to The Iveagh Hostel to see if they had any vacancies but they were full up.

I might have gone to a few others. But they were also full up.

So I went back to The Simon Community and told the lady I had no luck finding a place.

I think she then gave me a 24 hour emergency homeless phone number.

Thanks for being so compassionate.

I left and called the homeless emergency number from a public phone box.

I was told there was a bed available in The Morning Star Hostel; it sounded more like a morning newspaper.

I got there eventually. The place was very run down. I began to have doubts about staying there after waiting a while.

I decided to go home.

I asked the men across the road in another smaller hostel, could I use their phone to ring for a taxi?

No, our phones don't work that way. You can only make incoming calls. Don't kill yourselves, I thought to myself.

It must have taken a couple of hours to get home, maybe even longer; it was the damn heavy shoulder bag I was carrying that gave me most problems.

However I was delighted to be home with my mother.

I think a few weeks later I made my last effort to leave home.

I made an appointment to see a bedsit in Dun Laoghaire on the other side of Clarinda Park; it was much posher.

There was an Irishman and I was second and then an American came to look at it as well.

When we went into look at the bedsit, the American man skipped the queue ahead of me instead.

I said nothing as usual.

The place wasn't too bad. The heating was on full blast.

However I decided not to take it.

I think this was the last time I would leave home until I got my one-bedroomed bungalow from Dun Laoghaire Rathdown Co. Council in June 2007.

I don't remember much of the early summer of 1998.

Although I must have got a letter earlier in the year for an appointment to see a dermatologist.

I think I went in late August or early September 1998 to see Dr. O'Stalpeton in St. Bernard's Hospital, Dublin.

I had to undress into my underwear; then I was examined by a student doctor from Denmark for moles and other abnormalities.

Then I was asked my medical history.

Which I stupidly told her everything from my first admission in a General Hospital, which as St. Sebastian's Hospital, Co. Dublin, in early 1982.

After that I was taken to a bed or stretcher.

I can't remember exactly whether it was two or three moles that had to be removed.

While I was waiting to be seen to.

The student nurse asked me was I cold? I said yes. Then she pulled the blanket over me to keep me warm.

This is the only time a student nurse who actually cared for me.

I was deeply touched by this. As I never experienced it before and I never would again.

Then I was given a few local anaesthetics and then the male doctor had what I would call something like a soldering iron for fixing broken circuit boards.

I thought his methods were primitive.

As I thought they were going to be using laser beams and all sorts of science fiction technology.

But I was living in a make-believe world yet again.

He removed the skin moles with surgical scissors.

Then he used the heat from the soldering irons to seal the wounds.

Dr. O'Stalpeton supervised all of this.

A few minutes before the doctor was finished he asked, could I feel anything?

In the last minute or so I could feel the heat of the soldering iron.

However his job was done.

I was told to come, I think, in about six weeks or so for a check-up.

I came back about six weeks later and they and I were very pleased with my small operation.

That Christmas 1998 I was meant to send Dr. O'Stalpeton a Christmas card thanking her for doing a good job.

However I never got around to it.

Dr. O'Stalpeton must be retired a long time ago by now.

I don't remember much of Christmas 1998.

***

Now my 25th birthday, 12th of February 1999.

I think at this time I was taking about 90mg of Dalmane and Olanzapine I'm not sure how much of that.

So I was getting a reasonable amount of sleep.

That's why there is very little complaining from me at the moment.

Even though I had been treated worse than an animal by the so-called health system in this country. I was willing to let it go.

Even though I would get many flashbacks.

Also there was no point in complaining because as you can see you get absolutely nowhere because the system does not work for malpractice in this country.

I don't remember much of 1999 for some reason as it went by very fast.

Obviously Christmas 1999 was big, being the last Christmas of the 20th century and the end of the Millennium.

I can't even spell it right (but my editor will sort it out).

I remember some people were scared of the end of the world or computer systems crashing.

However none of this occurred.

I can't even remember the New Year celebrations.

The New Millennium January 2000.

In these doldrum years I usually spent every second week going for drives with my baby uncle Michael - he is four and a half years older than me.

Mostly down the country. I tried to walk as often as possible during these years.

My 26th birthday, 12th of February 2000.

I'm sorry I don't remember much of that either.

The next big thing I can remember is October 2000; it just came back to me today.

I tried to rekindle an old flame.

I wanted to go back to the good old days.

So I wrote a few letters to Niamh from primary school days.

Whom I knew. When I was 10 and 11.

It was a big mistake.

I tried my best to explain why things happened the way they did and that it was not her fault but mine.

I tried my best to explain I had no interest in any girls at that age because I had not gone through puberty yet.

I know I really hurt Niamh badly. I'm sorry. Please forgive me.

One evening in that October 2000.

The phone rang but I was cleaning my teeth.

My youngest brother told me, there was a phone call for you from a woman called Niamh.

I rang her parents' phone number back and I gave her da all of my details, my full name, address, telephone number. He wrote it all down.

Then a short while later the phone rang and I answered it.

It was Niamh. The anger in her voice! If she could have strangled me on the telephone line that night she would have done it there and then.

If I were to write any more letters she would call the gards.

I said I don't mind going to prison for you.

Then I got the message plain and clear.

That was 15 years ago.

Goodbye.

To be honest I got off lightly after the way I had treated her when I was 10 years of age and 11 years of age.

I got off lightly.

I knew then I had lost her forever. I have never tried to get in contact with her again and I never will.

I went on my first holiday abroad in December 2000 to Spain with my uncle who had bought a two-bedroomed villa there in Alicante.

There were no direct flights to Alicante from Dublin back then I think - I could be wrong.

So we had to go to Malaga in the very south of Spain.

This remains today the most enjoyable holiday of my life.

He had hired a very small car; I think it was a Fiat Cinquecento - I know I spelt that wrong.

It was dark as we left the airport at Malaga.

The roads got darker and darker as we went away from major towns and villages.

It became too dangerous to drive on the roads as we could not see where we were going.

We had to stop for the night in a hotel.

The lady at reception thought my uncle was American.

His passport had an American rubber stamp mark on it.

That's what must have caused her confusion.

The next morning. When we checked out of the hotel.

We got a fright; we had nearly driven off a cliff.

Which we knew nothing about until that morning.

How close we had cheated death.

The car did not even have a radio in it. I did not mind as we could talk forever.

My uncle must have driven over 700 miles to get to his villa in Alicante.

The landscape was amazing; it was like something out of a spaghetti western. I could visualise Clint Eastwood on horseback in the distance.

The mountains were totally barren and it was a semi-arid climate.

The weather for early December was amazing.

Totally blue skies every day with temperatures around 19 or 20 degrees Celsius - just perfect weather for holidaying.

The nights were a little chilly. However that is to be expected in early December.

We went for a stroll around late evening, getting back to my uncle's villa around 9.30pm or 10pm.

We spent a week there.

When we arrived at Dublin airport my uncle was getting worried that we might not be collected at the airport by my other uncle Joe.

I thought my bottles of alcohol had broken in my luggage, even though I had them well wrapped in bath towels.

My large luggage bag was wet. I said to my uncle I think the bottles of alcohol got broken by baggage handlers.

My uncle said they're just wet from the rain and then told me to shut the fuck up.

Sorry for the bad language. I had never heard my uncle speak like this to me before.

I was in shock.

Instead my da arrived and brought my uncle and me home.

My da kept on speaking about Tenerife; that was his favourite at the time since he had recently been there and thought it was the greatest place on earth.

He kept on talking about it all the way home.

When I tried to mention how lovely the scenery and landscape was in Spain.

He said I've already heard that. He was his rude self as usual.

However he kept repeating time after time about the same thing about Tenerife and I had to listen to it till I eventually got home.

I don't remember much of Christmas 2000.
Sorry about that.

My 27th birthday, 12th of February 2001.

Today Wednesday 29/04/2015.
I was like an antichrist today.
I took it out on my mother.
Sorry ma.
I'm still waiting to get my medical records from St. Bernard's Hospital, Dublin.

It's turning into another nightmare.

This is the second letter I've had to send again.

I need photo ID even though I told them I mislaid my passport.

I had to get a photocopy of my Travel Pass today at the local post office in Ballybrack Village, Co. Dublin.

I just hope it's good enough for them as usual.

However even if it suffices, I could be waiting at least a month to get my medical records at the earliest.

It may even be longer.

Some of the information in it could be extremely important for this book of mine.

But I can't remember what's in it.

Except Dr. Caitlin O'Larkin Devlin saying I have delusions about hairlessness.

I really wish it were true

My eyes today are paining me like hell. Today Wednesday 29/04/2015.

I was shouting and giving out to my mother about the way I have been treated by doctors and nursing staff over the last few decades.

I'm really worried about my heart as it keeps slowing down and then beating rapidly.

I'm in a real hurry to get this book finished before I'm dead.

I'm going tomorrow to see a hypnotherapist.

I've run out of options.

I'm becoming increasingly desperate.

May God help me.

I'm trying my best to speed up writing this book as quickly as possible.

***

Back to 2001.

I can't remember much of that year either.

I must have been on Dalmane 90mg and Olanzapine - I don't know how much.

My 28th birthday on 12th of February 2002.

I don't remember much of that either.

In fact something just came back to me.

I remember the summer of 2002 was very dry, including September 2002.

Sorry I'm trying to remember, did I get stung by a dying wasp that year?

Well if I did.

This is what happened to me.

It was either late September or early October 2002 or 2003, I'm not exactly sure.

I was in Dun Laoghaire walking past the entrance to St. Michael's Roman Catholic Church.

I felt something on the back of my head.

It felt like a fallen leaf of a tree on the back of my head.

So I tried to brush it off with my left hand.

So I brushed it off with my left hand and I felt an enormous pain in one of my fingers.

I knew I had been stung by a wasp.

It was the most intense pain imaginable.

I wanted to scream out loud but I was unable to because Dun Laoghaire was full of hundreds of people out shopping.

And I did not want to draw attention.

As I said I wanted to scream - the pain was that bad.

I managed to control myself.

It took nearly half an hour before the pain subsided.

The next day I went to my GP Oisin O'Devlin and told him.

What had happened to me.

He joked, I hope you killed that wasp?

I think this was the first time in my life I had ever been stung by a wasp.

Or if it wasn't, it was the worst ever sting imaginable.

I got stung by two more wasps in the next two or three years around the same time of year.

Which I may mention.

I'm not exactly sure but I think Dan in the old folks home passed away in late September 2002 or early October.

Now I could be wrong; it may have been the following year in 2003; it was either one or the other.

You will have to check records to confirm that to be a 100% sure.

My da happened to be in St. Sebastian's Hospital, Co. Dublin.

With a heart complaint, around the same time.

Because one day when I came in to visit him.

I said Dan in the old folks passed away.

Oh, Dan passed away and da said it to some of the other patients there.

It was the first time I heard of Dan's surname.

That's how I remember.

Dan was a harmless man.

I think I mentioned in 1984 I went rabbit hunting with him and his ferrets and got nothing. Only wet feet.

I think my da was there in St. Sebastian's Hospital for about a week or so.

He mentioned they were giving him rat poison to thin the blood.

He thought it was funny.

I'm not exactly sure, I think the name for it is Warfarin. I might be wrong or spelt it wromg.

I think he discharged himself.

I know exactly how he felt. They do nothing for you and you just want to go home as quickly as possible.

I've done it so many times myself.

However beginning in early October 2002 it started to rain a lot.

I think it rained nearly every single day for nearly two months until the end of November 2002.

I think the river Tolka in Dublin flooded its banks.

It was the wettest two months I had seen for a long time.

I remember we had to go to a snooker exhibition match in the Helix in Dublin City University.

It was my first time ever there.

My brother and I got the Dart into Tara Street and then a bus from the city centre out to DCU.

I had my Travel Pass with me.

Although it was nearly 6.30pm.

The bus driver showed no mercy.

You'll have to pay your fare. So I did.

It seemed to take forever to get out there.

I can't remember who Ken Doherty was playing in this exhibition.

My brother is a big Ken Doherty fan.

After the matches were over it got very late.

There was no public transport available.

So I called a taxi.

Luckily for me I was waiting for the taxi to come on The Collins Road and it came swiftly.

My brother had thought I was mad waiting for the taxi.

I was justified in the end.

The taxi must have cost a lot since we were travelling from the Northside of Dublin to Shankill in south Co. Dublin.

I remember the taxi driver telling me.

He had played a friendly against Tony Knowles years ago and nearly beat him.

I was impressed. I can't remember what the taxi driver's break was.

It must have been impressive.

As I would not be mentioning it now.

So we eventually got home late. I can't remember how much we paid the taxi driver.

I must have been getting my Dalmane 90mg and Olanzapine - I don't know how much.

And I could have been on other drugs as well, I just don't know or remember.

My 29th birthday on 12th of February 2003.

I don't remember much of that either.

I remember going to see my first every professional snooker tournament in Citywest, Saggart, Co. Dublin.

In March 2003 the Irish Masters tournament.

Getting out to that place was like a nightmare.

I think my brother and I got the first Dart into Tara Street, Dublin city centre.

We must have gotten in there early as I remember it was no later than 6.30am in the morning.

When we were waiting for the bus to Saggart I can't remember the number of that bus now.

It seemed to take forever; not only was there morning traffic to deal with.

It must have taken the scenic route.

I asked the driver to let us know when we got to Citywest Hotel.

As I'd never been there before.

The bus driver let my brother and me off as close as possible to the Citywest Hotel.

Then we walked up this long driveway and got there eventually.

We had no breakfast.

So we went to get breakfast in the dining room.

To our surprise it was full of our snooker heroes.

Stephen Hendry, Mark Williams, Joe Swail, Ken Doherty. I can't remember them all.

But most of the snooker legends of the early 2000s were there.

Oh, including John Higgins.

After we had our breakfast.

We thought we got away without paying for our breakfast.

The manager there made sure we paid for our breakfast.

I think it may have been around 10.50 Euros or punts; I can't remember now.

When the new European money was introduced here in Ireland. I've totally forgotten.

We bumped into Steve Davis. I asked him for an autograph as he is one of my greatest heroes of all time.

He obliged and signed his signature.

I must still have it somewhere.

They always say you should never meet your hero and they are right.

That morning my brother and I had tickets for Steve Davis, against who I can't remember.

However Steve Davis won the match.

When the first frame got under way.

My brother and I got the giggles.

I could not stop laughing as a mobile phone had gone off with a very annoying ringtone.

It belonged to a famous Irish person.

Which even made it more funny.

My brother was smarter than me.

He covered his mouth while laughing.

While I did not.

Steve Davis saw me and said, do you want to leave or not?

I was mortified. I gave the signal I would keep quiet.

I was very embarrassed by this especially as he is my hero, of all people.

One of the ladies there who was a big Steve Davis fan.

After the frame was over said did you hear Steve Davis saying something during that previous frame?

I said he was referring to me and I apologised yet again.

Thank God anyway Steve Davis won that match and so I could not be blamed if he had lost.

I met Steve Davis after the match while he was signing autographs.

I then apologised yet again.

Telling him it was I who was laughing in the audience because of the funny incident with the mobile phone in the audience.

He accepted my apology and said it could happen to anyone.
He was philosophical about it.
As I've said before, never meet your heroes and now you know why.

***

The next match we had to see was not until the late evening.
So we went walkabout.
We saw Mark Williams playing golf at Citywest Hotel Golf Course.
Then we bumped into John Higgins' wife.
I did not recognise her. It was my brother who did.
He asked her.
Are you John Higgins' wife? She said yes.
Mrs J. Higgins had a child in a buggy.
It was obviously one of John Higgins' children.
My brother and I watched another match that night.
I can't remember who they were.
I don't know exactly how my brother and I got home that night.
It was either a taxi or maybe my da. I just don't know.

I'm sorry. I'm totally burnt out today.
I went today to see hypnotherapist, Cormac Colleran Thursday 30/04/2015.
I really just hope he can help me.
As he is my last hope.
I told him everything, including my private life.
Anything to get some sort of help.
It cost me 150 Euros in cash.
I'm nearly smashed.
I don't care how much it costs me.
As long as I get better.
I have a receipt from him.
I better keep it in a safe place.
Not like most other important things that I have a habit of losing.
Please God, may he help.
I do not mean this in a blasphemous way.
I'm sorry about my poor spelling (changed – Ed).

The next big thing I remember was going to my first pop concert in May 2003.
My all-time favourite musician and hero Paul McCartney was playing

at the RDS, Dublin 4 I think.

My da was supposed to come with me. As he had a ticket also.

However he gave it to my sister instead.

So my sister and I went to the concert.

I got the impression my sister did not share my enthusiasm for this concert.

I think my sister and I got the Dart to Landsdowne Dart station or some other nearby Dart station.

While we were making our way to the entrance.

I saw Sean Kenny and his wife there.

They were getting out of a car.

Eventually my sister and I found our seats.

I saw four men dressed in Sergeant Pepper uniforms getting their seats.

I was really disappointed with seats we got, considering how much the concert tickets had cost.

I also badly scalded my mouth with very hot thick chips.

My mouth was in pain for the next two weeks after that.

Before the concert started there were some weird dancers on stage for maybe no longer than half an hour.

Then the concert started.

It was amazing, like everything else Macca does. He never fails to deliver.

Before the concert was even over, my sister wanted to leave to catch the Dart home.

I was going to say something. Like the concert isn't even over yet.

Paul McCartney has to sing Yesterday yet.

However we left.

When my sister and I were walking to Landsdowne Dart station I could hear Paul McCartney still singing.

Then I heard him singing Yesterday.

One of the greatest songs of all time.

I was so disappointed. That I had missed this.

My sister wasn't bothered at all.

Since she had gotten the concert ticket for free and had not my enthusiasm or interest in Paul McCartney.

The ticket I had bought cost around 100 Euros.

Which is a lot of money in anyone's books.

I felt like I had been robbed and cheated out of seeing at least the last half an hour of the concert and Paul McCartney's most popular song Yesterday.

I never said anything to my sister about it. As I did not want to start a fight.

That night or the next day.

My oldest brother told me.

That night of the concert. My mother kept saying I hope your sister is all right a number of times.

My brother said. What about Paul? It's his hero that's playing there tonight.

Why are you not worried about him?

I was not surprised by this. For most of my life.

My mother always did this. I hope your sister is okay.

Don't worry about Paul.

My mother does this without even realising it all the time since I can remember.

I've had to leave my sister's name out of this as I do not want to cause her embarrassment.

I don't remember much of the rest of 2003.

I was still on Dalmane 90mg and Olanzapine and maybe other medication as well.

It was enough just to get me by.

I still had most of the same complaints, losing hair and so on.

However I was still getting enough sleep to get by.

I don't remember much of Christmas 2003.

My 30th birthday on February 12th 2004.

I got my first birthday cake at home since my 8th birthday on 12th of February in 1982.

It came as a total shock to me. As I was not expecting anything.

My mother and sister came in with a big white box and then opened it and inside was a cake.

Saying on it 'Happy 30th Birthday Paul'.

I have never forgotten. I just mentioned it again to my mother two days ago.

I was really touched by this act of kindness.

I think my mother and sister had it specially made in SuperValu, Shankill, Co. Dublin.

That supermarket there has long gone.

It was made out of fresh cream. It was lovely. I really enjoyed it.

Thanks ma and my sister and the bakers at SuperValu.

It must have been about a week or a few weeks after my 30th birthday.

That my uncle and I were going to Spain in Alicante in his villa.

I was frightened to go as I had just turned 30 years of age and I thought it might be a bad omen.

If I travelled by airplane to Spain.

I could see the headlines in the newspapers.

Young man turns 30, dies in plane crash.

I said to my uncle I was really nervous about this flight and the reasons why.

He reassured me everything would be okay.

Eventually he won me over and we took our flights to Spain and everything went fine.

I don't really remember anything about our holiday in Spain.

I don't remember much else of 2004; nothing much happened that year. Nothing strange or unusual.

My mind has gone blank. Now it could come back to me later.

I don't remember much of Christmas 2004.

My 31st birthday February 12th 2005.

I don't remember much of that birthday either unfortunately.

I did a Tenancy Course on the 9th of March 2005 for Dun Laoghaire Rathdown County Council.

How do I know this? I have the certification on my bedroom wall in front of me - that's how I know.

I would not get a one-bedroomed council house until June 2007.

The summer of 2005 was extremely dry. As far as I remember it, virtually didn't rain a drop in Shankill, Co. Dublin.

In June, July or August, it was also very hot.

I knew myself that 2005 was the driest year I could ever remember in my life, even drier than the year 1983.

I was right yet again.

I heard a year or two later. That the year 2005 was the driest year ever recorded and I was not surprised.

I got stung by a wasp yet again in September 2005.

I was out walking one evening.

When I felt something hit my arm. I'm not sure which one.

I looked at it and knew yet again I had been stung by a wasp.

A big red rash appeared on my arm.

I went to my GP Oisin O'Devlin and told him what happened.
He gave me a prescription for cream for my arm.
Even he was shocked by the large red rash on my arm.
He said if that does not get better within a few days come back to me.
I said I will.
It gradually cleared after about a week or so.

I almost forgot that Christmas in 2005.
My sister was over with her friend in Rathsallagh, Shankill Co. Dublin.
When my old primary school friend Hazel got talking to her.
Hazel said to my sister, I saw your brother Paul O'Brein walking in the cold in his T-shirt in the evenings a few months ago.
That was around the time I got stung by a wasp.
As I've just mentioned.
I didn't even know Hazel was still living in Shankill.
It brought back times of nostalgia for me and when we were kids going to St. Anne's, Stonebridge Road, Shankill, Co. Dublin.
I said to my sister if you see Hazel let her know that I'm still available.
My sister then laughed.
Hazel still holds a special place in my heart and always will.
The next time I would get in contact with Hazel.

Would not be until April 2011 on Facebook

That year my mother wanted me to do a course.
I decided to look for one that would really be close to me.
I found a course in Shanganagh House, Rathsallagh, Co. Dublin less than a five minute walk from me.
I got a leaflet from Choices on Quinn's Road, Shankill, Co. Dublin.
These guys were really lazy.
You had to do all the work.
The lady there thought she was great just pointing out the leaflet to me.
That was basically a full day's work for her.
All they seemed to do in that place was chat and pretend to be busy typing on computers.

My mother has the same opinion of them.
A few years later she went there to try and find was there some jobs available.
They were not much help to her either.

So it's not just me. Who thinks this about them.

This place closed a few years ago. I don't know how it even stayed open so long in the first place.

I got a place in Shanganagh House, Rathsallagh, Shankill, Co. Dublin.

The lady in charge was Carmen Rodriguez. I used to know how to spell it.

It's a Spanish name. As she is from the north west of Spain.

Carmen Rodriguez is a lovely and kind lady.

I have nothing bad to say about this woman.

There were other teachers: Maeve Stafford, Bernardine McGowran and Toni McDermot.

Carmen Rodriguez taught Spanish.

Maeve Stafford taught Art.

Toni McDermot did Communications.

Bernardine McGowran did IT Skills.

***

Of all the subjects I did there, I benefitted the most from IT taught by Bernardine McGowran.

Without her I would not be able to type my story on this computer.

I hold this woman in high regard and always will.

I started my course in late September 2005 I think.

SHANKILL VTOS
Provisional Timetable September 2005

Times of Subjects:

Monday to Friday:
Subjects from 9.30am to 11.00am

Break 11.00am to 11.15am

11.15am to 13.00pm

Finish at 1.00pm

I think I got an extra 25 or 30 Euros more in my Disability Allowance for doing this course.

Once a week.

I met obviously some new people; I knew some members of the families.

Rachel - I knew her brother from secondary school in St. Brendan's, Woodbrook, Bray, Co. Wicklow.
She was from Shankill as well.

Sinead, also from Shankill.

Elizabeth Gamill, from Greystones originally.
However then living in Shanganagh Cliffs as well.
No longer lives there, for a number of years.

Gabrielle originally from Cashel, Co. Tipperary, now living in Shanganagh Cliffs.

Jurgen from Munich, Germany; he only came in for art.
He was naturally good at this subject.

I might have been the only man at the beginning this course; I might be wrong, I just don't remember any other man there except myself.
I just remembered Jurgen from Munich; he was only there for art.
Any other time I think I was the only man there for a while.

I know one or two others joined a few months later.
I think that is everyone at the moment.

We all got talking to each other in the first few weeks, asking each other where we came from.
At lunch break time mostly.

I asked Gabrielle if her blonde hair was natural. She said yes.
I said, you're a bit of stunna.
Rachel said something like, I'm not blonde so I'm not a stunna?
Not at all, I said.
I've said before, women from Co. Tipperary are very beautiful.
I asked Gabrielle where she was originally from. Tipperary, she said.
There, proves my point.

I noticed Jurgen had an anti-Catholic feeling from certain remarks he made.
I would never go his country, Germany, and make anti-protestant remarks there.
First of all, I wouldn't do it in the first place.
If I were to do such a thing, I would be run out of the country and rightly so.
As it's none of my business. What protestants do in Germany.

A lot of foreigners come to my country and tell me how to live.

A lot of these foreigners make anti-Catholic remarks in my country.

Which is none of their business and these foreigners are still doing this today.

Is it me or is there something seriously wrong with this country?

When it comes to foreigners telling me what I should and shouldn't do in my own country.

I tried my best at Spanish.

However I am terrible at it.

It's got nothing to do with Carmen Rodriguez as she is a brilliant teacher.

If it happened to be German, straight away I would have a great interest in it and also be very keen.

Out of all the classes I did, IT was the best and I learned the most from it.

Mainly down to Bernardine McGowran. Who was and still is a brilliant teacher.

Although in the first couple of months she nearly loss her patience with me.

I could not even turn on a computer.

I did not know what most of the keys on the keyboard were for.

I could not even send an email.

I thought people who sent emails were some sort of computer geniuses.

We got our mid-term break at Halloween 2005.

Then I went back in early November 2005.

I think the weather was very cold that day as a minor cold snap, a strong northerly wind from the Arctic, came down to Ireland.

This minor cold snap lasted no more than two or three days, tops.

I think in early November we all went into Dublin city centre to get our mature student cards.

Which helped us get student discounts, mostly around 10% or so, and some other benefits.

I'm not sure whether Daragh was with us or not.

We got our cards and went our separate ways.

I hung around with Daragh for a while.

I could have the years mixed; it could have been 2006 when Daragh joined. I'm not 100% sure.

We had our first Christmas party that year, on Christmas 2005.
Before we went up to Mickey Byrne's or Brady's Pub in Shankill Village, Co. Dublin.
Carmen Rodriguez brought in some Spanish dishes - paella and Spanish ham and bread rolls and some wine.
I hated the paella.
However the Spanish ham and rolls were lovely.
The wine was okay too.
Bernardine McGowran came into the room I was in and said, you're being looked after well and laughed about it.
We all enjoyed the meal and desert in Brady's Pub, Shankill, Co. Dublin.

I don't remember much of Christmas 2005.

January 2006.

My 32nd birthday on 12th of February 2006.
I don't remember much of that either.

I remember something in Toni McDermot's communications class.
I mentioned the low birth rate in this country.
She got smart, I don't see you doing much?
It never occurred to her that I might not be well for a considerable length of time, since I was a teenage boy.
That is why I never had a girlfriend in my entire life.
So I could not have any children.
Not because I didn't want to.
However because I am so ill.
Thanks to the great health service in this country.
I was never given a choice.
Whether to get married or not.
Since I can barely look after myself as I'm totally burnt out and exhausted.
No woman in her right mind would touch me with a barge pole.
Thanks again to the great doctors and nursing staff in my own country.

I remember it snowing in either late March or even April 2006.
It did not stick on the ground at sea level.

I think the next big thing that happened was around May 2006.
I think I got a visit or phonecall from Eithne O'Kelly Regan from Naomh

Theodores, Co. Dublin.

She was the community nurse there I think.

She paid me a visit in my mother's house.

If I had any sense I should have told her to get lost.

It had now been nearly ten years since I was last in St. Gregory's Hospital.

I should have stayed away from that place forever if I had any sense.

After talking to me for a while.

Eithne O'Kelly Regan convinced me to go back to St. Gregory's Hospital.

As I've just said, I should have said No?

I yet again thought these doctors and nursing staff.

Would perform miracles.

However I would be quickly brought back to reality, not for the first time or last.

That May 2006 was one of the wettest on records as the previous year 2005 had been the driest year ever recorded.

So there was a lot of making up to do.

It was raining cats and dogs the day I was admitted to St. Gregory's Hospital, Co. Dublin.

I asked Eithne O'Kelly Regan if she could give me a lift into hospital.

She said, yeah okay.

So she brought me in and then the nightmare began again.

As I've said when I was In St. Pius' Ward in May 2006 it rained very heavily, non-stop, day after day.

There was a young man from Scotland, a patient.

One day looking at the weather he said, this is worse than the Scottish Highlands.

That will give you an indication what the weather was like that May 2006.

All of a sudden my Dalmane 90mg was cut straight away to 30mg.

The very day I arrived there.

Even if you're going to be reducing somebody's medication, especially if that patient has been on it for a number of years.

It's necessary to reduce it gradually.

However in my case from a large amount of medication to a considerable less amount straightaway.

Have these doctors never heard of cold turkey, being huge withdrawal symptoms.

These guys are supposed to be psychiatrists.

They of all people should know this.

I wouldn't mind if you had somebody to talk to or to look after you.

As usual the nursing staff were nowhere to be seen.

Not that any of these lazy uncompassionate ruthless nurses ever cared.

All they ever seemed to do.

Was hang around at the nurses' station talking and laughing and not much else.

If you were to put a bomb under them.

They wouldn't move.

In fact they did move occasionally for their lunch break, that's about it, and to go home.

Yet again I would be much better at home.

Eventually I got moved to St. Breda's Ward on the top floor.

I was in bits.

I was totally burnt out and exhausted.

I could not survive on just 30mg of Dalmane alone a day.

I was going through hell.

Only on the next day did one of the staff nurses say to me.

I see your head moving from side to side as you're sitting in the chair.

You look exhausted

You should go back to bed.

I can't because Dr. Liam O'Mullen Dempsey would not like me to lie down on the bed during any time of the day.

Two nurses I recognised from the past.

Staff nurse Sorcha Bangahan, who I knew from way back in November 1988 and then again in the summer of 1994 in St. Ludwig's, St. Bernard's Hospital, Dublin.

She did not recognise me.

As I had put on about six and a half stone since she last saw me from the side effects of the medication - the Anafranil.

Also I had aged rapidly.

And lost most of my hair.

Staff nurse Sorcha Bangahan didn't even know who I was.

I explained to her that I last saw her in 1994 in St. Bernard's Hospital, Dublin.

Obviously I made a lasting impression on her.

Then the real evil; lazy vindictive ruthless heatless rudest nurse in the world was still there.

Staff nurse Winifrid. She hadn't changed a bit.

As I've said before, the bad apples always hang around.

There goes my proof yet again.

I used to go to bed early, not because I could sleep, just to keep away from that lazy evil monster.

One of the patients there Kevin O'Mulligan from Swords North, County Dublin.

Said to me one evening about lazy evil staff nurse Winifrid, nice job if you can get it.

She had a duvet on her last night in the nurses office.

He stayed up late as I normally went to bed early to avoid her as much as possible.

I said I know what that staff nurse is like. She's always been like that.

I never mentioned it to him.

How she had treated me in late 1996.

Like I was the lowest form of life on earth.

As I've said before and I'll say again, the rudest and laziest person on earth, and still nothing has changed.

I would not be surprised if she is still there in St. Gregory's Hospital.

If I were to go in one evening I might actually still find her there.

If she has not taken early retirement.

Although if you asked me.

She had retired before she had even started.

I got fed up of the place again.

I was going through cold turkey and no one cared even though I was supposed to be in a hospital.

I could not cope on 30mg of Dalmane.

So I decided yet again to sign myself out.

I contacted my brother and asked him, would he collect me?

He said yes.

So I got taken home by my brother.

This is where the trouble begins. Dr. Liam O'Mullen Dempsey started putting pressure on my GP Oisin O'Devlin to rapidly reduce my Dalmane intake.

This I knew would have dire consequences later in my life.

When all of my reserves and supplies of Dalmane would run out.

I would be in serious trouble.

Like I am right now.

It's okay for Dr. Liam O'Mullen Dempsey to rapidly reduce my medication.

As he's not the one.

Who has to live my life.

With chronic insomnia and eyes paining 24 hours a day all year round and losing all your hair.

I would like to see Dr.Liam O'Mullen Dempsey spend a few months in my body and see what he then thinks.

It's like if I were a doctor and somebody had severe arthritis and was in severe pain 24 hours a day all year round.

And that doctor decided to reduce that patient's intake of painkillers and anti-inflammatories.

The doctor isn't the person that's going through hell but the patient.

The doctor is living a great lifestyle on a huge salary without a care in the world.

***

I must have got back out of hospital in June 2006.

I bumped into Elizabeth Gamill one morning, a student form my course in Shanganagh House, Rathsallagh, Co. Dublin.

I said to her, not to say anything to anyone on my course.

As far as I know she didn't.

I'm not sure when my niece's baptism was.

I think it was in June 2006; now I could be wrong.

I was my niece's God Father.

A few months earlier in March 2006 my sister helped me pick out clothes for my niece's baptism.

In June 2006 I was God Father for my niece in St. Anne's Roman Catholic Church, Co. Dublin.

The weather was nice that day.

It went smoothly.

Although I was disappointed that I was left out of most of the photographs, maybe even all.

I could be wrong. There might not even be a photograph of me and my niece on her christening day.

I remember that evening.

My brother and I walked with my auntie Anne from Raheny to Shankill Dart station.

So she could find her way home.

I had taken a few Dalmane 30s the previous night so I would be refreshed for the christening.

Also that June 2006 my next door neighbour passed away from CJD or mad cow disease.

I think he was only 25 years of age or 26 years of age; I'm not a 100% sure.

One day maybe in July 2006 Eithne O'Kelly Regan, community nurse from Naomh Theodores, visited me.

My mother was also with me.

In the conversation I asked could I be given rohypnol to help me sleep. She said no.

I said I might have to try and buy it from drug dealers or on the black market.

She said that some may have rat poison in them and other harmful ingredients.

Then she said that it's a date rape drug and if you do buy some you'll be reported to the Gardai.

I said to her all I want it for is to get some sleep.

Nothing else.

I was telling the absolute truth.

Never would I date rape any woman.

The other factor is. I have no contact with any women.

Because there have been no women in my life.

This is because of my severe debilitating illness.

Thanks to the great doctors and nursing staff in this country.

I think this was the catalyst or spark that made me do.

What I did next.

I think within an hour after Eithne O'Kelly Regan, community nurse, left the house.

I picked up some small rocks near the beach and filled them up in my small back pack that I used in my course in Shanganagh House, Rathsallagh, Co. Dublin.

So I got the Dart to Dun Laoghaire, Co. Dublin.

Got the bus from outside the Dart station up to St. Gregory's Hospital.

I started throwing those small rocks at the big reinforced steel windows at the entrance to that so-called hospital.

I cracked a lot of them.

However as they were reinforced with steel. They did not break.

One of the brothers saw me and said I will get into a lot of trouble.

I left walking because I was too exhausted to run.

Got the bus outside the hospital keeping an eye out for anyone.

Just as the bus was pulling out I saw the security man.

I found out a few days later.

That a new patient happened to be there.

When I was throwing the small rocks at the windows.

The old lady at reception, or someone else, said.

I think that's Paul Byrne and they were right.

It's a pity they were not better at diagnosing patients instead.

I'm sorry I can't spell that fancy word.

I got back home and told my mother and brother.

What I had done at St. Gregory's Hospital.

My brother said, are you mad and he was right.

I said, it's too late now, it's done, I can't go back on it.

Around 6pm or 6.30pm Dr. Liam O'Mullen Dempsey rang and asked me.

What had happened? I told him the truth.

Then he said, do you want to come back in this evening to St. Gregory's Hospital?

I said okay. I'll try and get there as fast as possible.

I think my brother might have given me a lift back into hospital.

As it would have taken all day by Dart and bus.

I was admitted in St. Gregory's Hospital.

For the last time in my life.

I think it was either mid or late July 2006.

I was put in the most secure ward, St. Pius.

This place is worse than a prison.

I think late that evening Dr. Nuala Fitzsimons O'Denehy.

Gave me a few health checks.

Breathing or respiratory and testing me looking at her finger to see if my eyes could follow her finger with my eyes moving from side to side.

I think I spent at least a week or ten days in that hell hole.

I often broke down crying, not that anyone noticed, certainly not any of the nursing staff.

I made friends there with Dion from Mount Merrion Gates, I think a very posh area.

He seemed a nice guy.

He told me he had worked for Allianz Insurance for over 30 years.

He said he spent too much of his life working there.

Although he was now retired.

He was still in his fifties and looked a lot better than me.

Although that would be not difficult.

There was a guy there from Rathsallagh in Shankill, Co. Dublin.

I knew the name.

However I will not mention it.

In case I get the crap beaten out of me.

I think for a few days, maybe only two days.

They gave me a small amount of rohypnol - it made no difference whatsoever,.

As I could still not sleep.

One day I found out I was been taking off rohypnol and asked, could I see a doctor.

I saw a doctor all right.

However it was all in vain and a waste of time.

Dr. Caomhe O'Dempsey Higgins came into my room. I asked her, could I still be given rohypnol?

No, she said. I begged but it made no difference.

Dr. Caomhe O'Dempsey Higgins is like some sort of god in that place and also at Naomh Theodores.

I have often seen her on TV giving her great advice.

She should listen to it herself.

I used to stay up at night as late as possible since I could not sleep.

The few that were up were usually sent to bed at 1am or 1.30am at the latest.

Of course the Gards were brought in to question me about the cracked windows.

I told them everything, to the minutest detail.

It's a pity St. Gregory's Hospital is not has quick with dealing with much more serious health concerns.

If they were as quick with everything else, the whole system would be much better.

I had a short friendship with Jack from Dun Laoghaire.

I fell out with him a day or two before I got moved St. Pius' Ward.

I used to tell lots of jokes while I was on that St. Pius ward to break the ice

The staff nurse in charge on St. Pius ward was Bronach.

She told me she had worked as a general nurse in St. Breda's Hospital, Dun Laoghaire, Co. Dublin.

I said I know the place since I'm from south Dublin.

I knew she had chosen the psychiatric nursing so she would have a much lighter work load.

I pretended I didn't know this.

She was not too far away from retirement.

She must have been at least 60 years of age back then.

So she had only five or six years before retirement.

So it was a handy number.

I noticed when she was taking my blood with a syringe; she was doing it wrong.

I said nothing.She was not wearing gloves.

This practise had been going on at least since I was first there in November 1988.

And all of the nurses since then.

All had been taking blood by syringe negligently.

I can't tell you, the reader, what it is because when this book gets published.

They will be tipped off by my divulgence and will change the way they take blood by syringe.

So I will look like I'm wrong in my serious accusation.

I told my auntie Ann in Deansgrange, Blackrock, Co. Dublin, about this practise and she was shocked.

I got moved into the biggest room for male patients.

The smell out of my wardrobe was unbelievable.

I kept spraying it with body deodorant.

However it made no difference whatsoever.

I was amazed at the patient from Rathsallagh, Shankill, Co. Dublin.

He slept like a baby.

He went to bed at around 10pm or 10.30pm latest and snored for most of the night and he did not even have his curtains pulled around his bed.

He never got up for breakfast as he was still fast asleep.

I have to admit I was jealous.

If I slept like that I could take over the world.

I think he got up around 12 in the afternoon or even later to eat dinner.

I almost forgot; one day I asked staff nurse O'Caroran, could I have my shaving razor?

I tried to help by showing what it looked like and to help her find it.

When I started to walk into the office.

She turned around and roared at me like some sort of prehistoric monster.

I jumped back with fright.

I quickly got out of there.

I was going to say, I was only trying to help. Sorry!

As I've learned never to help any nurses no matter what they're doing.

Whether they're carrying something or something else.

As you will get your head bitten off you.

There is no place for chivalry in this day and age.

I told Dr. Liam O'Mullen Dempsey about this incident before last Christmas 2014 with my mother present.

He said I think O'Caroran still works nights there.

I remember a day or two earlier I heard O'Caroran boasting about how much time she had spent as a nurse in England.

I think it was five years.

Well the one thing they didn't teach her over there was manners.

That's one thing no hospital can teach, manners, in Ireland or England for that matter.

As I've said many times before, the bad apples always hang around.

I wanted to report staff nurse O'Caroran the moment I got discharged from hospital.

However I could not because of the broken windows incident.

The moment St. Gregory's Hospital had of gotten my complaints about nursing staff.

The very next day I would get a bill in the post threatening and looking for money to pay for the broken windows.

That's how these guys work unfortunately; it's all about the money.

Not, are you okay or can we help?

They're not interested in your illness; it's all about the money and it always will be.

Eventually I got moved to St. Ludwig's Ward.

There was an English nurse called Helen or Helene; in fact I think she was on both St. Ludwig's Ward and St. Pius' Ward.

While I was there.

She told me she was an agency nurse from the north of England.

I think she had gotten married to an Irish man.

I asked her where he was from. Blackrock, she said.

I noticed she had a cold. I mentioned it to her.

She said, yes I do.

As I've said before, the work load is so light that you could have influenza.

And find it no problem working in these hospitals.

As the so-called work load is so light.

I told her I had chronic insomnia.

Not that I got much compassion from her.

I find it hard to sleep the last few weeks.

That's because there's one of the hottest and highest humidity at nights in the last two weeks.

So anybody would find it difficult to sleep in these sultry conditions.

I was going to say to her.

Try having this at 15 years of age tossing and turning every night without a wink of sleep and then dragging that into months and then years.

And on top of that having a male sexual problem, masturbating several times during the night that you haven't slept a wink.

I call this double tired.

But I wasn't going to waste my breath.

One day I was going to show her the hospital charter.

You might find it strange, startling, even peculiar.

Care Compassion Dignity Excellence Justice Respect Trust.

Yes they are written on a big wall chart in nearly every ward in that so-called hospital.

I told my brother about it.

He said they're only words, that's all.

And he's right.

I would not be hanging around here for long; I was already making my plans to go home.

As I had enough of bullshit.

I'm not 100% sure; it may have been the first day I was there or the second day.

I was queueing up for medication, maybe 15 or 20 minutes.

When it came to my turn to get my medication.

The kind and compassionate nurse there said, you have been taken off Brufen.

I said I did not know that.

I had not been informed of that.

I said I'm in a lot of pain.

Well lie on your bed.

Wow! You nurses are amazing, where did you learn that from. In case you can't tell, I'm being sarcastic.

You went to university to tell me that load of rubbish, I was going to say.

Even a ten year old kid could come up with something better than that, I was going to say.

I should of lay on my bed and came back later and said.

Wow! I feel brilliant after lying on the bed.

All the pain in my body has gone away. Yippeeh.

In case you can't tell, I'm being sarcastic.

I told my youngest brother about this incident and he couldn't stop laughing.

This is what I would have done if I was that staff nurse in question.

Wait until I have given all the medication out to all the other patients.

I would then try and get the doctor on call to see if he can give you anything for your pain.

If not I can only give some paracetamol instead.

I will try my best, that's all I can do.

However none of any of this happened.

Because this nurse was lazy and just didn't give a damn what was wrong with me.

And simply wasn't bothered.

As I've said many times before, this has happened time after time and still hasn't changed and never will unfortunately.

That night I decided I would be leaving the next day.

I had had enough by now.

So the next day I saw Dr. Liam O'Mullen Dempsey; I asked him, could I go home and be discharged.

I tried to make a joke out of it.

By saying I had overstayed my welcome and I just wanted to go home.

He said you can be discharged this evening. That's fine, I said.

So I got my last meal that evening but I was interrupted by a foreign doctor from Africa.

It was the usual rubbish.

Then she told me before I left.

Mid-August or late August 2006.

That my mother and I had to go back to Naomh Theodores the following week.

As a matter of urgency.

I didn't really want to.

However I said yes.

Being the idiot I am.

As it was a matter of urgency maybe they were going to do something this time to help me.

However I would be in for a nasty shock yet again.

The following day my mother and I had to get the bus to Naomh Theodores, Co. Dublin.

My mother did not want to go.

So I had to try hard to persuade her to go.

I said it's urgent; I think they're going to do something for me this time.

However my mother was right all along.

When we got there my mother was interrogated by the African doctor, asking my ma very personal questions.

I could hear my mother getting upset.

I was being interrogated by Dr. Muirin O'Twohig I think her name was.

More like Dr. Wrong I was going to say.

I was trying my best to tell her what was really wrong with me.

However it was all in vain.

How come this hasn't happened to other men?

I might have said to her, forget about it.

I'm going, I've had enough of this.

My mother had just come out of the other interrogation room.

She saw Dr. Muirin O'Twohig and was not impressed. Later when my ma and I were coming on the bus.

My mother said to me, Dr.Muirin O'Twohig isn't a proper doctor, and I totally agreed with my ma.

My mother was right all along; it was a total waste of time yet again.
I had been told by that African doctor that it was a matter of urgency.
And I believed her.
As usual, with doctors especially, they will just talk you to death and ask lots of personal questions and do absolutely nothing for you.

As I've already said, I wanted to make complaints about staff nurses Winifrid, O'Caroran and that staff nurse who told me to lie on the bed.
However I couldn't because the moment they would get my letter of complaints.
The very next day they would send the bill for the broken windows.
That's how caring and compassionate the place is.

I have never been to that St. Gregory's Hospital since.
And I have no intention of ever going back there.
It's nearly nine years ago now and I hope it stays that way.
Please God.

I knew from now on my days were numbered.
Dr. Liam O'Mullen Dempsey and Naomh Theodores wanted to put me on as low as possible a dose of Dalmane, 30mg, as soon as possible.
How very concerned they were for my welfare.
If they had done their job properly in the first place.
I wouldn't need any Dalmane or any drug.
I wouldn't even be writing this book in the first place.
However due to their gross negligence incompetence, rudeness, uncompassion, stupidity, ignorance, vindictiveness, laziness, lack of respect, I've lost all dignity whatsoever over nearly 27 years of hell since the age of 14 years old.
My life is in a mess.
Thanks to the great doctors and nursing staff in this country.

I worked it out.
With my reserves of Dalmane 30mg and other drugs including Olanzapine.
I might only have two to four years left before my Dalmane would run out and then I would be in serious trouble.

I also knew it would not be long before my old GP Oisin O'Devlin would retire from practise.
As he had now nearly reached retirement age.
He retired from the Medical Card Scheme in 2010 I think.

He then fully retired a year or two later forever.

He must be at least 70 years or more of age.

I knew once he would retire I would be finished for good and I was correct yet again.

I managed to get by for the next few years on my reserves of Dalmane 30s and also some from my old GP Oisin O'Devlin.

I went back to my course in September 2006 at Shanganagh House, Rathsallagh, Co. Dublin.

I got my mid-term break for Halloween 2006.

My cousin Tina was in the Theodore's Clinic, Co. Dublin, for an operation at that time.

So I tried my best to visit her every day that late October 2006.

I can't remember what the operation was for now.

Since I've forgotten by now.

All I remember is my cousin Tina saying that men were ten times more likely to get it rather than women.

So she considered herself to be very unlucky.

I went in sometimes with my auntie Frances, her mother.

My auntie Frances was staying in my mother's house for about a week or so.

I had one or two meals in the Theodore's Clinic, Co. Dublin.

The food was okay; of course we had to pay for them like anyone else.

Although it is a private clinic I was not overly impressed by it.

I mean it's okay.

However the brilliant reputation it has is exaggerated.

Sometimes my auntie would get a bus in from Shankill at the Bus Stop across the road from St. Anne's Roman Catholic Church Shankill Co. Dublin.

Then late in the evenings my auntie Frances would get a taxi home to my mother's.

After about a week my cousin Tina was discharged from the Theodore's Clinic.

However she still seemed to be in a lot of pain from the operation.

I was really worried about her.

I only found out a couple of weeks ago speaking to my mother.

I said to my mother Tina should have been in hospital for at least another week because she was not well enough to come home.

Then my ma said, she discharged herself early, that's why.

I didn't know that back then until you now whe my Ma told me.

So I'm writing in this book now.

My cousin Tina and my auntie wanted to go back to Co. Wexford as soon as possible where they had relatives living there on both sides of the family.

I kept making lots of phone calls that day.

I can't remember who or what?

I tried my best to look after my cousin Tina as possible.

I made her tea and toast and asked did she like marmalade or butter.

There was nothing else in the house as my mother needed to do the weekly shopping.

So that's why the cupboards were bare.

My da called in the evening.

He happened to be heading down to that part of the country and asked my auntie Frances and my cousin Tina did they want a lift to Gorey, Co. Wexford.

They both took the lift.

My da took the carrier bags. Even though he was a strong man.

He said the weight of the bags.

I used to say the same thing to my auntie Frances. How can you lift these bags? I'm a man and they are even too heavy for me.

A few days later after my da drove my auntie Frances and Cousin Tina to Gorey, Co. Wexford.

He told my ma that Tina had been shivering all the way down to Gorey.

I was not surprised by this.

As I knew she was still not well from the operation.

I tried to phone my cousin Tina to see how she was.

However she never answered her phone.

I sent her a text message.

She said she was fine and eating tacos in the local fast food restaurant, one of her favourite dishes.

She also told me she got very strong painkillers from the local GP and was doing fine.

I tried for the next several weeks to keep in contact with my cousin Tina.

However it was in vain.

As she and my auntie Frances never answered their phones.

This is not unusual for them.

As they still do the same thing today.

Shankill VTOS Christmas Dinner 2006 in Shanganagh House, Shankill, Co. Dublin.

Before the Christmas holidays 2006 my colleagues and I had dinner in Brady's in Shankill, Co. Dublin.

Like the year before.

I don't remember much of Christmas 2006 other than.

My mother got a lovely letter from my auntie Frances.

It was worth more than all the money in the world.

My auntie Frances thanked her for all that she did for keeping her in my mother's house while my cousin Tina was in hospital and for everything else.

It was beautifully written.

My mother still has that letter of thanks from my auntie Frances till this day.

That's about all I remember of Christmas 2006.

It just came back to me today.

The beginning of January 2007.

The World PDC Professional Darts Championship Final.

Between Phil Taylor and Raymond van Barneveld.

The Greatest Darts Final of all time.

I think it went sudden death.

My youngest brother and I.

Were both too scared, nervous and afraid to watch the last couple of legs of the darts.

I remember my brother was on his mobile phone asking for the results.

Who had won the final and it was Raymond van Barneveld.

The next day it was all over TV.

The final leg.

Phil Taylor got to throw first at the bulls-eye to see who would throw first for the final leg of the match.

As far as I remember Phil Taylor's first dart landed in the 25 circle around the bulls-eye.

Raymond van Bernaveld asked for the dart to be kept there.

He was able to use this dart as a guide or marker to the bull-eye.

Which he took advantage of that and got the bulls-eye.

So he was able to throw first on the final leg of the match.

Which of course gave him a great advantage over Phil Taylor.

He went on to win the leg and the match.

I could be wrong with my memory of that match.

So I stand corrected.

If anybody reading this book knows different.

I know Phil Taylor would have won that match if he had the first throw in that final leg.

However he didn't and Raymond van Barneveld won it fair and square.

And you can't take that away from him.

I don't think that final will ever be matched or equalled again.

Now I could be proved wrong on that.

However it waits to be seen.

Congratulations and well done to Raymond van Barneveld again on that great victory.

Over eight years ago now.

Well done yet again Raymond van Barneveld.

***

My 33 rd birthday, February 12th 2007.

I don't remember much of that either.

The next big thing was I got a letter in the post saying I was being offered a one-bedroom council house in Loughlinstown, Co. Dublin.

I'm not sure whether I had to accept straight away or not before even looking at it.

I must have said, yes I'll take it.

It was June 13th 2007 when I got see my new home.

The weather that summer 2007 was very wet.

It was raining the day I went to see my new home.

I was of course early for my appointment.

There were two young lads talking to me.

While I was waiting to see my new home.

I only remember one of the young lads, Adam is his name; he was eight years old then.

He is my next-door neighbour's son.

If my maths is correct he will be 16 years old this year and he still lives beside with his ma and da and brothers and sisters.

Then men from the Dun Laoghaire, Rathdown Co. Council arrived with the keys to my bachelor pad.

Of course the house was boarded up with steel sheets.

After they had taken them down.

A glass fitter from Richmond Glass fixed a broken window pane.

I knew these guys from St. Gregory's Hospital.

Since I had received a huge bill running over maybe 6,500 Euros or maybe 7,500 Euros.

From St. Gregory's Hospital.

As I've said before, they don't wait long before sending you a bill.

However when it comes to anything else like supposedly looking after you or any complaint about doctors or nursing staff.

You hear absolutely nothing.

As I've just said, I saw my new home for the first time on June 13th 2007.

I took it.

I had no choice I think in the matter.

They gave me all the keys I needed for house door, bedroom door, shed door and side gate.

It took me altogether about two months to settle in.

I had to buy furniture, carpets, lino, laminated flooring and household appliances.

I had to get the electricity connected first.

I had to make a down payment of 300 Euros to get the electricity turned on.

I had to see the welfare officer; luckily he was based literally just down the road.

In St. Theodore's Health Centre; Co. Dublin.

I told him I had just gotten a house from the council.

He said he'd have to take a look at it after lunch before he went back to work.

I said I'll be waiting for you and sure enough he arrived.

He looked around at the bare house I had just now got.

A few days later social welfare cheques arrived in the post for me.

So I could buy furniture and appliances for my home.

I mentioned to him one day.

That I needed to pay 300 Euros to get the electricity turned on.

Well you got a cheque for 250 Euros, you can do whatever you want with that.

So I used the cheque and added 50 Euros of my own money and got my electricity turned on.

So that was a start.

I bought most of the furniture from Des Kellys or Bargaintown.

I used to spend the whole day it seemed waiting on deliveries.
I seemed to be always left last on their list.
I kept having to make mobile phone calls, often several times a day.
Asking where the hell they were?
They often did not arrive until after 4.30 pm.
My diet was poor in those days while waiting.
I just kept eating big packs of Snickers bars with plenty of cups of tea.
That was basically my diet back then.
Eventually after about two months most of the furniture and appliances arrived and I moved in properly.

I remember in August 2007 I still had no heavy curtains for the windows or was it net curtains.
So I had not much privacy until eventually I had all of my curtains.
Thanks mainly to the help of my sister.
Around this time some teenage brat kept giving me grief.
He often pounded my front door and ran off.

***

I also think Shankill VTOS co-ordinator Carmen Rodriguez left.
As far as I know she had an argument with some woman.
I don't know who she was; that's all I heard.
I never saw Carmen Rodriguez again. I guess she must have gone back to Spain with her husband and child.

***

I remember seeing a photo of her daughter on her desk.
I asked her what her daughter's name is.
She said, Roisin. An Irish name, I said?
Carmen Rodriguez put me to shame.

She spoke fluent Irish and knew all the different dialects: Ulster Irish, Connacht Irish, Leinster Irish and Munster Irish.

Then some time in mid or late September 2007 I had put my green bin out early that night.

I heard a sound near the front of my door like somebody lifting the cover of the sewage pipes from my toilet and kitchen.
I was going to go out and investigate.
However I did not want to bring attention or cause trouble.

The next evening my sewage system overflowed.

He had taken waste paper from my green bin and had stuffed it in the sewage pipes.

So now they were overflowing.

I had to get the council out to clear it.

After a few days they came out and cleared it.

I made a complaint to Dun Laoghaire Rathdown Co. Council about unsociable behaviour.

The man on the phone from the town hall asked me, did I know the individual's name.

I said no. If I knew that I would have not have called your department in the first place.

I would have it sorted myself.

This has been going on for months I said.

Do you know where he lives or his name, again.

Look, I said he doesn't leave a calling card in the letter box every time he causes trouble.

If he did I would not be making this complaint.

Well we can't do nothing he said.

I thought you were meant to sort out anti-social behaviour; isn't that what your department is for?

Well I can't do anything he said. End of call.

As usual, another waste of my time.

The last real trouble I got from this spoilt teenage brat.

On Halloween 2007 he was firing fireworks directly at my house.

I also knew he aimed one at the exhaust for fumes from the gas boiler.

I could hear it hitting close by because the next day one of the young lads told me.

Some guy was aiming fireworks directly at your house and nearly hit your exhaust pipe for your boiler.

I asked what was his name and what he looked like.

However nobody seemed to know.

This sort of harassment lasted another couple of months and died out and then they've left me alone since.

I hope it stays that way.

That Halloween 2007 bonfire was directly across the road from my house on the green.

I really enjoyed it every Halloween.

Until the last bonfire was in Halloween 2011 I think.
Then it died out.

Bernardine McGowran took over as co-ordinator in Shankill VTOS.
Although I asked several times, was she taking over and she said no.
However I knew in the end she would take the job.

***

We had our Christmas Dinner 2007 in Bradys in Shankill again.
I think this was the last time Rachel was with us.
Or she may have already left by then.
Because the last time I ever saw Rachel was around Christmas 2007 in Dunne's stores in Cornelscourt, Co. Dublin.
I have never seen her since.
Even though she only lives about a mile and a half away from me, well no more than two miles.
I often pass her house on the number 7 bus.
Somebody lives there because the windows are often open.

I must have gone down for Christmas dinner to my mother's and then come back to my place late that evening or night.
That was how I spent Christmas Day 2007.

January 2008.

My 34th birthday was the 12th of February 2008.
I don't remember much of it.

I started getting fed up of going to Shankill VTOS in early 2008.
One day Bernardine McGowran called me on the phone and said would you not give it one more try.
I said okay I will.
I was delighted I gave it one more go because I began to enjoy doing IT especially as Bernardine McGowran was a brilliant teacher.
We had to move to Choices on Quinn's Road, Shankill, Co. Dublin.
As they were renovating Shanganagh House, Shankill, Co. Dublin.

There was an office we were able to use in Choices on the top floor.

I spent the last few months of my Shankill VTOS course there and finished in June 2008.
With a FETAC Cert for my troubles.
As I've just said, if it hadn't been for Bernardine McGowran I would

not be typing this book today.

I would not know how to write and save letters on my computer.

How to send emails and many other things I learnt from her.

Many thanks Bernardine. You're the best.

Keep up the good work.

As she still works at that.

The summer of 2008 was very wet.

During the summer the young lads would come around nearly every week looking to cut my garden.

It wasn't even big and they did a terrible job, and I think it cost me nearly 10 Euros every time.

However I never complained as I just wanted to keep the peace.

I had some money saved in an envelope to do some DIY on my house.

However when I opened the envelope, most of my money was gone.

I had originally 1,000 Euros saved in it; now there was only 350 Euros.

It may have been a couple of months earlier. As I remember my sister asking me to let my brother, who had taken all of that money, to let him off 100 Euros as it was his 21st birthday.

So I did.

However his 21st birthday was in March 2008.

So I must have discovered he had taken my money a few months earlier.

I only remembered now. That's why I'm telling you this now.

He slowly paid me back, 50 Euros a month here and there.

My mother a few years earlier.

Had told me that money of her's had gone missing and she thought my baby brother was behind it.

I did not believe her.

He wouldn't do anything like that.

However, he did and then stole my savings as well.

When I first found out he had taken my money.

He said I thought it was ma's not yours.

So my mother was right all along.

I don't remember much of the summer of 2008; only it rained a lot.

In fact something came back to me today.

I'm not a 100% sure.

However I think Sean Heinz painted the outside of my house in mid or late July 2008 or it may been 2009.

It was either year.

I just don't know which one now.

He was painting my neighbour Melissa's house.

I had already brought masonry paint in Woodies for this exact job a few months earlier.

I even had a large tin of Hammerite for my gates.

I even had plenty of brand new paint brushes and rollers.

I had everything for this job.

I asked Melissa who was painting her house?

She said a relative of her's.

I asked her could I talk to him and see if he could paint my house too.

I got talking to Sean Heinz.

He said he would paint my house too.

I asked how much would it cost?

I think he said 400 Euros; now it might have been a little more.

Or it's spot on.

After talking to him for a while.

I found out he was from Monkstown Farm, Co. Dublin.

I said I had relatives from there too.

I asked him did he know them?

He said yes.

My great aunt's maiden name is Heinz.

So I then found out we were both distantly related to each other.

However this did not mean I got a discount for the work.

I still got charged the same amount, family or no family.

He gave me his mobile phone number.

So I could think about it and call him.

If I wanted him to do the job.

One evening I called him on the phone.

Is that Sean Heinz?

Who's this, Paul Byrne? Are you the one who lives beside Rhona?

Yeah that's me. When can you paint my house for me?

His daughter was doing Irish dancing that evening.

When I called him on the mobile phone.

From what I heard his daughter is a good Irish dancer.

I can't remember what he said next.

It must have been no more than a couple of days.

Till he started painting my house.

It must have taken a couple of days to paint the whole outside of the house and my two gates.

I have to admit he did a good job.

The house looked like it was brand new.

Rhona made a joke one day passing my house in her car.

You showing the rest of us up?

I just laughed.

In September 2008 my sewage pipes got blocked again.

I was really worried.

I thought yet again that teenage brat was up to his old tricks again.

I remember Terry Junior, my next door neighbour, made jokes about all the shit in my front porch and I remember Terry Junior making fun about the shit outside my porch and garden, thinking it was funny.

I'm glad you can see the funny side to it.

The council came out again to clear my sewage.

They found the culprit this time.

I had been putting too many toilet wipes down the toilet and that's what caused the blockage.

I learned a lot from that.

Never put more than one toilet wipe down the toilet after each flush.

To my relief.

That teenage brat had not returned.

I don't remember much of Halloween 2008.

Only that the bonfire was straight across the road from me on the green.

Most of the neighbours including myself would all have a chat watching the bonfire and make a joke or two.

Christmas 2008.

I must have gone down to my mother's for Christmas dinner and came home that night.

New Year January 2009.

I don't remember much of that either.

My 35th birthday on 12th of February 2009.

I'm sorry yet again I don't remember anything special about that.

The next big thing was in the summer of 2009.

I decided to get my front and back garden covered in pebbles.

So the young lads would stop hassling me to mow my garden nearly every week during the summer.

And they never did a good job.

It was also costing me a lot of money.

Since they charged 10 Euros every time they mowed the garden.

I had had enough.

I remember walking all the way out to Bray as the number 45A bus did not make an appearance that day.

I also had to walk even further because I had to go up to the back of Fassarow in Bray, Co. Wicklow.

It was like being out in the countryside.

I looked at the different types of pebbles available.

None were really the ones I was looking for.

I decided I'll have to pick a certain type.

So I did .

Beggars can't be choosers.

I must have paid for them there and then.

I'm not 100% sure.

The hardest part was digging the back and front gardens.

My brothers and I did it the old-fashioned way, by mostly shovel and pick.

My brother and I worked tirelessly for hours.

It was usually one brother at a time.

When I was working.

There were old concrete slabs which weighed a tonne each.

I had to walk and pick each one up.

Slab by slab.

My back was killing me.

I was in a lot of pain.

Rhona my neighbour asked me if I needed young Terry Junior to help?

I said, I'll be alright.

There was very big thorny tree in the back garden.

It took a while to get rid of it.

The front garden was also full of nasty surprises.

Hidden under the earth.

Where red bricks were in the form of a wall going around the garden.

This was also a nightmare for my brother and I.

However, eventually we got the job done.

There were a few nosy people around especially when I was lifting the slabs into the skip.

I remember one man who I originally saw delivering shopping from SuperValu in Shankill, Co. Dublin.

A few years earlier before it closed.

I haven't seen him since then.

The way they were looking at me.

You'd think I was murdering somebody.

I had to buy membrane for underneath the pebbles so no weeds could grow in the garden.

One day I needed to go to Woodies to pick up a few more rolls of membrane to finish the garden.

When I was walking to the bus stop.

Rhona my neighbour was passing me by in her car.

And asked did I need a lift?

I said I'm heading down Sallynoggin to Woodies to pick up a few things.

She said I'm heading that way with her young son Darragh to a party.

After leaving Darragh at his party.

She gave me a lift to Woodies in Sallynoggin, Co. Dublin.

I asked her could she wait for me.

I'd be back in less than 10 minutes.

She said okay.

I have a feeling she thought I would be much longer and had regretted saying she would wait for me.

However I knew what I was looking for and was finished in a little over five minutes.

To her surprise.

As we live beside each other.

She drove me home.

I thanked her and brought my stuff that I bought with me.

My brother had to use a whacker to flatten my front garden before we could put the membrane on.

He gave out to me one day, saying the skip I got was too small.

I had originally wanted to get a bigger skip.

However he told me I didn't need one that big.

And now he was giving out about it in the first place.

I said nothing as usual and kept my mouth shut.

It was a lot of hard work; it must have taken one to two weeks to get the job done.

However everything worked out fine in the end.

I still have my front and back garden covered in pebbles.
However when the weather gets warmer, some weeds still grow.
So during the summer once a month is usually enough to keep the garden in shape.
However at the moment my front and back garden do need weeding.
However, since I'm trying to write this book.
I haven't got time to do that yet.

Halloween 2009.
The bonfire was straight across the road again in the green.
It stared to rain very heavily in early November 2009
I'm not 100% sure; I think in November 2009.
I think there was flooding on the River Shannon.
I think the dam at Ardnacrusha Dam had to release large volumes of water.
Which caused heavy flooding further downstream, mainly in Cork City I think.
Now I could be wrong with this information.
As it's coming out of memory alone and nothing else.
So I may stand corrected.

In mid or late November 2009 it snowed.
It snowed when I was in my uncle Michael's in Deansgrange, Blackrock, Co. Dublin.
That night when it snowed.
My da happened to be there too.
He was taking photos of the snow falling
It was very beautiful.
I stayed that night in my uncle Michael's.
I left early that morning.
My uncle Michael phoned his friend Patrick.
Who was heading to work out in Little Bray Co. Wicklow in his car and I asked could he pick me up on the way out?
He said yes.
I waited on the main road near Deansgrange Cemetery.
To my surprise a bus passed me while I was waiting for Patrick to collect me.
I could have gotten the bus home instead of waiting for him to pick me up.

However since it had been arranged I decided to keep with my appointment and not let him down.

Eventually he arrived and dropped me off near The Commons Road in Loughlinstown, Co. Dublin.

And I walked home the rest of the way.

I'm not 100% sure how long this snow and cold snap lasted.

However it must have been five days or a week before the thaw set in.

As I remember walking in the snow a couple of times to my mother's.

***

I had bought a ticket to see Paul McCartney in concert in the old O2 in Dublin.

This was around the 19th of December I think in 2009.

The last pop concert I was ever at.

I got the number 7 bus into Dublin city centre.

I asked the driver when was the last number 7 bus leaving for Loughlinstown?

He said I think about 11.30 pm at O'Connell Bridge, Dublin.

Thanks for that I said.

I got the Luas to the O2 or Point near East Wall, Dublin.

The Paul McCartney concert was brilliant as usual.

Even Henry McCullough was there.

As Paul McCartney pointed him out in the crowd.

Henry McCullough had been with Paul McCartney in his early years after The Beatles had split up.

In the early 1970s.

Henry McCullough performed on some of Paul McCartney's early stuff.

However they fell out over musical differences including guitar playing by Henry McCullough.

I think around 1980 Henry McCullough was in an accident and severed the tendons in one or both of his hands and could not play the guitar for a number of years.

However I think he's doing fine now and back playing guitar.

What he loves doing best.

Paul McCartney played Simply Having a Wonderful Christmas Time.

He said he normally never played this song.

However since it was nearly Christmas he'd decided to perform it that night and he did a great job.

After the concert was over.

I was worried I would miss the last bus home.

I thought the Luas would not get me back in time for the bus.

So I literally ran all the way along the Quays; I noticed patches of frost and ice.

So I had to be careful I didn't slip and fall.

I was totally out of breath by the time I made it to the bus stop on O'Connell Bridge, Dublin.

I think I made it with about two minutes to spare for the last number 7 bus home.

While I was waiting a lady asked me to show her the Paul McCartney concert programme.

Which I had bought at the concert.

She told me she was at the concert too.

How did you get here so fast? I said.

I got the Luas.

I ran all the way here.

If I'd have known that, I would have got the Luas too.

Why did not someone tell me that? I said to myself.

Well a minute later the number 7 bus arrived and I got off at the last stop near where I live.

It must have been after 12.30am.

When I eventually got home.

Christmas 2009.

I must have spent Christmas Day in my mother's for dinner.

And then went home that night.

January 2010 went to Berlin.

My last trip abroad.

My uncle and I had booked a long weekend in Berlin in January 2010.

I would remember it for all the wrong reasons.

We must have gone on a Friday I think and stayed for three nights.

That's Friday, Saturday and Sunday nights I think.

During the flight I picked up tonsillitis; it must have been from the air-conditioning in the plane.

I think they recycle the air nowadays.

In the past I think they nearly always used fresh air.

However to cut costs they do not do that anymore unfortunately.

By the time I got off the plane in Berlin.

I felt dreadful.

I had to stand for nearly two hours maybe.

As they were very strict, checking everyone's passport thoroughly.

Including mine.

As I've said, I found it hard to stay standing that long due to severe tonsillitis.

I don't remember how we got from the airport to Kurfurstendamm.

We must have been walking more than two hours to try and find our hotel.

I was really finding it hard to walk this length of time on my feet.

As my tonsillitis was taking over my whole body.

We were walking around in circles, really we were.

We kept coming back to the same place.

I got tired of this and I said to my uncle I'm getting a taxi, I don't care how much it costs.

So I put my hand out for a taxi.

My uncle gave the name of the hotel.

Even the taxi driver had to look at a map at first to find it.

In less than five minutes we got to our hotel

I think it was 3-star hotel.

However it did the job.

I was now very ill coughing and shivering with headaches - just feeling absolutely awful.

My uncle got fed up of me complaining.

Do you want to go home now?

I said no.

My uncle could quickly lose his temper when he wanted to.

He did not seem to realise.

How ill I really was.

I was doing my best not to complain and to try and put a brave face on everything.

I remember seeing some ice floating on the River Spree or maybe a smaller river or canal.

If there are any canals in Berlin.

Kurfurstendamm is Berlin's answer to O'Connell Street, only a lot longer; I don't know exactly how much longer.

However it must have been three or more times longer than O'Connell Street in Dublin.

Now I could be exaggerating as I was very ill and even a five-minute walk would have nearly killed that long weekend.

I think we got our breakfast in the hotel.

There is a famous bakery on Kurfurstendamm.

Where even the local wildlife comes in for a snack.

Little birds would fly in each day we there, into the bakery.

My uncle ate some very rich pastries, maybe Danishes.

They were too rich for me.

I ate just light apple pastries instead.

I was like a coughing machine.

No matter how hard I tried my best not to cough, I could not stop.

I was also shivering and had terrible headaches to go with it.

Every time I coughed my throat felt like it was being torn apart - like a jagged thing for mixing a cake with jagged teeth tearing my throat apart.

I kept taking as much paracetamol as possible in 24 hours.

This made absolutely no difference whatsoever; it was like a glass of water or a placebo.

One day we went to a pharmacy in Berlin.

The lady there spoke little English.

I tried to explain I had tonsillitis.

She ended up giving me something for my thyroid gland instead.

Of course this was absolutely useless too.

I tried my best not to complain and put a brave face on things while I was in Berlin.

All of the taxis in Berlin were Mercedes-Benz cars.

They have good taste in cars in Berlin, especially taxi drivers.

We got a tour of a nuclear bomb shelter in Berlin.

Which very few people knew about.

You would never think it was under the streets of Berlin.

It was obviously built during the Cold War.

I bought a few souvenirs including a model of the Brandenburg Gate.

Which I still have on my mantelshelf till this day.

My uncle later regretted he hadn't bought one.

I bought Irish Moss aftershave for the name.

I think it means an English Irish Moss aftershave.

I still have it in its original box.

I have never used any as I don't use aftershave.

Since I regard that as vanity.

At night I had to wear a fleece in bed in the hotel because I was shivering from my heavy dose of tonsillitis.

The day we were going back to the airport in Berlin.

We got a double-decker train.

I had never been on one before.

I thought it was brilliant; of course we went upstairs.

We nearly got away without paying for a ticket for the train.

Until the lady conductor came to us with only two stops to go.

We were totally honest with her.

We told her what station we got on and where we were stopping.

I think it was two Euros and something for each ticket for my uncle and I.

Then we got the plane back to Dublin Airport.

I was glad to be back and I also think my uncle was as well since he had no longer to put up with my condition.

The next day I had to go to my old GP Oisin O'Devlin with my tonsillitis as it was not getting any better.

He gave me antibiotics. I think they were called Calvepen.

Now I could be wrong with that name.

After a few days I started to improve and when I finished the course of antibiotics.

I had made a full recovery.

My 36th birthday on February 12th 2010.

I don't remember much of this either.

Some time in 2010 my old GP Oisin O'Devlin retired. I had been expecting this for a long time and now it had happened.

I definitely knew now I was in serious trouble since my Dalmane would be seriously reduced with dire consequences.

My new GP was Dr. Blathnaid McManus.

More than likely the moment I started attending her surgery.

She must have started reducing my Dalmane.

I could do nothing about it except make a token gesture complaint to her.

I might have visited Naomh Theodores no more than three or four times in that entire year of 2010, maybe even less.

It was just the usual rubbish: a psychiatrist looking at a computer screen and telling you what medication you should be on.

Then that psychiatrist would send an email or letter to your GP insisting in a reduction of the Dalmane as quickly as possible.

However they did not come with any new ideas how to get some sleep, if any.

Thanks for your compassion, care, trust, excellence, dignity and understanding.

In case you can't tell, I'm being sarcastic yet again.

I don't remember much of the summer of 2010.

Halloween 2010.
The bonfire was lit straight across the road again on the green.

Some time in November 2010 I asked Dr. Blathnaid McManus if she could give me something to help me sleep.

She suggested slow release Melatonin; as it's a hormone it's not covered under the Medical Card.

So you have pay for it like anyone else on private health insurance.

I'm not exactly sure how much you actually get in a packet.

I think it was around 20 Euros for two or three weeks supply.

It worked for the first few nights.
However it then wore off.
I kept my GP Dr. Blathnaid McManus informed of this.
One day she asked, have you tried hypnosis?
Yeah I tried twice before and I couldn't be hypnotised.
She just looked at me.

I think in early December 2010 the first snows fell.
We were in another cold snap.
This period of snow lasted a week or ten days.
After that spell of snow had gone.
My neighbour Rhona mentioned it to me.
I said, Rhona the winter isn't over yet. I would not be surprised if we got more snow again before the month is out.
And I was right yet again.

About a week later it snowed again.

I remember looking out my kitchen window.
Some of the neighbours were giving Rhona's husband's car a push as it was skidding on the ice.

Christmas 2010.
I think I went to my mother's for Christmas dinner as usual and then I

stayed the night and went home on St. Stephens Day.

The place was lethal with ice; I had to tread carefully home.

However a thaw was setting in that day and a day or two later.

The snow cleared for good.

Although Christmas Day 2010 was snowy.

It wasn't an official White Christmas as no snow had fallen on Christmas Day.

So Christmas Day 2010 wasn't an official White Christmas.

Despite the fact the ground was covered in snow.

My 37th birthday 12th of February 2011.

I don't remember much of this birthday either, sorry.

The next big thing I remember was going for a long weekend on a coach to Cobh in Cork and going To Kilkenny City on the way back and the Rock of Cashel.

This was in April 2011.

We went on a cruise liner for a couple of hours docked in Cork harbour.

My uncle and I.

They were very strict with passport checking, going on board and leaving; maybe in case of stowaways.

They were giving out free wine at dinner I think.

I loved the lemonade; it was old-fashioned lemonade American style.

It was ice cold and full of lemon bits.

As much as you like from a big machine.

It remains till this day the nicest lemonade I've ever had.

We then got to our hotel.

It wasn't great.

The TV must have been at least 20 years old and you only had a couple of TV channels with poor reception.

Then the next day the coach brought us to the Rock of Cashel which had some work being done to it.

As there was scaffolding around.

There was very little in the town of Cashel.

Very disappointing.

Then we went to Kilkenny City; we got a tour of the Kilkenny castle.

I had been here before as a school kid in 1983.

However I had not been inside the castle itself.

After a few hours in Kilkenny we headed back to Dublin and were left at a hotel.

I can't remember which one.

I got the number 7 bus home to Loughlinstown and my uncle got the bus to Deansgrange instead.

About a week later my uncle emailed me some of the photos taken in Cobh.

When I saw the big belly on me.

I was in for a shock.

I decided I would be willing to do anything to lose it, no matter how hard it was.

I used up or threw all of my junk food out.

***

I got in contact with Hazel on Facebook.

I told her who I was.

That's me you saw walking in Shankill back in 2005.

Don't forget to say hello if you see me again walking.

I won't bite.

That was the last time I was in contact with Hazel in April 2011.

That's now just over four years ago.

I mentioned nothing about going on a diet.

In case I could not stick to it and end up giving up and then looking like an eegit.

So I kept it to myself and said nothing.

***

My diet started on the 27th of April 2011.

Officially May 1st 2011.

I kept at it up until mid to late October 2011.

Today Monday 04/05/2015.

I feel absolutely dreadful today not only am I burnt out and exhausted.

The pain in my eyes is killing me.

I had to take painkillers 10 minutes ago for the pain in my eyes.

I saw a reflection of the big bags under my eyes in my cheap mobile phone.

They are even worse than I thought.

Since I have had big bags under my eyes since I was 15 years of age.

I've gotten used to them.

However sometimes I'm brought back to reality.
Like today.
My receding hair line is also even worse.
Than I had thought.
I just looked in the mirror over the fireplace.
I was also brought back to reality.

Now more than ever do I want to get this book finished.

My diet officially began on May 1st 2011.
I started walking several miles a day.
My diet consisted of eating tuna or mackerel in cans or tins every single day.
I had Oatibix every single morning for breakfast.
I only used low fat supermilk every single day.
I had just bought a few weeks earlier a digital weighing scales.
I started weighing myself, every single day at first.
Then once a week.
Since you would notice a relative drop in body weight, maybe sometimes up to two kilos, in a week.
If I really did well.
The first six weeks were the hardest.
My lower back was killing me.
I had to go through the pain barrier every single day.
This lasted about six weeks.

Eventually after about six weeks the pain in my back went away.
This was around mid-June 2011.
I know what was causing the pain in my lower back.
It simply was all the weight I was carrying when I started to exercise so much.
By walking around five to six miles per day on average.
Sometimes I even walked further.
I got lucky with the weather that summer of 2011.
Not only was it dry.
It was one of the coolest summers in years.
It was perfect weather for plenty of exercise and walking.

Some of the neighbours near my mother said to her one day.
Anytime I see Paul. He's out walking.
I think my mother said, he's trying to lose weight.

Some time in July 2011 my big steel side gate broke.

It was one of the big steel hinges.

I knew I needed a welder to fix it.

There was a man near St. Anne's School, Stonebridge Road, Co. Dublin.

He was Mrs McGarry's son.

I think his name is Michael.

I asked Laura who lives a few doors away from my mother.

Do Mrs McGarry's sons still do welding up near St. Anne's School?

Laura said yes, he still does work there.

Thanks Laura for that.

I'll walk up to see him.

Laura said, you're not walking up there now are you?

Yeah I am? And then I'm walking up to Loughlinstown.

All you seem to do is walk all the time? Laura said.

As I've just said, I was on my diet.

So I was doing a lot of walking that summer 2011.

I went to Michael's.

I told him I knew his mother.

When I went to St. Anne's School, Stonebridge Road, Shankill, Co. Dublin.

Back in the early 80s.

I asked him, could he fix my gate?

I told him what the problem was.

He asked me where I lived.

I told him where. And how to get there.

I asked him, how much would it cost?

I think he said 40 Euros?

I said that's okay.

A few hours later he arrived at my house.

He got his welding equipment and had to plug something in my house.

So he could do the welding.

I think it took around five or 10 minutes.

Then he was finished.

My side gate scuffed of the wall.

So he adjusted it for me.

I never asked him to do that.

However he was just helping me out.

I paid him 40 Euros and that was the last time.

I ever saw him.

I was now on my diet for nearly two months.

I must have been losing at least a stone a month or maybe a little more.

I think I must have been over 16 stone when I went on my diet on May 1st 2011.

However, when I ended my diet in mid or late October 2011 my weight had to around 10 and half stone.

The diet lasted nearly six months in duration I think.

From May 1st 2011 to late October 2011.

I noticed every week weighing myself on my digital scales.

I was losing over two kilos every week.

Now I could be wrong.

I might not be 100% accurate.

On into September 2011.

I was still on my diet.

I was still lucky with the weather.

As far as I know it was the coolest September since 1994.

And it was mostly dry I think.

My clothes were now starting to get loose on me.

Into October 2011.

One day I was walking through Cromlech Fields, Ballybrack, Co. Dublin.

Through the path on the football pitch.

When I bumped into Gillian, my neighbour.

She said to me, don't lose any more weight.

It now began to dawn on me.

That I had nearly accomplished my job to lose weight.

I was now feeling a little more confident.

I ordered a cowboy outfit with poncho, hat, spurs, gun belt, cigar.

From the Sergio Leone spaghetti westerns to look like Clint Eastwood.

What made me do this?

Halloween was coming up and also I had lost so much weight.

That I just wanted to make an effort this Halloween 2011.

I even started growing a beard to look the part.

One day in early October 2011.

I got the bus to Dun Laoghaire.

I got talking to a man on the bus.

He told me he had worked in Germany for many decades.
I said I love Germany, especially its history.
After talking for a few minutes.
We got talking about God.
He said I don't really believe in that.
I'm a Roman Catholic I said.

I've lost all belief in that he said.
Especially the Catholic Church.
As I've said before I've noticed this anti-Catholic feeling from foreigners living in my country and also so-called Irish people.

After a week or two I shaved off my beard.
As I looked terribly scruffy.
Then a week or two later.
I had to grow a beard again.
Since I would be dressing up as Clint Eastwood out of the Fistful of Dollars trilogy.

I think I had got my weight down to 10 and a half or 11 stone by now.
So I was happy.

***

Halloween 2011.
It was the last time.
The bonfire would be across the road from me on the green.
I dressed up as a cowboy like Clint Eastwood in the spaghetti westerns.

I noticed a woman standing in front of my house looking at the bonfire.

She used to work in Post Office, Co. Dublin.
I knew she had been unhappy there.
From her body language.

I said to her, don't I know you from somewhere?
Did you used to work in Post Office, Co. Dublin? Yes, she said.
I don't work there anymore.
I think she had finished in early October 2011.
I asked her where she was from.
Gilian is from there.
I know that, she said. I'm a friend of her's.
What part of Shankill are you from? I said, St. Anne's Park.

She said, really I know a lot of people from there.

Do you know? I asked and I mentioned so and so or this person.

I can't mention their names as I do not want cause offence or embarrassment.

She knew all the people I mentioned.

I said I'm originally from Shankill too.

That was about as much as I was going to get out of her.

It was like extracting teeth.

This lady would be great at keeping secrets.

Even the Gestapo wouldn't get anything out of her.

I have never seen her since then.

It will be four years exactly this Halloween.

She is a very beautiful woman.

I would be afraid to even pay her a compliment.

As I know from trying to talk to her.

I would get nowhere.

She had absolutely no interest in me whatsoever.

I'm not good-looking or rich.

So I don't fit into her category of a man.

Like all of Gillian's female friends - they are all very beautiful.

A few months ago.

What was the name of that lady with you?

I think she used to work in Post Office, Co. Dublin.

She's from Shankill.

You mean Brigitte, she said. I think that was the name Gillian mentioned.

I may be wrong.

It's a very usual female name.

I've rarely heard of that name before.

It's the type of female name an American would give to their daughter.

My mother asked me one day after I had lost all of that weight.

Did your GP Dr. Blathnaid McManus say anything to you about it?

No, I said. She never mentioned a word about it to me.

I don't think she even noticed.

Or maybe she did not want to say anything in case it may cause offence.

Or just simply didn't notice whatsoever.

I used to go up to Dr. Blathnaid McManus once a month for my prescriptions in late 2011 into 2012.

And she never once mentioned or noticed anything about losing my weight.

As usual if you want anything done, as the old saying goes.
You have do it yourself.
The doctors didn't help me lose my weight.
I had to do it all myself; nobody else did it for me.
Even recently my mother said, the doctors did nothing for you in losing your weight.
Yeah I said. I had to do it all myself as usual.
No thanks to any of the doctors.
Even though they were responsible for me putting the huge amount of weight on in the first place.
After I was put on Anafranil in September 1995 I must have put on at least six and half to seven stones in weight.

In the winter of 2011 into 2012.
Dun Laoghaire Rathdown Co. Council were painting all of the council houses in Loughlinstown and Ballybrack.
I'm not sure what month my house was painted; it was either November or December 2011 or January 2012.
I remember the painter had a tin of Dulux Weathershield when he was painting my house and also my neighbours' houses.
This was the last time I got my house painted.
I've noticed some of the paint has been flaking off in the last few months, near my front door for example.
I almost forgot. I think I got new double-glazed windows and a new front door around the same time.
Everybody in the area also got this work done.
Including my neighbours.
This has been the last great effort by the council to maintain the houses.

The men doing most of this work.
Kept most of their tools and equipment in large containers in the local council estates.
And also had their lunch breaks too.

***

Christmas 2011.
I must have gone down for Christmas dinner and went back late that evening again.

The winter of 2011 to 2012 was the driest ever recorded I think.
I already had a good idea.
Since I never experienced such a dry winter before.

It barely rained at all from November 2011 until late April 2012.
The weather was mainly cloudy and very windy and cool but dry.
There were warnings of low water level in reservoirs and of a drought and the warning of water shortages.

***

My 38th birthday on February 12th 2012.
I don't remember much of this birthday either.
Nothing special.

I think some time in February 2012 I went to.
Magic Hair in Dublin.
I don't know.
What made me go to this place.
Since I don't have male pattern baldness or generic baldness or alopecia.
It cost a fortune.
It was well over 100 Euros for consultation, if you can call it that.
I had to pay for shampoos.
Which were also very expensive, between 30 and 50 Euros I think.
Then I went to a lady in the same building.
She used an infra-red light beam comb or something like that.
Then rubbed my hair with some sort of shampoo.
Then I had to go home on the bus.
With a very strong smell from my scalp and hair.
It was a very long journey home on the bus.
From Dublin city centre all the way to Loughlinstown, Co. Dublin.
Not only had I to contend with the strong odour from my scalp and hair.
It also looked scrawny and dirty.
I had to keep washing and washing and drying nearly every day.
It seemed to take forever.
This went on for two or three weeks.
Then I had enough and never went back.
By the way they gave me a small discount of maybe 10 or 20 Euros top.
Since I was on disability allowance.

How very kind of them.
As usual I was just wasting my money again.

Will I ever learn from my mistakes?
I don't think so.

As I already said.
I'm sorry but I'm going to have to be explicit.

***

If I masturbate my scalp gets hot and itchy and then greasy and darkens in colour and my hair falls out.
This has been going on since I was 15 years of age and now I'm balding.
Thanks to the great doctors in St. Bernard's Hospital, Dublin.
Also the great doctors in St. Gregory's Hospital.
There was nothing they could do for me.
In Magic Hair, Dublin.

The name sounds great.
Like they're going to do all sorts of wonderful magical things.
However that's cloud cuckoo land.

The spring of 2012 was also very dry.
However in late April 2012 the weather began to change.
By early May the rain became very heavy.
It tended to rain in the Dublin area, mainly at night.
Some night up to three inches or more of rain fell.
This went on for a couple of months.
I remember the local Shanganagh River would nearly be bursting its banks.
I can still remember how high the water level was.
Even though they had a few years earlier built new flood defences for that area.
If it hadn't been for them, the roads around there would have been continuously flooded.

Also walking in Shanganagh Park, Co. Dublin.
Became very tricky as most of the big paths were covered in big pools of water.
Also the children's playground was flooded.
I can still remember the huge volumes of water in the playground.
I can't remember how long this wet period of weather lasted.
However it had made up for the driest winter of all time just several months previously.

Halloween 2012.

There was no bonfire across the road from me on the green.

This was the first year without the bonfire being there.

However there have been no more bonfires across the road since.

And I don't think there ever will be.

I have to admit I really miss them.

I never thought I would be saying that to you right now.

The nearest bonfire I think is on the edge of the football pitch in Cromlech Fields, Co. Dublin.

These Halloweens.

The next big thing was my father passed away in November 2012.

He was making his way to the Murphy Clinic in Helenscourt to see the doctor.

However he never made it.

He collapsed and was taken to St. Bernard's Hospital, Dublin.

I think he was given no more than two days to live.

He had some blood clot.

If they operated, he had a 95% chance, or maybe even more, of dying during the operation.

So it was too dangerous to operate as he would die during the operation.

I was hoping he would say 'sorry' to me.

However he never did.

Or 'I love' You.

However, he never did either.

If he had have said just one of those words.

It would have meant everything to me.

All the times he had beaten me up, insulted me, and humiliated me, and generally run me down.

Just to hear one of those words from him.

Would have meant everything to me.

After all of this time.

My father still loved me.

However it never happened.

My da was treated appallingly there in St. Bernard's Hospital, Dublin.

I was not shocked or surprised by this.

As I had experienced far worse many years ago.

When I was younger.

He was made to sit in a chair with a big hole in the foam part.
With just a bare piece of wooden board to sit on.
So he didn't get too comfortable there.
Also he was made to stand up for a long time.
Until they changed his bed.
Even though he was extremely ill and could barely stand.
While the nurses were laughing and joking with each other.
My mother was appalled at his treatment there.
I wasn't.
This had been going on for years since I was a patient there in the summer of 1994.
Well I told you so ma, I said to her.
Now do you believe me?
What goes on in these so-called hospitals.
I haven't been making any of this up you know.

The last time I saw my father alive.
I had just left.
Leaving the hospital grounds, in my sister's car I think.
When we all got text messages saying my da had just passed away.
His brother was with him when my da died.

My da passed away on November 13th 2012.

At the age of 63 years.

He enjoyed his life to the full.
I have to say that.
Even my mother says that.
Just before my da's funeral I had bought my first suit.
It was a black suit just in case of a relative's funeral.
However did I know I would get my first use out of it so quick.
For my da's funeral?
I had of course a couple of good black ties to go with my suit.
My father's body was looked after by O'Donovan & Son's Funeral Home, Sallynoggin, Co. Dublin.

***

The Funeral Mass was at the Holy Family Church, Kill O' The Grange, Co. Dublin.
I think there was a beautiful harpist playing the harp at the Funeral Mass

and singing like an angel.

Now I could be wrong with that.

I might be getting that mixed up with my granda's a year earlier.

I may stand corrected.

Outside the church after the Funeral Mass was over.

I saw lots of relatives.

Giving my mother Funeral Mass cards.

My da's coffin was taken to Mount Jerome Cemetery to be cremated.

I did not like this grisly end.

It was what da wanted.

I think he was thinking of saving money on funeral costs.

As burial plots in Dublin can be around 10,000 Euros or more.

My mother hated it too.

She still talks about it today and it gives her the chills.

I hope when I die. My mother says don't cremate me. Make sure I get buried in a proper cemetery.

The afters were in The Graduate, Killiney, Co. Dublin.

We all had dinner and a few pints.

Well I did anyway.

I decided to head home on my own.

By getting the bus outside the Graduate to Loughlinstown, Co. Dublin.

I was freezing at the bus stop.

As I only had my black suit on.

No coat whatsoever.

About a week later.

I had an appointment at St. Bernard's Hospital, Dublin.

With Dr. Seamus O'Carrol Maguire, dermatologist.

However I saw two female doctors.

Who looked like surgeons.

I'm usually always early for my appointments.

I was again.

However somebody had cancelled and I was taken next.

I came in and had to lie down on a bed.

Where two young female surgeons.

Well that's what they looked like to me.

Removed some warts and maybe something else on my abdomen.

I was impressed by their professionalism.

They looked like identical twin sisters.

They were clean and well groomed.

I had told them that my da had passed away about a week ago in St. Conon's.

Oh I know St. Conon's.

I think the doctors thought I meant St. Conon's hospital.

I meant to correct her and say St. Conon's ward here in St. Bernard's Hospital, Dublin.

However I did not want to go into details with them and I let them get on with their work.

I sent Dr. Seamus O'Carrol Maguire a Christmas card saying thanks for doing a good job that Christmas 2012.

Also I changed GPs again sometime in mid or late 2012.

Dr. Blathnaid McManus said to me.

That she was moving to a different practise.

As she was not getting enough patients at her surgery in Ballybrack, Co. Dublin.

I said it's not because of me you're leaving?

No it's not.

I'm moving to a new practise in Rathgar, Dublin.

I was then given a new GP on the Medical Card Scheme.

Dr. Meadhbh O'Cullen,
Co. Dublin.

I have been with her about nearly three years now I think.

Now I could be corrected again.

I think my old GP Oisin O'Devlin,
Co. Dublin.

Made a full retirement this year 2012.

Finishing with his last private patients.

Now I could still stand corrected on that.

***

I should have made a letter of complaint about the way my father had been treated in St. Bernard's Hospital, Dublin.

The reasons I didn't.

I had left on bad terms with my father before he died.

As I've already said he used to beat me up, insult me, laugh at me, humiliate and generally run me down.

Most of my life.

You also have to make a complaint within six months or it's out of the time frame.

Even if I'd made a complaint straight away, nothing would have been done anyway.

I'm a veteran of the health system in this country and I know what I'm talking about.

Nothing ever happens; it's quickly forgotten and swept under the rug forever.

I actually mentioned my father's bad treatment there.

In the last several months

Both to the Minister for Health and to St. Bernard's Hospital, Dublin.

It was never mentioned even once in my replies from both parties.

So there's your proof.

I did tell you that.

That's how the health system works in this country and it's never going to change.

I told my mother after my father had passed away.

I was going to ask my mother: did she want me to make a complaint?

Then I told her the reasons why I did not.

And she totally understood.

***

Christmas 2012.

I must have gone for dinner to my mother's for Christmas Day 2012.

I went home late that evening.

January 2013.

My 39th birthday on February 12th 2013.

I don't remember much of that either.

Nothing special must have happened.

***

My Auntie Madge passed away in June 2013 I think.

We were all shocked.

As it came like a bolt out of the blue.

My uncle Larry got worried she had not been answering her phone calls.
He husband happened to be in hospital at the time.
So she was on her own.
My uncle Larry started getting more worried.
Called to the house and got no answer.
I think he then called the Fire Brigade and maybe there was an ambulance as well.
The fire men had to break in the door.
My auntie Madge was found dead in her bed.
I think she was either 80 years of age or 81 years of age; her birthday was just a few months away in September.
So she would have turned 81 or 82 years of age in September that year.
If she had been still alive.
As I've just said, we were all shocked.
I thought my auntie Madge would have lived into her 90s.
She had a healthy lifestyle.
She ate small meals, took her time eating.
Always did plenty of exercise.
And was very religious all of her life.

The funeral Mass was in the local Catholic church in Donaghmede, North Dublin.

The church was only a couple of minutes from her house.
I spoke a few sentences at the funeral mass.
Then I think she was buried in Fingal council cemetery.
Now I could have the name of the cemetery wrong.
I stand corrected yet again.

We all had to wait at least three or four months for the post mortem or autopsy.
My uncle Larry gave a copy of the Death Certificate to my mother.
Eventually when the final results came back.

I was shocked at what I saw in it.
She had heart disease.
She died from a cerebral haemorrhage.
She did not suffer.
She more than likely died instantaneously.
My question was:
How did she have heart disease?

Given her healthy lifestyle.
Only God knows the true answer.

As I've said, my uncle Jim in Donaghmede was in hospital at the time.
He was diagnosed with cancer.
He's fighting it at the moment.
He can't eat or take his medication properly.
He's at home at the moment.
Making occasional trips to hospital.
He has to be fed using tubes and also for his medication as well.

I got the inner wall of my house insulated in the summer or early autumn of 2013.
So did everybody else in my area including parts of Shankill and other parts of Dun Laoghaire, covered by Rathdown Co. Council.
Most of the insulating happened in the year 2013.

***

Halloween 2013.
No bonfire across the road from me on the green this year either.

Christmas 2013.
I must have gone for Christmas dinner to my mother's and went home late that evening.

January 2014.

My 40th birthday on 12th of February 2014.

A big milestone in my miserable life.
I went for dinner in The Martello Tower for my 40th birthday.

The next big thing was The St. Patrick's weekend 2014.
My cousin Jacqueline was running in the Tralee Marathon.

I promised I would go down to Co. Kerry to support her.
I was by now rationing my sleeping tablets for special occasions only.
Like going to Tralee in Co. Kerry to support my cousin there.
My cousin had booked the Central Hotel in Tralee before Christmas 2013 for all of us.
My mother and I, her mother and my uncle Larry and my cousin Kevin.

So we got the train from Heuston Station Dublin to Tralee, Co. Kerry.
My mother and I and auntie and uncle and cousin.

My uncle and I and my cousin passed the time playing dominos.

I had never played them before.

However it was great fun.

The time passed very quickly.

It must have taken over three hours to get to Tralee, Co. Kerry.

We kept asking for directions to the Central Hotel in Tralee.

When we eventually got it.

It was closed, to our horror.

I think there was a note on the entrance saying it was shut.

I also noticed a lot of junk mail on the floor.

Which looked like it had been there for a while.

Then, as we were walking back down the lane into the main town.

My uncle said I think I see Jacqueline and it was her.

We told her that the Central Hotel was closed.

She checked also and then believed us.

It was one of the busiest weekends in the year and we were literally homeless.

The only other hotel we could find was The Grand Hotel.

My cousin Jacqueline got very upset and started crying and became very upset.

Strange though it may seem, I didn't panic.

I had a feeling everything would work itself out and it did.

The Grand Hotel management were great.

After a while we all got accommodated.

I shared a room with my cousin Kevin.

My mother shared a room with my cousin Jacqueline.

And my aunt and uncle were together since they are a married couple.

So everything worked out fine.

I had my spare sleeping tablets, barely enough to get me by.

However they did the job that weekend.

I think the Tralee Marathon was the next morning at about 9am or 9.15am.

My cousin is a vegan.

So she's a little fussy about what she eats.

I think she had a fruit salad that morning and other vegan meals.

We waited to see Jacqueline finishing the marathon.

We were waiting for over an hour or more to see her finish.

At the time she was coming in the last half kilometre or so.

By poor bad luck at around the time my cousin Jacqueline was finishing.

My uncle and I and my auntie and cousin Kevin happened to move back for a few minutes to give ourselves a rest.

When my cousin Jacqueline happened to be going by at the same time.

So we ended up missing her finish the Tralee Marathon.

Only my mother saw her finish the marathon.

As she had made her way a short while earlier nearer the finish line.

Of course my cousin Jacqueline was disappointed.

We didn't see her finish except for my mother.

I apologised to my cousin Jacqueline for not seeing her finish the Tralee Marathon.

That's why we had all come in the first place.

I think the St. Patrick's Day parade was on the next day in Tralee, Co. Kerry.

We all looked at some of it.

We were very well treated in The Grand Hotel in Tralee, Co. Kerry.

The food was great and everything else.

We thanked all the staff in The Grand Hotel the day we were leaving.

My cousin Jaqueline got a different bus than us.

As she was getting a plane to London, England.

As that is where she lives and works.

For some reason the train to Mallow, Co. Cork, was cancelled.

So we all had to get the coach to Killarney train station, I think.

We just made the train on time.

It was kept waiting for all of the passengers.

My auntie wouldn't stop complaining.

I'm never going here again.

Eventually we got back to Heuston Station, Dublin.

We then got the Lusa to Connolly train station, Dublin.

My mother and I were heading southbound.

While my aunt, uncle and cousin Kevin were heading northbound.

We jumped a diesel train going to Pearse station and then Bray.

My mother and I smartly decided to get off at Pearse station to check what time the next dart was and it was due in a couple of minutes.

So my mother and I waited for the Dart and got home eventually.

Back in Shankill, Co. Dublin.

I promised my cousin Jacqueline that I would do my best to get a copy of the Kerry's Eye newspaper.

There is a famous corner shop in Co. Dublin that sells many local newspapers from all over Ireland.

So the next day I went into Co. Dublin.

I asked him, had he got a copy of the most recent Kerry's Eye newspaper?

He said it should arrive tomorrow.

I asked him to keep a copy for me.

He said he would.

So the next day I went back into Dun Laoghaire again.

I asked him had the Kerry's Eye newspaper arrived and it had.

I checked to see if the Tralee Marathon results were in it and they were.

I checked to see my cousin Jacqueline's name was in it and she was there.

Her time and results.

I can't exactly remember what time she finished at - it was between 3 hours and 38 minutes or 3 hours and 48 minutes or somewhere between those times.

The next day I posted the copy of the Kerry's Eye newspaper with her results in it.

In a big white A4 or C4 envelope to England.

A few days later she got it.

She was of course was delighted with it.

Both her time and results were printed in black and white.

This was the last time I actually enjoyed myself.

Thanks to nearly the last of my emergency supply sleeping tablets.

I had a couple left for very important occasions.

During the coming year.

After the trip to Tralee, Co. Kerry.

My health rapidly deteriorated since I had no more reserves of sleeping tablets left.

By the end of March 2014.

I checked a few of the GPs on the Primary Care Team; most of their practises were full up.

Eventually I found one.

I think the doctor's name is:

Dr. Aislin O'Flanagan Carroll,
Co. Dublin.

Now I could be wrong with that certain GP.

All I do know is it was in Co. Dublin, past the church, just a little further down.

Now I may stand corrected.

If that is the wrong GP.

My deepest and sincere apologies.

Well if it was the right place.

All they seemed interested in yet again.

Was my Medical Card details.

I waited maybe half an hour to an hour.

Eventually I got to see.

Dr. Aislin O'Flanagan Carroll.

I told her I had chronic insomnia.

Since I was 15 years of age.

She asked me what medication I was taking.

I told her what I was taking.

Then she suggested Ambien or its more scientific name Zolpidem.

I had already heard about this sleeping tablet.

It was another substitute for Dalmane.

That was basically it.

That was my consultation.

No more than a few minutes.

I had to get the bus to Dun Laoghaire and then back again.

All for that.

That's the great HSE.

Primary Care team.

Co. Dublin.

That was over 13 months ago.

And do I feel great.

After that.

In case you can't tell, I am being sarcastic yet again.

I was in bits for the next few months.

Burnt out and exhausted.

I didn't want to leave my house anymore.

Around late April or early May 2014.

Many brats were jumping in an out of my garden, sometimes for up to an hour at a time.

I pretended I didn't see them.

I just wanted to be left alone in peace.

Then I heard a loud banging noise in my back garden and shed.

Then I heard Rhona my neighbour shouting.

What are you doing?

Some young lad about 10 years old or 11 years old.

Had a screwdriver and had been hitting it against my shed window.

It was made out of Perspex.

He then broke it.

Rhona got him.

Then I went outside and I asked what was going on?

I then saw what had happened.

His mother had just arrived.

I asked her was that her son?

She said yes.

I said you will have to pay for my broken window.

Or have it fixed.

Her husband then arrived.

He told me he would fix it.

I said okay then.

I can't remember exactly how long I had to wait to get it fixed.

It must have been a couple of days.

The day he was supposed to fix it.

He never turned up.

It took me over half an hour to find his house.

I knocked at the door.

However nobody was in.

So the next day at 6pm I called again.

And this time he was there.

When his wife opened the door.

He had a piece of Perspex and a hammer and small saw and maybe some other tool.

Well he did a good job.

It's now nearly exactly a year to the day.

Just by coincidence.

The kids this evening are going mental.

Screaming and shouting like animals.

My sister got married in June 2014.

It was a civil ceremony.

I told my sister before the wedding I didn't really approve.

However it was her special day.

And she can have it.

Anyway she likes.

I was picked to bring her into the civil wedding ceremony.

I did not think much of it at the time.

However a few months ago.

My brother and I got talking.

Then he said to me.

My sister chose me instead of my two other brothers.

I never even realised that.

Until he said it to me.

Then I realised how much my sister.

Wanted me to be there on her special day.

I would not even have noticed if one of my brothers had been chosen instead to be there for her.

As I was not one to get jealous.

So thanks for choosing me.

My beautiful sister.

My sister's friend is a good photographer.

He took nearly all the photographs for the wedding.

My sister gave me a choice of the best photo of me taken at the wedding.

I don't look great in any of them.

I'm going totally bald.

According to the great doctors.

I'm suffering from delusions.

Or it's all in my imagination.

I really wish it was.

Believe me.

My sister did all the organising of the wedding.

I have to admit.

She did a brilliant job.

The dinner was great.

There was a chocolate fountain with profiteroles with brown and white chocolate.

I couldn't eat any more.

I think I got the Dart home at around 9.30pm or 10pm.

My sister went on honeymoon to Morocco I think.

Germany won the World Cup in July 2014.
My heroes did it again.

My cousin in North Dublin. Her new baby girl was getting baptised in mid or late August 2014.

I think it was in Killester Roman Catholic Church.
I took a few sleeping tablets the night before.
So I would look like I managed to get a night's sleep.
The dinner was in a hotel near Bayside or Sutton I think.
It may have been called The Marine something Hotel.
Now I could be wrong.
I may stand corrected.
So if I'm wrong.
Please correct me.
That August was very cool and showery.
The weather had been very hot in June and July 2014.
However, August 2014 was lovely and cool.
My auntie Ann's birthday was around the same weekend as well frm Deansgrange Co. Dublin.
It was a big birthday for her.
When I got off the Dart at Shankill Dart station on the way home from the christening.
My Auntie Ann called me to thank me for sending her money and a card for her birthday.
I said no problem and she thanked me again.

I had no more sleeping tablets now left.
My health was getting worse day by day.
I kept complaining to my GP Dr. Meadhbh O'Cullen.
She referred me to Naomh Theodores, Co. Dublin.

I went there in November 2014.
I'm not 100% sure which doctor I saw first.
I think it was my old consultant Dr. Liam O'Mullen Dempsey.
While I was talking to Dr.Liam O'Mullen Dempsey.
My mother got a little upset.
I didn't even notice it at the time.
Until after my mother and I left.
My mother said to me, Dr. Liam O'Mullen Dempsey was rude to me.
He basically told my mother to shut up.

Or he would ask my mother to leave.

Or he would have her taken out.

Or even worst call the Gards.

I said to my ma I didn't even notice that.

I'm used to far much worse than that.

Sort of treatment over the years.

I told him about Dr. Caitlin O'Larkin Devlin.

When I was in St. Bernard's Hospital, Dublin.

I said to Dr. Liam O'Mullen Dempsey. When I asked her for a second opinion, she said No.

I said to Dr. Liam O'Mullen Dempsey. When I asked her if I could I see a male doctor, she said No.

I said to Dr.Liam O'Mullen Dempsey. When I asked her if I could I see a dermatologist, she said No. Yet again.

Then Dr. Liam O'Mullen Dempsey said, well that's wrong.

I said, I know that.

You're entitled to a second opinion if you asked for one, Dr Liam O'Mullen Dempsey said to me.

If you asked to see a male doctor, you're entitled to see one, as well.

I said, I know that.

However I was denied both requests.

He said that was wrong.

I said, I know that.

However I have never even got an acknowledgement of this in any of my complaints I've made to St. Bernard's Hospital, Dublin.

Till this very day.

And I never will.

I think I was there for 45 minutes or maybe close to an hour.

I then went home with my mother.

Very disappointed again.

I'm not exactly 100% sure whether I saw Dr. Eoghan Rogan a week before Dr. Liam O'Mullen Dempsey or a week after.

I do remember Dr. Eoghan Rogan putting me on sedatives and some other drugs to help me sleep.

One of them is Tevaquel XL.

It took my body a few weeks to get used to some of its side-effects, including low blood pressure.

Which makes your legs weak and you get a little unstable on your feet.
After about two or three weeks this side-effect wore off.
The biggest problem I have at the moment with this drug is very severe constipation.
My bowels have barely gone in nearly five months.
Yes, you heard right, five months.
I don't even know.
How I'm still sitting here right now.
I have tried the strongest laxatives available and none of them work.
Or high fibre foods either.

I'm going to my GP Dr. Meadhbh O'Cullen to try and get the most powerful drug to flush out my bowels.
If I don't get this drug.
I could be in serious trouble.
I dare not think.
How my bowels are at the moment.
It doesn't bear thinking about.
The only thing I can say about Dr. Eoghan Rogan.
He was brutally honest with me.
This powerful drug I'm putting you on.
Might not work.
Well at least he's honest.

I've been on these drugs now for nearly five months.
I'm in bits.
My life is a total nightmare.
I'm totally burnt out and exhausted.

I met Dr. Eibhlin O'Kooney I think twice before Christmas 2014.
I told her everything that was wrong with me.
What caused my illness.
Everything about myself.
Very personal things including my sexual history, including puberty.

The only good thing I can say about Dr. Eibhlin O'Kooney.
She did not judge me.
She did not insult me.
She did not laugh at me either.

***

Christmas 2014.

It was the worst Christmas since 1994.

I felt absolutely awful.

I was talking to Rhona my neighbour on the evening of the 23rd of December 2014.

I told her I hadn't slept a wink for days.

I'm in bits Rhona, I said.

We must have been talking for about 45 minutes.

I wished her Happy Christmas.

She said the same to me as well.

I went to my mother's that night on the 23rd of December 2014.

I managed to get a little sleep that night in my mother's.

I called up to an old friend Rosaleen on Christmas Eve 2014.

I brought a bottle of Bailey's Irish Cream.

Her favourite.

She had a friend of her's from Germany.

We walked her to the local Shankill Dart station.

Rosaleen's friend was a little nervous having to go home late at night.

However she only had to wait a few minutes for the Dart to arrive.

When I got back to Rosaleen's house.

I asked her if she wanted to go 10pm Christmas Eve Mass in St. Anne's Church, Shankill, Co. Dublin.

She said yes.

I said to her, they don't do Midnight Mass anymore unfortunately.

Too many drunks turn up at Mass at midnight.

So that's one of the reasons why they stopped doing that I think.

I was surprised.

The church was packed.

Well that's a good sign, I said to myself.

They sang lovely Christmas carols including Silent Night.

After Mass.

We went back to Rosaleen's house; her mother and brother were there too.

I left after some time after midnight.

There was a fox walking straight across the road from Rosaleen's house.

I didn't sleep a wink Christmas Night 2014.

The next day I felt awful.

I was terrible company that day.

My eyes were paining me.

I felt absolutely awful.
I said to everyone at dinner.
I'm sorry, I'm not much good today.

I stayed with my mother until the New Year.

I must have left on January 3rd 2015 to go back to my place.

***

January 2015.
Another terrible year for me yet again.

I think I saw Dr. Eibhlin O'Kooney In January 2015.
My mother was asked to go with me there too.
Dr Eibhlin O'Kooney spoke to me first.
Then my mother.

After, we left Naomh Theodores to go home.
My mother told me.
She asked Dr. Eibhlin O'Kooney, could I get meals on wheels.
Dr. Eibhlin O'Kooney said to my mother.
She would get the social worker to arrange meals on wheels for me.
I said to my mother.
That's never going to happen.
I can guarantee you.
I'll never hear from any social worker or meals on wheels.
My mother said, give it a week or two.
Well I'm telling you now.
I won't be hearing anything.
I'm a veteran of these sorts of things.
I've heard it all before.
They promise a lot but never deliver.
My mother said yet again, give it a week or two.
Well, all right, let's see then.
A week passed by and then another week and still absolutely nothing.
I told you, ma, that I'd hear nothing. Wasn't I right yet again?
I call it chasing.
Where if you want anything done.
You have to constantly chase for it.
If I'd done some chasing and made a few phone calls to Dr. Eibhlin O'
Kooney.

She would say, I forgot.
I'd say, you didn't forget, you just weren't bothered.
I've been dealing with this level of incompetence all of my life and always will be.

I was supposed to be getting meals on wheels In January 2015.
It's now May 2015 and I'm still waiting.
My dinner now must be getting cold.
Or maybe it's even gone off by now.

My 41st birthday on February 12th 2015.
My worst birthday since February 12th 1995.
My mother wanted me to go out for dinner for my birthday.
I said I won't be going anywhere for my birthday.

I'm wrecked; I can barely stand.
I don't even want to leave my house.
I feel like shit.
I'm totally burnt out and exhausted.
I never want to go outside again.
For the rest of my life.
That's how bad I still feel.
And nothing still has changed.

I got a surprise visit on my birthday from my mother and sister.
I was in my house.
When there was a knock on the door.
I thought they were travellers selling pillows.
I answered the door.
And I got a surprise.
It was my mother and sister.
I said to them.
I thought you were travellers selling pillows.
They just laughed.
They bought me cream cakes.
I also got an Adidas polo neck T-shirt.
And a few other small gifts.

My sister was in a hurry to get back for her son from school.
So she left in a hurry.
My mother stayed with me for a few hours.

One day, maybe a week or two later.

My mother came up to visit me.

After a while she began to realise.

How ill I really was.

I'm sorry ma, I'm cracking up.

She broke down crying. It's alright ma… I said

You don't know.

What I'm going through on my own.

As I live on my own and you would have to live with me to really understand.

What I'm really going through.

I met Dr. Eoghan Rogan in either February or March 2015.

My mother and auntie Ann came with me.

My auntie Ann was very good.

She spoke quite eloquently.

However it made no real difference whatsoever.

My auntie Ann drove me and my mother home.

She stayed for a while.

When we were talking.

My auntie said to me, you look totally exhausted. Would you not go to bed for a while?

I said to my auntie, I won't sleep a wink.

It doesn't make any difference whatsoever.

I went to:

HELLS, Co. Dublin.

To see Dr. Eibhlin O'Kooney.

It was the last time I would be interviewed by her.

I think now I could be wrong.

I may stand corrected.

She asked me mostly the same questions.

I had already answered.

There was a male psychiatrist or psychologist with her, asking the same questions.

Then when it came to the end of our conversations.

The male psychiatrist or psychologist asked me, do you think you have schizophrenia?

I said to him, can you explain the term schizophrenia?

I can't remember now what he said exactly?

My reply was, no I don't think so.
Then our session was over.

After I had just left the building.
It dawned on me yet again.
Wasn't it their job to tell me.
What was supposed to be wrong with me.
In the first place?
Not me making my own diagnosis.

My last appointment with Dr. Eoghan Rogan was on Friday 3rd of April 2015, 12.00pm.

I have it in front of me in black and white, sent from Naomh Theodores, Co. Dublin.

I think I was with my mother.
He basically told me to keep taking the same medication.
Then I asked him.
To send my prescription for my medication to my GP.
However, I only want to go to see her as little as possible.
So can you ask her to give me a three-monthly prescription.
So I can see as little of her as possible.
As I want as little as possible to do with any of the medical profession.
In fact if I never have to see another doctor, that would be great.
As I'm totally fed up with the lot and that goes for any of the hospitals as well.

I wish I could be allowed to write my own prescriptions instead and have nothing to do with any of them.
Ever again.
He said, I'll pass that on.
I said please make sure of that. As I don't want to have to come back again.
And start giving out.
Okay?

I went to see Dr. Meadhbh O'Cullen on Thursday 7th of April 2015.
To get my prescription that day.
I get something to stop the real physical pain in my heart.
It's caused from severe anxiety, anger, hatred, impending doom, worry, and it's all caused from my severe illness, being burnt out and exhausted from chronic insomnia; my whole body feels like I'm a very sick 101-year-old man.

Also my bowels have not gone properly since November 2014.

None of the laxatives work, even the strongest ones unfortunately.

After I told Dr. Meadhbh O'Cullen what was wrong with me.

I was surprised.

What she did next.

She typed a letter with what medication I'm on and wrote other details on it as well.

She must have written.

What I described was wrong with me.

Then she said, bring this letter to the Emergency Department in either St. Breda's Hospital, Co. Dublin or St. Bernard's Hospital, Dublin.

I was shocked.

I just expected to get a prescription for a drug to ease the anxiety and stress on my heart.

Also a drug to flush out my bowels.

Then I would go up to the pharmacy.

Maybe Dr. Meadhbh O'Cullen is not the monster I made her out to be after all.

There is still some compassion in her after all.

I just hope I can patch up my differences with Dr. Meadhbh O'Cullen.

I hope our doctor patient relationship can return.

Now it could change dramatically again.

I hope not.

Instead of having been enemies.

Maybe we can still be friends.

So I got the number 7 Bus to Co. Dublin.

Stopped outside St. Breda's Hospital, Co. Dublin.

Walked into the Emergency Department.

Waited about five minutes to talk to the lady at reception.

Gave her my details and the letter from my GP and next of kin.

Then I asked her, where could I get some water?

She said, there's the water cooler over there in the corner of the waiting room.

I just got my plastic cup of water and nearly finished it.

Then my name was called.

I thought I'd be waiting at least an hour or two.

I was brought in, took my jacket and T-shirt off, put on a small dressing gown.

Then they stuck small stickers on my chest and legs and arms.

Then the doctor took an ECG of my heart.

Then a nurse took some blood samples in a syringe.

The doctor asked me.

What my complaints were?

I told him about the pain in my heart.

I also mentioned my bowels had not moved properly since November 2014.

He took notes.

Then a short while later they sent me to the Radiology Department.

Sorry, is that were they take x-rays?

Now I could be wrong and I'm prepared to stand corrected.

I was brought down on the trolley by a porter.

I said to him:

I'm usually complaining about hospitals not doing enough to help me.

There's no need for this fuss.

I can walk down to Radiology if you want me to.

No, I was told to bring you down.

Well okay, I said.

The radiologist asked, was I able to stand and walk to the radiology room?

I said yes.

Then she took an x-ray of my chest.

Then an x-ray of my chest sideways on, also.

I had just told her I had chronic insomnia since the age of 15.

She was shocked by this.

Then I was brought back by trolley.

While I was waiting for my results.

I needed to use the bathroom.

So I asked where the toilets were.

One of the doctors said down the corridor on your right.

When I got there.

The toilet was engaged.

I waited about five minutes.

It was still engaged.

So I went back to the room where I was.

And asked, are there any other toilets?

The doctor said, they're the only ones.

So I went back again.

However the toilet was still engaged.

There are only two toilets in that Emergency Department at St. Breda's Hospital, Co. Dublin.

One for able-bodied patients and one for wheelchair users.

I had no choice but to use the wheelchair toilet instead.

I then went back to my bed.

I had to wait about 10 minutes.

So I turned back on my mobile phone for a minute.

To send a text message to my hypnotherapist.

That I would not be able to make my appointment since I was still in hospital.

Then as I was turning off my mobile phone.

The doctor came in and asked me more questions about my heart condition.

He said all of the tests showed no signs of any serious problems.

He then said he would write me up a prescription and a letter for my GP.

I asked him for his name.

I said to him:

This is the first real positive admission in hospital in my whole life.

I always had very bad experiences in hospitals.

He said, I'm sorry to hear that.

However this time it has been the total opposite.

I just want to say that to you.

I asked him his name.

I said don't worry I'm not going to sue you.

He laughed.

He gave me his name.

He wrote it down for me.

I think it is.

Dr. Peadar O'Kane Twohy.

I thanked him again.

He gave me my prescription and letter for my GP.

Then I did a little shopping.

Then I just had to wait a couple of minutes for the number 7 Bus.

I got off at Co. Dublin shopping centre.

To collect my prescription.

I asked, did I have to pay for any of the things that were written on the prescription from St. Breda's Hospital, Co. Dublin.

She said I think it's around 23 Euros.

I said just let me think about it for a minute.

Then I said I'll go ahead and buy it.

I also had the second of my three monthly prescriptions.

I came back about 10 or 15 minutes later.

One of the men working asked me if I was okay?

I said I'm waiting on my prescription.

I had to wait about 10 minutes.

Then the pharmacist brought me over to a different counter.

For more privacy.

I asked him how powerful stuff to flush out your bowels works.

He then told me.

I asked about the other medication prescribed for me.

By the doctor in St. Breda's Hospital, Co. Dublin.

He said it was a painkiller.

I said I thought it was something to relax me and ease the anxiety and stress that's causing my heart to race and slow down and it keeps paining me for several hours some days.

No, the pharmacist said it was a painkiller.

I think the name of the drug is Toradol, 50mg caps, one to be taken three times daily when required.

I said, that's not going to work because I need something close to Valium to relax me.

That's not going to make it better.

I'll still have the same problem.

The pharmacist said, you will have to talk to your GP or psychiatrist about that.

Then I asked him how much altogether for everything?

I have the receipt in front of me now.

The total was 38.39 Euros.

Which of course I paid.

Then I got lucky again.

I saw the bus coming in the distance.

I ran to the bus stop just past the Church; I managed to catch the bus and got home very quickly.

I really got lucky yesterday with the buses.

I wish it was like that all the time.

Before I finish this book.

I would like to thank all the nursing staff and doctors in St. Breda's Hospital Emergency Department, Co. Dublin, for looking after me.

Maybe not all of the medical staff in Ireland are monsters after all.

If I had not gone into St. Breda's hospital yesterday.

My experience of hospitals in Ireland.

Would have been appalling.

However, maybe there are still some good doctors and nursing staff out there.

Maybe I have been very unlucky and just met the very bad out there.

I was talking to my mother last night about.

What had happened to me.

I had said to her before that I have been put in the wrong hospitals.

All along.

I should be in general hospitals instead of psychiatric hospitals.

Which I have been going to nearly all my life.

Whether it's been to St. Gregory's Hospital or the psychiatric ward in St. Bernard's Hospital, Dublin.

I've always said that I should be sent to a general hospital not a psychiatric hospital.

This just proves my point.

If it had not been for my experience yesterday.

I would have condemned all hospitals to the scrap heap.

However maybe there is still some hope left.

The only thing I noticed in St. Breda's Hospital, Dun Laoghaire, Co. Dublin.

Was the lack of Irish nurses.

I only saw I think two Irish student nurses there.

The rest were mostly Philippinos.

Now I'm not criticising the Philippino nurses.

They did a great job yesterday looking after me.

I've heard stories of many Irish nurses going abroad and it must be true.

I hope things will improve and maybe in time the Irish nurse will return back home one day.

If you have read my book (if it gets published and that's a big IF).

Everything, to the best of my knowledge, is 100% accurate in my autobiography.

I had to tell my true story.

If I'm to die not long from now.
Now you will know why.

If I have caused offence to any member of my family.
Without the intention of doing so.
I deeply apologise sincerely.
If I hurt or offend anybody innocent, I again apologise sincerely yet again.
Any innocent member of the health system in Ireland, both doctors and nursing staff in the last 27 years or present.
Who I have never come across or passed by during my hell (which I'm still going through).
I do not want tar everybody in the health system in Ireland with the same brush.

***

Who to thank for writing this book?
I know this might sound selfish.
I really only have to thank myself and nobody else.
Except for the two hours of work that Pat Forde did for me.
Which I had to pay for out of my pocket.
Other than that I did everything myself.

I have an appointment on Friday 15th of May 2015 in Naomh Theodores, Co. Dublin at 12pm.
With Dr. Eoghan Rogan.
He will be moving on to a new post somewhere else.
I think my mother is going with me there too.

I know little of what's in my medical records in St. Bernard's Hospital, Dublin.
All I remember in them is:
He has delusions about hairloss – 'He' being me of course.
Written and signed by Dr. Caitlin O'Larkin Devlin.
What else is in it?
I do not know.
I can only speculate.
There could be other damning and critical information in it.
It may also be even more shocking.
I can only speculate at the moment.

I will have to wait at least a month to get my medical records from St. Bernard's Hospital, Dublin.

I wish I had requested them six months ago.

However I was waiting on replies from letters of complaints over the last several months and that's why.

That's why I waited so long to get my medical records.

I really wish I had written this book at least six years ago.
However I didn't and that's my own fault and nobody else's.

It took me the best part of five to six months to write this book.
Literally blood, sweat and tears.

As a Roman Catholic I'm entitled to justice.
Which I have been trying to get for nearly 20 years.
However I'm still looking for justice and I think I always will.

As a Roman Catholic I cannot seek revenge or vengeance as it's one of the seven deadly sins.

I will leave it up to the reader of this book to judge and to come to their own conclusions.

Although it is really up to God to judge in the end.

***

God Bless.

Paul Byrne.
Dublin.
Ireland.

Friday May 8th 2015.

THE END?